PARTY POLITICS IN INDIA

The Development of a Multi-Party System

Party Politics in India

The Development of a Multi-Party System

Myron Weiner

PRINCETON, NEW JERSEY
PRINCETON UNIVERSITY PRESS

1957

MYRON WEINER prepared this study while he was associated with the Center of International Studies at Princeton University. He did his research in India in 1953 and 1954. He is now Assistant Professor of Political Science at the University of Chicago.

TO SHEILA

Foreword

Two features about this book seem especially noteworthy. In the first place, it is concerned with the developing political character of the recently emerged nation of India. In view of the mounting importance of this country in world affairs, we need to know as much as we can about the political processes operating within it. Otherwise we will not be in a position to evaluate the strengths and weaknesses of its institutions or estimate the chances of its future political stability and democratic character. Participation by the masses in the political life of India is of course a very recent thing, and the effort to adjust Western democratic procedures to the needs and conflicts of this ancient people provides some fascinating material for those interested in political management. The author provides us with an insight into the way India is seeking to work out a political system which in some manner responds to the great variety of interests, classes, and loyalties of its vast population, and at the same time preserves the essential basis of national unity.

In the second place, the author makes fruitful use of recent advances in the comparative study of political systems and parties in different countries. This interesting development opens up new opportunities for the construction of theory in the field. On the basis of the data collected in India, he formulates a number of hypotheses about the stability of political parties under the conditions existing there. These should be of great value for purposes of comparison with studies of political parties in other non-Western countries.

This book is part of a continuing program of research in comparative politics and parties, carried out under the auspices of the Center of International Studies. The Center was established at Princeton University in 1951. Its basic purpose is to bring to bear on the elucidation of foreign policy problems the full resources of available knowledge and modern methods of analysis. To this end it engages in and publishes research directed toward the development of systematic, disciplined, and comprehensive appraisals of the varied aspects of international relations, with special emphasis on the foreign policy of the United States. The members of the Center work at all times in close association, but each member is free to formulate his research project in his own way and each published study represents an individual analysis of a problem.

FREDERICK S. DUNN
Director

Center of International Studies
Princeton University
April 9, 1957

Acknowledgment

A large part of this study has been based on intensive interviews with Indian political leaders. In the Praja Socialist Party I am especially grateful to Asoka Mehta, Jayaprakash Narayan, Acharya Kripalani, Prafulla Ghosh, and Suresh Banerjee. In the Marxist left parties, Tridib Chaudhuri, Saumyen Tagore, Bishwanath Dubey, S. S. More, and Amiyanath Bose were extremely helpful. So were N. C. Chatterjee, Dr. N. B. Khare, V. G. Deshpande, Ashutosh Lahiri, L. B. Bhopatkar, and Veer Savarkar in the Hindu Mahasabha; and Mauli Chand Sharma, Vasanta Rao Oak, K. R. Malkani, and Din Dayal Upadhyaya in Jan Sangh. In the Congress Party, S. N. Agarwal, U. S. Malliah, Harekrushna Mahtab, Surendra Mohan Ghosh, and Syed Mahmud were of assistance. I was also fortunate in having a lengthy interview with Rafi Ahmed Kidwai before his unfortunate and untimely death. In the Communist Party, interviews were granted to me by Ajoy Ghosh, A. K. Gopalan, and Jyoti Basu. There were many other political party leaders and rank-and-file members who, in the great tradition of Indian hospitality, freely gave me their time and assistance. Wherever possible, I have acknowledged such help in the text. However, I received a considerable amount of information and opinions which for obvious reasons it has not always been possible to acknowledge.

In addition, materials were made available to me by the Indian Council of World Affairs in New Delhi, the research and press sections of the All India Congress Committee, the Diwan Chand Political Information Bureau in New Delhi, the *Kesari* Library in Poona, the Sarat Bose Academy in Calcutta, the office of the Praja Socialist Party in Bombay, and the Parliamentary Library in New Delhi.

I am exceedingly grateful to Professor Humayun Kabir, Lakshmi Jain, and K. R. Malkani, who read and commented on parts of the manuscript, and to Professor C. J. Chacko of Delhi University, who was my Fulbright adviser in India.

I also want to extend my thanks to Professors Gabriel Almond and Dankwart Rustow of Princeton University, Professor Lucian Pye of the Center for International Studies of the Massachusetts Institute of Technology, and Professor Sigmund Neumann of Wesleyan University for their advice on portions of the manuscript.

To Professor William Lockwood of Princeton University, who read a large part of the manuscript and made many valuable suggestions, I am especially indebted.

Others who have assisted in one way or another include Patricia Wohlgemuth, Andrew Westwood, Bidyat Sarkar and many of my friends at the Indian Cooperative Union in New Delhi.

This study was made possible by a Fulbright grant and by assistance from the Ford Foundation and the Center of International Studies of Princeton University. They are not, however, to be understood as approving by virtue of their grants any of the statements made herein. I am alone responsible for any errors in fact or interpretation.

Finally, I am indebted to my wife, Sheila, for her perseverance in reading, rereading and then rereading again this manuscript through its many drafts and for doing so much to make this readable to others.

M. W.

Chicago, March 1957

Contents

Part III

Tables

Maps

The maps were drawn by R. S. Snedeker

PARTY POLITICS IN INDIA

The Development of a Multi-Party System

Introduction

Like many other nations of Asia, India, with its 370 million people, is attempting to adjust to the technological, social, cultural, and political impact of the West. Those of us in the United States with a growing recognition that developments virtually everywhere in the world impinge upon American policy are particularly concerned with the outcome of this attempt to graft Western political institutions into a non-Western setting. Essentially, this is a problem of introducing people into a new kind of political process. We want to know how successful the Indians have been, and in particular how stable a government is developing within the democratic framework.

The process of non-Westerners' learning to participate in a Western-type political system is a complicated one. This is a study of one aspect of this process: *party development, the role which party leaders and members play in the development of a multi-party system in India and the effect of that system upon the prospects for political stability and democracy.* In short, this study is concerned with the *internal* characteristics of the party system rather than the relationship between the parties and the government or between the parties and the voters.

Although it does not offer any general theories as to the process of political formation, it is hoped that this study of one major aspect of party formation in a single country will in some small way contribute to a general theory. This hope is based on the belief that too many of our current generalizations in the field of politics (and in other social science disciplines as well) are made solely on the basis of Western political experience. And if "general" theories are too elusive, further studies in non-Western areas may at least call our attention to the limitations of many of our existing concepts.

Essentially, this is a series of case studies on the obstacles to the growth of a strong opposition party and to the achievement of unity among the opposition parties. In these case studies the focus is on the role of party leaders and party "militants" in the splits and mergers which have affected the growth of opposition parties. The case studies are framed by three chapters. Chapter 1 describes in a cursory way the setting within which the events described in the case studies occurred. Chapter 11, which follows the cases, attempts to make some estimate of the factors which have affected party splintering. The final chapter explores some of the consequences of the present splintered party system and discusses the prospects for the development of an opposition party system which can provide stable government.

Although in terms of the central problem in this study it would have been most logical to arrange the chapters in terms of those cases dealing with splits, then those dealing with mergers, this has not been done. Instead, in order to make for continuity in reading, the arrangement has been in terms of keeping together those chapters which deal with related parties. Chapter 2 briefly describes the background of the Praja Socialist Party, the largest of the opposition parties in India today. Chapters 3, 4, and 5 examine in greater detail the origins of the Praja Socialist Party: the split of the Congress Socialist Party from the Indian National Congress in 1948 (Chapter 3), the split of a group of Gandhians from Congress in 1951 to form the Kisan Mazdoor Praja Party (Chapter 4), and the successful merger of the Socialist Party and the KMPP in 1952 to form the Praja Socialist Party (Chapter 5). Chapter 6 gives a brief summary of the background of the Marxist left movement and Chapter 7 describes the unsuccessful attempt by the Marxist left parties of Bengal to unite in a United Socialist Organization. Chapter 8 briefly summarizes the background of the Hindu communal parties, while Chapter 9 describes in some detail the creation in 1951 of Jan Sangh, the largest of the Hindu communal parties, and Chapter 10 describes the attempted but unsuccessful merger of Jan Sangh and the Hindu Mahasabha, another major Hindu communal party.

These cases were selected for several reasons. First, they involve the major opposition parties—that is, those with the largest popular support and with the best-known political leaders. Second, the studies cover the political spectrum, from the "communal" to the "secular," from the conservative "right" to the more radical "left." Third, the cases are recent enough so that materials on them are readily available; most of the participants are alive, and the events fresh enough so that the memories of those involved can be relied upon. Finally, these are the parties and the leaders most likely to be on the political scene in years to come; an understanding of their behavior and motivation at this time will be of considerable help in assessing their motivation and behavior in the future.[1]

In each of these six case studies our aim has been to find underlying behavior patterns. In the three studies dealing with splits we have been concerned with uncovering what the links were which originally tied the factions together and why these links broke down; in the three studies dealing with mergers we have been concerned with understanding what kept the parties apart to begin with, how and why the question of merger arose, what forces of repulsion and attraction were involved, and, finally, whether the forces of attraction or that of repulsion was stronger and why. In all six studies we are concerned with the role and attitudes of both the leadership and the rank and file. Conceivably, leaders may form a party for one set of reasons, party members may join for another, and voters may lend their support for still other reasons. The cases in this study are limited to an examination of the behavior of the leadership and their party followers. They try to answer the question: How and why is a party formed in India? They do *not* deal with the motivation of voters. For this reason, this study of India's multi-party system is inconclusive and will remain so until a large number of voting behavior studies are available. Until we understand why the

---

1 Since the Communist Party of India has not had any major splits since independence nor attempted to merge with any major groups (although a few very small groups have merged themselves with the CPI), no case study on the Communists has been included here. However, insofar as the Communists were involved in the problems of trade union unity and the unity attempts of the Marxist left parties in Bengal, they are discussed. How the Communists, in spite of enormous internal differences since 1947, have been able to avoid splits resulting in the creation of rival parties is an important and fascinating question, but one which is beyond this study. Readers interested in the Communist Party of India will find an exceedingly useful account in John Kautsky's *Moscow and the Communist Party of India* (Cambridge, Mass.: Technology Press of Massachusetts Institute of Technology, 1956). A study is also being prepared by Gene Overstreet and Marshall Windmiller of the University of California.

voters give their support to a wide range of parties, we cannot know why a two-party or a multi-party system exists. On the other hand, the question cannot be answered either unless we know why political leaders and their party followers create one kind of party system rather than another. In this study, therefore, we have confined ourselves to one aspect of the problem of adapting Western institutions to a non-Western area—the role of leaders and party "militants" in opposition party formation, and the impact of the resulting party system on political stability in India.[2]

[2] Since the events dealt with in this study occurred largely before the reorganization of the Indian states in November 1956, the older names of the Indian states have been retained. For a clarification of the present position of the states discussed in this study, the reader is referred to the maps on pages 9 and 267.

PART I

1. Parties in Indian Politics

India entered an age of mass politics in 1920 when Mahatma Gandhi launched the first national civil disobedience movement. Ever since, politics and government have been a part of the central core of Indian life. The popular coffee houses in Bombay, Calcutta, and the other urban centers are meeting places for the educated young and the politically minded, who are one and the same. For the educated young are as politically minded as were their parents a generation ago. Just as a generation ago their fathers entered the Congress movement, today's young people most often enter the opposition parties—the Communists, the Socialists, one of the Hindu communal parties, or one of the many Marxist groups. Here then is a conflict not only between two generations but within the younger generation itself. While the last generation of youth was united by the cause of nationalism, today's youth is divided by the varied ideas of what a national government means and how its power should be utilized.

THE IMPORTANCE OF POLITICS

To gain an accurate perspective of political parties, the reader must first understand the intensity with which Indians participate in politics. Partly, the current importance of politics is related to the central role which the nationalist movement played in the lives of virtually all educated Indians. Large sections of the educated community were organized around the task of achieving self-government; the way to one's goals, including status and prestige, was through political rather than economic activity. National prominence was achieved not through sports or the cinema (although the ubiquitousness of the cinema has managed to thrust some film stars into national recognition, especially since independence) or even by amassing wealth (which could make one infamous) but rather by suffering and sacrificing for the national cause of independence. The need for such sacrifice no longer exists, but politics and sacrifice continue to remain prime routes to status and prestige.

This striving for status through politics is intensified by the fact that party workers in India come from urban areas, where traditional values have been disrupted and where the traditional social structure has been breaking down. Young party workers have often broken from the tightly knit organization of their village, their caste, and even their joint family. The party thus provides both an alternative set of values and an alternative social structure.

There are few outside loyalties to temper the intensity of party membership. Unlike party workers and members of interest groups in the United States and Great Britain, who are at the same time members of their family, business and church groups, trade unions, veterans' organizations, and so on, Indians do not generally have multiple group memberships. Party workers therefore tend to be uncompromising in their attitudes toward other parties. They are often more concerned with maintaining the identity of their group and its ideology than in increasing their prospects for achieving political power by working more closely with others. Indian parties are frequently torn by two desires: on the one hand they want to work more closely with other parties or even to merge in order to improve their electoral prospects, but on the other they fear that the identity of their group will be lost. The result is often a vacillating policy of uncompromising attacks against other opposition parties and passionate calls for unity.

Adding further to the intensity with which Indians take part in politics is the fact that job opportunities in business, social work, education, and even government service have not kept up with the growing number of university graduates. A study by the Lucknow University Anthropology Department showed that about 25% of the students who received their master's degree from Lucknow University in arts, science, commerce, and law between 1949 and 1953 are still unemployed. The survey also reported that about 47% of the liberal arts students, 51.4% of

INDIA BEFORE THE REORGANIZATION OF STATES

For a map of India since the reorganization, see page 267

the science students, 7% of the commerce students, and as many as 85.7% of the education students said they joined the university to have the necessary qualifications for government service. About 51% of the degree holders concluded that university education is a "waste of time."[1]

Much of the political party recruitment, especially among the opposition parties, is from these educated unemployed—largely young people whose expectations are not being fulfilled and who consequently feel alienated from society. The opposition parties, with their *Weltanschauung* and their tightly knit organization, provide alternative outlets.

The importance of politics in the daily lives of educated Indians is also related to the fact that politics provides the language and symbols which serve as a unifying force. This proposition may first appear absurd and even contradictory when one thinks of the divisiveness of politics, the petty squabbles, the factional disputes, and the enormous ideological differences between political groups. None of this is irrelevant. No one can deny that politics divides. But it also unites those who have no other basis for union. Members of the educated elite who are otherwise divided by the traditional barriers of caste, language, and provincialisms of one kind or another, find in the symbols of politics a unifying link. Members of the Hindu Mahasabha, for example, whether they are Brahmans or Kshatriyas, from Bengal or Maharashtra, find in their language of Hindu communalism a unifying *culture* without which there would be no communion of feeling. The horsetrading of special interests, the logrolling and bargaining, which are so characteristic of American political parties, are not enough to unify a party in India, for a larger umbrella of values does not exist as it does in England or the United States. The sense of rootlessness and purposelessness which a Westernized elite feels can in part be mitigated through a language of politics and by the patterns of relationship which a political party can provide, but which the traditional forms of society no longer can.

[1] *Statesman*, November 27, 1955.

Before 1947 the political struggle was between the British bureaucracy in India and the national movement; after 1947 the political arena centered around conflicts among Indian political parties. This remark no doubt seems commonplace to the Western reader, but it involves a phenomenon in Asia and Africa almost unique to those countries which lived for many years under foreign rule. In Thailand and Japan, countries which were not under prolonged foreign occupation, the response to the West came from an intelligentsia in the government. It was the bureaucracy, civil and military, which maintained a dominant position so that political struggles occurred *within* the bureaucracy. To the observer the political game was like stud poker, where the unseen cards were often most significant.

With the British in control of the bureaucracy in India, the "mediators" of the Western impact emerged from the professional classes—the teachers, the lawyers, the doctors—and the lesser government officials. It was from this group that the nationalist movement developed. The political struggle was thus against the bureaucracy, and the political arena was consequently open for all to watch.

With independence, there came to power a Westernized elite committed to creating a democratic, secular government, raising the standard of living of the masses, achieving a greater measure of social justice, and eliminating those features of the old social order which it felt to be anomalous. This elite set out to utilize the power of government to reconstruct society in its own image, and those in the society who cannot accept the new values are forced to wage their struggle in the political arena. In this sense the issue of Westernization is now even more of a political question than it was before.

POLITICS AS AN URBAN PHENOMENON

Maurice Zinkin has given an incisive picture of the differences between Asia and the West in terms of the respective importance of the village and the city.[2] The civilizations of the West

2 Maurice Zinkin, *Asia and the West* (London: Chatto and Windus, 1951).

largely grew in the urban areas, such as Athens, Rome, Florence, and Venice, while in Asia, especially in India and Southeast Asia, civilization emerged from the rural areas. The old cities of India—like Delhi—were less centers of commerce and culture than they were centers of government. Bombay, Calcutta, and Madras are new cities, the product of Western impact.

The ability of the urban areas in India to be initiators of change is enhanced by the fact that being relatively new they have no historical tradition to undo. Out of the cities and the larger towns of India have come the personnel of politics. Even the political recruitment of young people from rural areas takes place in the urban centers where they have gone to study or work.

It is often argued in India and outside that the crucial areas of the nation are the villages, where some 85% of the population lives; for there lies the antiquity of Indian culture, there is the greatest potential for discontent and revolution. But *satygrahas* (civil disobedience movements) of peasants are frequently organized by Socialist, Communist, and communalist leaders who come from the urban areas. Peasant protest is often mobilized and directed by one urban elite in an attempt to weaken or destroy the political power of another urban elite, for the urban areas are the centers of parties radiating their influence out to the villages.[3]

THE DEVELOPMENT OF POLITICAL PARTIES

There are many ways in which the development of political parties in India differed from their development in Great Britain and the European continent—not the least of which is that the struggle by parties for parliamentary institutions in India was not against an indigenous wealthy, aristocratic ruling class, but rather against alien rulers, thus permitting Indian big business, the intelligentsia, the urban shopkeepers, and the peasants to join together against a single enemy. But perhaps the single

[3] This raises several interesting questions beyond the scope of this study: What is the present political relationship between the rural and urban areas in India? To what extent are the rural areas developing their own leadership and their own political organizations which may become a threat to the present dominant position of the urban leadership?

most important difference is that of *timing.* Parties emerging today find ready-made ideologies waiting for them, while parties of the nineteenth century had to evolve their own ideologies to suit prevailing conditions. But even more important in the matter of timing is the fact that suffrage was introduced into most European countries gradually and after prolonged struggles; the process of broadening the political base was a relatively slow one, in most cases allowing time for various groups to adapt themselves to new political rules. Britain is the classic case of the gradual entrance into politics of new groups—labor being the most recent—who accepted the basic democratic framework. In India, as in other newly independent countries, universal suffrage has been introduced all at once in a society where interests are not clearly differentiated and organized. There is thus a measure of unpredictability in the behavior of these groups and consequently a degree of latency in Indian politics. So long as these groups have not organized themselves, they provide a fertile ground for organization by party leaders who seek to direct protest in ways that will gain political benefit for their groups or themselves.

The *suddenness* of independence—in the sense that Indian political groups did not gradually take over the apparatus of government, but took power all at once in 1947—meant that there was little time for a gradual adjustment to an entirely new political system. Most of the opposition parties which emerged after 1947 existed before independence, but they were largely political groups within the Indian National Congress functioning in a common cause as part of a national movement.

The national movement itself passed through three stages of development: first it was a pressure group, then a national movement, and finally a political party. The Indian National Congress, created in 1885, was largely a pressure group which sought to influence rather than control the government on behalf of the special interests of its members. "Its outlook," wrote two historians, "was urban rather than rural; it had no organic connection with peasants, labourers, or country traders. . . . The great majority of those who attended the Congress were lawyers, teachers or journalists, that is to say, they belonged to the three new professions which had grown up under British rule; a few Englishmen or Scotsmen gave substantial help in the early stages; the procedure was modelled on English practice; and the movement may justly be described as an attempt to influence the Government within the existing constitution."[4]

Until the 1920's the urban, professional intelligentsia which dominated the Indian National Congress had little communication with the masses of the country. The nationalist movement itself arose first in those areas where the Western impact was greatest: Bengal, Madras, the Punjab, and Maharashtra. The early Congress conferences were held in urban centers: Poona, Calcutta, Bombay, Karachi, Delhi, and Madras. British influence, wittingly or unwittingly, provided the impetus for a truly national nationalist movement. The unification of India by the British had facilitated the growth of a feeling of being "Indian." British higher education not only introduced Western liberal ideas and led to the emergence of professional classes, but also provided the language—English—whereby the educated elites of various parts of the country could communicate with one another. In the early days of the national movement there had been some mass participation, but it was largely confined to Bengal, which in 1905 in spite of the uproar of the Bengali population was partitioned by the British. The nationalist movement did not become nation-wide, however, until the 1920's when Gandhi successfully fused religious notions and political objectives and rallied the villagers behind him.

As a nation-wide nationalist movement, the Congress brought together a wide assortment of groups from business, labor, and the peasantry. Only communal considerations were able to substantially divide the national movement, with the Muslims, Sikhs, Anglo-Indians, and Parsees maintaining their own or-

---

[4] W. H. Moreland and A. C. Chatterjee, *A Short History of India*, 3rd edition (London: Longmans, Green and Co., 1953), p. 427. For a succinct account of the history of the nationalist movement in India see W. Norman Brown, *The United States and India and Pakistan* (Cambridge, Mass.: Harvard University Press, 1953), Chaps. 4, 5, and 6.

ganizations to act on behalf of their communities. The major opposition groups in India today were in pre-independence days part of the Congress fold: the Socialists, the Hindu communalists, the Marxist leftists, and the Communists. Although Nehru and many other Congress leaders were deeply committed to parliamentary institutions, there were many in the nationalist movement who were not. The Communists, the Marxist left, and the Hindu communalists all participated in the national struggle without favoring the adoption of Western democratic political institutions. Such was the wide diversity of outlooks tolerated within the nationalist movement.

The Socialists, who became the second largest party in India after independence, first organized in 1934 as the Congress Socialist Party within the Indian National Congress. The Hindu Mahasabha, the largest of the Hindu communal parties in independent India, was never formally a part of Congress, but until the 1930's many of its members were also members of Congress. The Marxist left groups evolved out of the terrorist organizations which had been formed in Bengal at the turn of the century. Most of these groups functioned within Congress until shortly before the beginning of World War II.

Of the various pre-1947 political parties, the Communists have perhaps the longest record of opposition to Congress. The Communist Party of India was organized in 1924 and until the mid-1930's opposed Congress leaders, including Gandhi, as tools of imperialism. In 1934 the Government of India banned the Communist Party, but later in the '30's the Communists joined in a popular front with the Congress Socialists. When war broke out in 1939 the Indian Communists opposed it as imperialist, but completed switched their line the following year as the Japanese advanced through Southeast Asia. By supporting the war effort the Communists alienated themselves from Congress, which opposed the war and was at that time urging the British to "Quit India." At the close of the war in 1945, Congress expelled the Communists on the grounds that they violated its policy.

With the achievement of independence in 1947, the political

setting in India underwent a drastic change. The Indian National Congress was now transformed from a national movement to a political party. This change was dramatically expressed in the new Party constitution which forbade Party members from belonging to any other political party. The Socialists, Communists, and others shifted their attack from the ruling British to the ruling Congress Party. A Constitution having been put into effect in 1950, the political parties began preparing themselves for the first national elections.

By 1951 four major groups of parties had emerged. One group more or less accepted the basic democratic, secular state provided for in the Constitution. This group included the Congress Party, the Socialist Party, the Kisan Mazdoor Praja Party, and several small state parties such as the Krishikar Lok Party in Andhra. A second group rejected the Western-type parliamentary Constitution and advocated instead a model based on the Soviet or Chinese political and economic system. Besides the Communist Party of India, this group included the various Marxist left parties: the Bolshevik Party of India, the Revolutionary Socialist Party, the Peasants and Workers Party, etc. A third group also rejected the existing state, but turned instead toward the Indian tradition for its inspiration. In this group were Jan Sangh, the Hindu Mahasabha, and Ram Rajya Parishad, the Hindu communal parties. A fourth group could be characterized as "indifferent" to the Constitutional framework, being primarily concerned with some provincial or communal interest. The Sikh Akali Dal, the Scheduled Caste Federation, the Jharkhand Party, and the Tamilnad Congress were in this group. These parties not only made demands on behalf of their own communities; they were carriers of a group consciousness, sometimes communal, sometimes provincial, and in a few instances tribal.

THE 1951 ELECTIONS AND THE ISSUES AHEAD

Somehow the Congress Party managed to survive the multitude of problems facing the new state after 1947. The normal difficulties involved in dividing the subcontinent into India and Pakistan were further complicated by widespread riots, violence, and the mass exodus of Hindus from Pakistan and Muslims from India. Furthermore, almost simultaneously with partition, violenc · and war broke out in Hyderabad and Kashmir. And in the midst of these birth pangs, the Communist Party of India launched its insurrection in Hyderabad.

In spite of these apparently insurmountable obstacles, the new Government of India continued to function. A strong administrative apparatus and a strong army, both legacies of British rule, stood behind the new government. But perhaps most important of all, the Congress Party leadership demonstrated that it could carry on, in spite of the assassination of Mahatma Gandhi in January 1948. The Congress leadership was able to deal effectively with the Communist insurrection, bring peace to Hyderabad, control the refugee situation, integrate over 500 princely states into the Indian Union, and avoid war with Pakistan. Furthermore in 1950 the Constituent Assembly, with a Congress majority, approved a new Constitution, and India was declared a Republic.

Even with a stable dominant political party, however, there were portents of political difficulties. Independence had not brought the anticipated new era, and there was increasing corruption, disillusionment, and loss of *élan* in the Congress Party. Factional disputes multiplied. The Congress Socialist party, which had up to this time operated within Congress, withdrew and set itself up as an independent opposition party, and a few years later a large group of Gandhians in Bengal, Madras, Uttar Pradesh, and Malabar likewise withdrew from Congress. In addition there were growing regional pulls, expressed in the increasing agitation for reorganization of the Indian states along linguistic lines, which puts strains both on the Congress Party and the government. And finally there was increasing recognition that the Congress Party was failing to recruit younger people and that no new leaders were developing inside Congress who could assume control when the elder Congress leaders withdrew from the political scene.

There was considerable curiosity and anxiety about the results of India's first national general elections based on universal suffrage: the largest elections ever held in a democratic state anywhere in the world. Although it was assumed that the Congress Party under Nehru would remain the major political force, there was still the question whether a major democratic opposition would emerge. From the point of view of traditional Western political notions about the function of political parties in a democracy, the growth of an opposition seemed desirable. This reasoning was based on at least two assumptions: first, that opposition parties, by providing an element of choice to the voters, are basic and essential to a democratic system; second, that the opposition would integrate those interest groups being neglected by the government and might be in a position to assume power and bring about a new public policy if the government failed to heed those interests adequately. The existence of a strong opposition, therefore, would serve as a check on the government and help insure responsibility in government. As the *New York Times* correspondent said several years later, there are many who "would like to see a second democratic party emerge strong in India, to provide stimulation and a feeling of 'running scared' for the Congress Party, to put forward new ideas and to give voters who are dissatisfied with the Congress Party a real choice."[5]

For those who looked forward to the growth of an opposition in India, a second question remained: Would there develop a two-party system as in the United States and Great Britain, an unstable multi-party system as in France, or a stable multi-party system in which compromises by various groups make stable government possible, as in Sweden? In short, what would be the relationship between the party system and political stability?[6] Whether an opposition which offered the prospect of alternative

[5] *New York Times*, January 2, 1956.

[6] Political stability is used in this study *in the context of democratic values* (there can of course be stability in non-democratic societies too) and refers to conditions (1) in which one or a group of political parties controls the government and performs the minimum socially accepted functions of government for a reasonable length of time and (2) where change in the governing parties occurs within the legally prescribed democratic rules and is tolerated by the defeated groups.

in a sufficiently strong position to provide the possibility of alternative stable government in the event Congress lost power. But this did not present any immediate difficulties. There were even some who argued that although a party system had not developed similar to that of a Western democracy (whether the United States, France, or Sweden), there were certain advantages to having a virtual "one-party democracy." It could, in fact, be argued that as long as there was a pressing need for rapid economic development planned by the state, such a program could best be carried out if a single party, with a minimum of opposition, led the country. If Congress and its leadership could organize the country around the Five Year Plan and minimize the many divisive tendencies in Indian society, many Indians felt that this was to the good. As long as free speech and the right of the opposition to organize exist and the ideal of a party system with a strong opposition remains, then the opportunity for such a system to develop remains open. Perhaps the process of getting non-Westerners to participate in a democratic framework could make most progress under the leadership of a single party which is capable of maintaining popular support even while allowing the opposition to operate. This, however, should be distinguished from a period of political "tutelage" in which one party maintains itself in power through suppression.

The Congress Party has been able, in fact, to maintain national political stability since independence by virtue of its dominant position and, at least for the moment, appears likely to continue to do so for some time. While there are advantages to such single-party domination, it is obvious that as long as the opposition has the right to organize, Congress cannot permanently remain in power. Moreover there are still no clear indications that the present leadership of the Congress Party has fostered the development of a younger crop of alternative leaders from within its own ranks; and it also remains to be seen what will happen when a new set of leaders do appear who do not have the prestige of being "the founding fathers." The real test of the stability of India's political system lies in the answer to the question whether power can be transferred to another group, capable of governing effectively within the democratic framework. This question must remain unanswered until Congress is defeated.

If this first disturbing feature for the moment appears to be remote, the second is nearer at hand. It concerns the impact of the party system on relations between the central and state governments. As long as India maintains a federal system, with considerable power in the hands of the states (including agriculture, education, and public health), then relations between the center and the states can have far-reaching consequences. As Sir Ivor Jennings noted, ". . . one must put up with the inevitable consequences of federalism, one of which is the possibility of a conflict between the State and the Federal Governments."[9] But can an underdeveloped country intent upon central planning for economic development afford the "luxury" of such conflicts? There is little doubt that conflict could stymie much of the development program. Paul Appleby in his report on public administration to the Government of India noted that there is in India "an almost complete dependence of the Centre on the states for administration of social-action programs."[10] And although there are ways in which the center can influence, if not control, state policy,[11] the effects are at best unpredictable and at worst deleterious to the development program.

The existence of widespread state-center conflict has thus far been precluded by one-party control of the central government and most of the states. There are, however, three conceivable developments in the various states that could affect state-center relations. First, it may be possible for an opposition party or group of parties to gain control of a state and provide effective

[9] Sir Ivor Jennings, *Some Characteristics of the Indian Constitution* (London: Oxford University Press, 1953), p. 69.

[10] Paul N. Appleby, *Public Administration in India—Report of a Survey* (Delhi: Manager of Publications, 1953), p. 3.

[11] The means by which the national government might influence state governments include power of the center to veto state legislation in conflict with national law, and, perhaps most important of all, the power of the center to take over the administration of a state and to make laws for a state when a Proclamation of Emergency is issued by the President and subsequently approved by both Houses of Parliament.

government with a minimum of conflict with a Congress-controlled central government. The Praja Socialist Party or other pro-democratic groups, for example, once having won state power, could be expected to cooperate to a greater or lesser degree with a national Congress government. A second possibility is that a party or a group of parties might be able to assume power in a state and provide a measure of law and order, but be in direct conflict with the central government. A state government controlled by the Communists and other anti-democratic groups or possibly some of the Hindu communal parties would be an illustration of this. Finally, there is the possibility that no one party or group of parties could form a stable state government. Local law and order might then break down. Such a situation occurred in the state of PEPSU in 1952. It then became necessary for the central government to implement the emergency provisions of the Constitution and apply what is known as "President's Rule" with the center passing and administering laws for the state.

It was with more than passing curiosity, therefore, that the election returns in 1952 were scrutinized to judge the trend of party development in the various states. In Madras, the largest and most populous of the South Indian states, Congress returned only 152 legislators out of an Assembly of 375; in PEPSU, Congress returned 26 out of 60; and in Travancore-Cochin, Congress returned 43 out of 108. An anticipated post-election crisis in each of these areas did occur, but through a combination of political maneuverings within the states and the use or threatened use of emergency powers by the central government, it was possible to establish a stable government dominated by the Congress Party in each instance. Nevertheless in PEPSU and to a lesser extent in Travancore-Cochin, stability did not come until after a period of considerable uncertainty and disorder. Thus as long as the opposition parties remain splintered, of the three possibilities for party development in the states, experience suggests that the third is most likely to occur—that a Congress defeat would be followed by the emergence of a number of parties, none of which has so far proved capable of forming either a stable government or a stable non-Congress coalition government.

The future of the opposition remains perhaps the single most challenging political question in India today. The prospects for democracy in India depend upon many factors, not the least of which are the extent to which the aspirations of people for economic development and social change can be provided for, and the extent to which the Indian government can provide national unity and maintain law and order. If we are right in assuming that the future of parliamentary and democratic institutions in India depends in large part upon the long-range development of a political party system which can ensure stability, then it is essential that we understand how far India has thus far gone in this direction. It is necessary therefore that we take a look at the development of the opposition parties and the factors which have led to their fragmentation, and then assess the prospects for the emergence of a stable party system. It is toward these two questions that the following chapters are directed.

PART II

2. Background of the Praja Socialist Party

The Praja Socialist Party is an amalgam of a number of political parties and is now the second largest in India and the largest among the opposition. The Praja Socialist Party was not created until after the 1952 general elections, but the three parties which created it together received 17.4 million votes in the elections, second only to the 47.6 million votes polled for Congress and far ahead of the 5.7 million votes which the Communists and their allies received. The Socialist Party alone, the largest of the three groups which formed the PSP, won 11 million votes. How did the Praja Socialist Party grow and what does it stand for? In this and in the three case studies which follow we shall try to answer these questions.

A BRIEF HISTORY OF THE PRAJA SOCIALIST PARTY

The Praja Socialist Party is the direct descendant of the Congress Socialist Party (CSP), founded in 1934 by younger leftist members of the Congress Party.[1] Socialist groups had already existed in Bihar, Uttar Pradesh, and Delhi, but not until 1934 were they organized as part of an all-India body.

The immediate issue which precipitated the formation of the Congress Socialist Party was the opposition of Congress Socialists to the growing willingness of Congress to participate in legislative activities although India was not yet independent.[2] More basic, however, was the feeling on the part of many of the younger members of Congress that the Party should pursue a more revolutionary leftist policy. The Congress Socialists subscribed to

[1] Two of the most useful accounts of the early history of the Congress Socialists can be found in the collected writings of Acharya Narendra Deva and Jayaprakash Narayan, the President of the first Congress Socialist Conference and the first Organizing Secretary respectively. See Acharya Narendra Deva, *Socialism and the National Revolution*, edited by Yusef Meherally (Bombay: Padma Publications, 1946); and Jayaprakash Narayan, *Towards Struggle*, edited by Yusuf Meherally (Bombay: Padma Publications, 1946).

[2] Deva, *op.cit.*, p. 26.

Marxism and declared that the economic struggle of the workers was an integral part of the national movement for independence. To unite the national struggle for independence with the workers' struggle for a better life was the aim of the new party.

The Socialists organized themselves as a party inside Congress, and actively tried to influence Congress Party policy. A number of the leaders of the CSP—Acharya Narendra Deva, Jayaprakash Narayan, and Achyut Patwardhan—were members of Nehru's Working Committee, the highest Congress Party organ, in 1936. The main efforts of the Socialists during the pre-war years were directed, first, toward influencing Congress against accepting office under the new 1935 Constitution granted by the British; second, toward launching a revolutionary movement to get the British out of India; and, third, toward injecting socialist economic ideas into Congress resolutions.

The Congress Socialist Party was not the only exponent of leftist views in the pre-war years. Pandit Jawaharlal Nehru and Subhas Chandra Bose had both become national spokesmen for leftist ideas. To a lesser extent so had M. N. Roy, a founder and onetime leader of the Communist movement in India but in the mid-thirties a leader of an anti-Communist Marxist group. A large number of leftist, formally terrorist groups had their own political parties, largely in Bengal. But of the organized leftist groups, the most important in the mid-thirties were the Congress Socialists and the Communist Party.

The Communists, until early 1936, had vilified the Socialists as they had vilified the entire national movement. But after 1936 the Communists began united front tactics and advocated a new policy of cooperation with the Congress Socialists, a policy which was later to have a major effect on Socialist thinking. The Popular Front reached its height in 1937 and 1938 when the CSP had two Communists as Joint Secretaries and two others on the Executive Committee.[3] By the time the CSP Executive

[3] M. R. Masani, *The Communist Party of India: A Short History* (London: Derek Verschoyle, 1954), p. 68. The most complete account of the Popular Front period can be found in Chapter 4: "Front Populaire 1935-1939." An even more complete account of Communist-Socialist relations can

expelled the Communists from the Party, in 1940, the Communists had successfully gained control of the CSP organizations in large sections of South India, including Travancore-Cochin, Andhra, and Madras, all centers of present Communist strength.

During the war, the Congress Socialists backed the Congress Quit India movement, and soon came to play a dominant role in many parts of India. After the war, for a variety of reasons which we shall deal with in the next chapter, Socialist relations with Congress grew strained until the two severed relations in 1948. As an independent party in opposition to Congress, the Socialists tried to rally around themselves other opposition parties which subscribed to their basic socialist principles. The Bolshevik-Leninist Party, a small Trotskyite party, accepted the Socialists' invitation and merged with them, but none of the major leftist parties were prepared to follow suit. Prior to the 1952 general elections, the Socialists arranged electoral alliances with a number of parties, but not until after the elections were any other mergers brought about. Finally, in 1952, the Socialists merged with the Kisan Mazdoor Praja Party (Peasants, Workers, and People's Party), which, with over 6 million votes, was the third largest political party.[4]

The KMPP was formed shortly before the elections by pro-Gandhian dissidents inside the Congress Party. Their strength was greatest in Mysore, Madras, and West Bengal, areas where the Socialists had had limited appeal. The merger, therefore, tended to make the Socialists more national in scope. A few months after the KMPP and the Socialists merged to create the Praja Socialist Party (People's Socialist Party), they were joined by the Subhasist Forward Bloc of West Bengal.

THE SOCIALIST PROGRAM AND TACTICS

The detailed program of the new Praja Socialist Party was first outlined at its convention at Allahabad in December 1953. The program adopted by that convention describes the objec-

---

be found in "Problems of Socialist Unity in India" by Jayaprakash Narayan, in his *Towards Struggle, op.cit.*, pp. 159-190.

[4] See Chapters 4 and 5.

tives for a Socialist central government, but does not, unfortunately, outline the policy of the Party for the state governments.[5]

According to the program, a Socialist government would aim to balance technological change with the need for maximum employment. In agriculture, mass voluntary labor would be recruited to increase the amount of irrigated land. A Food Army of a million persons would be raised to bring new lands under cultivation.[6] Lands would be redistributed, the maximum holding being three times the unit of land a family can cultivate without employing hired labor or mechanization.[7] In the industrial sector, emphasis would be placed on the development of industry based on small machines capable of use in villages and towns.[8] A Socialist government would demarcate spheres between large-scale and small-scale and small-unit decentralized industries.

Economic and social inequalities would be eliminated by imposing a ceiling on all incomes. The underprivileged castes and tribes would be given preference in the matter of land distribution, employment, and educational opportunities.[9] A welfare program in the fields of health, housing, and education would also play a major part in the program of a first Socialist government.[10]

In the administrative sphere a Socialist government would aim to decentralize authority. Control over police would be transferred to local bodies; greater legislative powers would be vested in the district and local village panchayats. The office of the Governor and Rajpramukh would be abolished as would the second chambers in state legislatures.[11]

Apart from some of their constitutional and administrative proposals, Socialist disagreements with Congress generally center around the speed and approach to economic development. The Socialists have been especially critical of what they feel is the Congress government's lack of speed in carrying through an agrarian program and what they consider to be the failure of

[5] *Governmental Programme for Socialist India* (Bombay: Praja Socialist Party, 1954).

[6] *Ibid.*, pp. 7-8.   [7] *Ibid.*, p. 6.   [8] *Ibid.*, p. 5.
[9] *Ibid.*, p. 12.   [10] *Ibid.*, p. 15.   [11] *Ibid.*, pp. 12-15.

the government to give adequate encouragement to cottage and other small-scale industries. In approach, the Socialists do not believe that large landholders ought to be compensated for confiscated lands, nor would they be as solicitous as they feel Congress has been toward princes and capitalists.

In foreign policy, the PSP places great emphasis on the "Third Force" approach which condemns both power blocs and seeks to develop a third group of nations in between. Many of the Socialists have been critical of Nehru's policy for its failure to be "neutralist" enough. The Socialists are considerably more critical of both the Soviet Union and Communist China than the Prime Minister is. While the Socialists, like the Prime Minister, have condemned SEATO and other Western-sponsored military alliances, they have also been critical of China's policy in Tibet. They have also differed with the Prime Minister on his policy toward Kashmir and urged that the issue be withdrawn from the United Nations and Kashmir be completely integrated into the Indian Union. They have also advocated India's withdrawal from the Commonwealth.

The methods by which the Praja Socialist Party could achieve power were outlined by the same convention.[12] The Party welcomed the move toward the consolidation of political parties which had developed since the general elections. The Party declared its opposition to both Congress and the Communists and said that it would not join a coalition government except in the event of a national emergency; or unless it were the largest party in the legislature and/or such a government were based on socialist policies and a socialist program.

The convention further said the PSP is opposed to totalitarian creeds and would prefer to work with democratic forces, but does not always have that choice. PSP candidates may also enter into electoral agreements with other parties opposed to Congress in order to avoid triangular fights.[13]

As for tactics, the PSP declared that it would emphasize both

[12] *Political Perspective and Programme of Work* (Bombay: Praja Socialist Party, 1954).
[13] *Ibid.*, pp. 7-8.

constructive work and struggle. Whether control of the government must come through the electoral process or whether power can be won through non-legal devices is not explicitly discussed. Presumably this is because there is considerable disagreement and uncertainty on this question within the Party.

In their approach to both domestic and international questions the Socialists have been faced with two problems: how to give socialism an Indian character, and how to have a program and ideology which are distinct from those of both the Congress and the Communists. The Indianization of socialism has gone a long way since the Party broke from Congress. Emphasis on decentralization, non-violence, Bhoodan, and other Gandhian notions has turned the Socialists away from their past preoccupation with solely Western writings as the basis of their ideology. But while there has been considerable effort to make the Socialists more distinctive, in practice their differences with the Congress Party have not always been clear to the public. The Congress Party declaration for a "socialist pattern of society" at its annual conference in 1955 has further increased the confusion.

Early in 1953, disputes arose within the Party which grew even more intense after the Allahabad convention. These disputes seemed primarily to center around the question of the attitude which the Socialists ought to have toward the Congress Party. While the Socialists generally agreed that the Congress Party was reactionary on economic matters and politically corrupt, there was some disagreement as to what extent, if at all, they ought to be prepared to work together. This was highlighted in early 1953 by talks between Jayaprakash Narayan and Prime Minister Nehru which were directed at increasing cooperation between the two parties on questions of national development.[14] Jayaprakash's offer of fourteen points as conditions for closer cooperation was rejected by Nehru, but the question of closer relations between the two parties remained an issue from then on and is still a major issue inside the PSP. Asoka Mehta, the

[14] *Nehru-Jayaprakash Talks* (Bombay: Praja Socialist Party, 1953).

General Secretary of the PSP, offered his thesis known as "political compulsions of a backward economy" in his report to the Party in June 1953,[15] in which he declared that the Congress belief in nationalism, secularism, and democracy brought it close to the Socialists. In a backward economy, Mehta argued, the Socialists had to be prepared to cooperate with Congress either by some kind of programmatic agreement between them or by delimiting areas of agreement and disagreement.[16]

This point of view was rejected by the Party rank and file and especially by Rammanohar Lohia, a member of the Party's National Executive and later the General Secretary. Lohia's belief that the Socialists are "equidistant" from both the Communists and the Congress was accepted by the rank and file. As elaborated by Lohia, this meant that in election fights the PSP should be equally prepared to make electoral adjustments with Communists or Congress, but that "in all areas where Socialists are strong and are becoming the alternative to the party of capitalism or mixed economy, there is no need for an electoral adjustment." The Socialists, he felt, should be prepared to tolerate but not to participate in Congress or Communist governments. "It should not think in terms of a coalition government unless it is at least the largest single party in assembly or parliament."[17]

The question of relations between the PSP and other parties was raised on the practical level during the February 1954 elections in Travancore-Cochin. In order to prevent a Congress victory in these special elections, the Socialists negotiated an electoral alliance with the Communists and two smaller leftist groups. When no one party won a majority of seats in the legislature, the Socialists were in a dilemma as to which party, if any, they should support. The National Executive of the PSP declared that although they had only 19 seats in a legislature of 117, they would be prepared to form a government. Rather than permit the Communists to form a government, the Con-

---

[15] *Report of the General Secretary to the Betul Convention of the Praja Socialist Party* (Bombay: Praja Socialist Party, 1953), pp. 6-9.

[16] *Ibid.*, p. 9.

[17] Rammanohar Lohia, "Need for an Electoral Adjustment," *Janata* (November 29, 1953), p. 7.

gress Party acquiesced and Pattam Thanu Pillai, the Socialist leader of Travancore-Cochin, was called upon to form a Socialist Ministry. Sections of the PSP were not happy about this, especially since it meant that the Socialist Ministry had to rely upon Congress support to remain in power.

Months later, when police fired on agitators demonstrating in Travancore-Cochin for a linguistic state, Lohia, then General Secretary of the PSP, immediately demanded the resignation of the Socialist Ministry. This precipitated a crisis in the Party, intensified by the refusal of the Ministry to resign, the subsequent resignation of Lohia as General Secretary, and a declaration by the National Executive of the PSP calling for an investigation of the incident and a reexamination of the Party policy but not calling for the resignation of the Ministry. The Party members were deeply disturbed by these developments—so much so that a special convention of the Party was held in November 1954 at Nagpur. (Precisely what the basic differences were we shall return to later.) The convention reaffirmed the decision of the National Executive and elected Acharya Narendra Deva as a new compromise Chairman for the Party. He was empowered to form a new National Executive which would contain representatives of the divergent elements in the Party. It should be mentioned here that the disagreements were not between the various merged units of the PSP but rather between elements of the former Socialist Party. The new National Executive of the PSP failed, however, to heal the breach within the Party, and a year later Lohia and his followers withdrew to form a party of their own.

SOCIALIST IDEOLOGY

The Praja Socialist Party is made up of three major ideological streams, Marxism, democratic socialism, and Gandhism. It would be a mistake to say that at any one time the Party was Marxian or that today it is Gandhian, since the Party has always been a mixture of a number of ideologies, although at some times one point of view has been more dominant than the other. Prior to the collapse of the Popular Front in 1940,

Marxism played the most prominent part in the thinking of the Socialist leadership and rank and file. During this pre-war period, pro-Soviet feelings and in some instances even sympathy for the communist outlook was a major element. At that time there was little sympathy for Gandhi's point of view. During the war and especially at the time of independence, the Socialists increasingly made democratic socialism their ideological mast. Members of the Party grew critical of the Soviet Union as a result of events in both India and the Soviet Union: the anti-national behavior of the Communist Party of India, the increasing number of disturbing accounts on the Soviet dictatorship, etc. There was a growing acceptance, especially among the Socialist leaders, of democratic methods as a means of winning power and in general a growing appreciation of the meaning of a society based on democratic rights. These changes were already apparent at the Party's convention at Nasik in 1948. At the Party's 1949 convention, a new Party Constitution was approved which in effect abolished the revolutionary-type organization under which the Socialists had previously operated. Membership was open to all and collective affiliation of organizations was provided for, somewhat along the lines of the British Labour Party. As Jayaprakash expressed the new outlook of the Party: "Democratic socialism involves acceptance of democratic means, peaceful methods and constructive approach, in the attainment of our goal."[18]

Along with the acceptance of democratic socialism, the influence of Gandhian thought increased within the Party. This influence was greatest upon Jayaprakash Narayan, but it was shared in one way or another by the bulk of the Party. There was an increasing emphasis not only upon non-violence, but upon many of Gandhi's economic principles. Rammanohar Lohia, for example, who tried to reformulate some of Gandhi's notions for the Socialist Party, emphasized the need for a decentralized economy based on cottage industries and small machines which would use maximum labor and minimum capital.

[18] *Annual Conference of the Socialist Party, Patna, 1949* (Bombay: Socialist Party, 1949), p. 50.

Decentralization became a central notion in Indian Socialist ideology.

The various ideological shifts within the Socialist Party can most clearly be seen through the changes which have come about in Jayaprakash Narayan, perhaps the best known of the Socialist leaders. Prior to 1940, Jayaprakash was a confirmed Marxist sympathetic to Soviet communism. As a student in the United States in the 1920's he became a staunch communist. Long after other Socialist leaders had turned against the Communist Party of India in the Popular Front days, Jayaprakash refused to break with the Communists. But when he did break in 1940, the break was severe. When the Socialists held their convention at Patna in 1949, it was Jayaprakash as the General Secretary of the Party who was the most outspoken advocate of democratic socialism.

The influence of Gandhism on Jayaprakash grew after Gandhi's death, until by 1952 he spoke in Gandhian terms as frequently as he did in socialist terms. He stressed the need for Gandhian constructive work on the part of the Socialist members, and declared his support for the Bhoodan Yagna movement of Vinoba Bhave, which seeks to bring about the voluntary redistribution of land. The appeal of the Bhoodan movement for Jayaprakash basically involved a new estimate of "human nature" and its relationship to socialism. Jayaprakash felt that traditional socialism had overemphasized the role of institutional changes and underestimated the value of a "change of heart." The Bhoodan movement, he felt, could help to change people's attitudes toward property. Jayaprakash became increasingly skeptical of the ideals of an industrial society and of material "progress" and was increasingly enamored of the religious values professed by Gandhi and his disciple Vinoba Bhave. Finally, in 1954, Jayaprakash announced that he was withdrawing from active political work and was going to dedicate his life to Bhoodan and constructive activities. He resigned from the National Executive of the PSP and declared that he would not accept any position of responsibility in the Party. This did not, however, mean that he was breaking with the Party since he retained his membership.

The three ideological elements represented in the Praja Socialist Party—Marxism, democratic socialism, and Gandhism—are most clearly personified by three of its leaders. Before his death in February 1956, Acharya Narendra Deva was the leading spokesman for Marxism in the party, although his anti-communist feelings were well-known. Asoka Mehta is perhaps the most outspoken advocate of democratic socialism, and, as we have already noted, Jayaprakash is the most outspoken of the Gandhians.

Present ideological disagreements do not, however, concern these traditional outlooks but rather revolve around the question of the role of the PSP as an opposition party. A major question has been whether the Party ought to be an agitational party protesting against injustices and building up mass opposition to Congress and support for the Socialists, or whether the Party should emphasize constructive work and legislative activity, in opposition to Congress when necessary but with it in its nation-building activities. Although on the surface this difference in approach has centered around varying estimates of the Congress Party—one group, led by Rammanohar Lohia, stresses Socialist differences with Congress, while the other, led by Asoka Mehta, emphasizes their similarities—more basically these groups differ in their attitude toward legislative power and the parliamentary system. Lohia and the bulk of the Party rank and file, who support him, have a basic contempt not only for Congress but for legislative power itself. They are, furthermore, less committed to the electoral system and more eager to be militant than are Asoka Mehta and the bulk of the Party leadership. Lohia said in November 1953: "Nothing but a general revolution, a revolution of the mind as well as a revolution in politics, can save India. Sooner or later the PSP will have to consider if it should not take the nation through another struggle of suffering and ascent. If it considers this question while there is time it can justify its existence."[19]

These differences have never been clearly articulated in these terms, but they played a major part in the dispute over

[19] Rammanohar Lohia, "Need for an Electoral Adjustment," *Janata* (November 29, 1953), p. 8.

the Travancore-Cochin Ministry. Many of the Party rank and file resented the fact that the Socialists had won power by what seemed to them political calculations rather than as the result of some mass upheaval; there was also some vague feeling that legislation was not the means by which socialism could be brought about and that in any event the Travancore-Cochin Socialist Ministry had failed to bring about any revolutionary change in that state.

POLITICAL STRENGTH OF THE PRAJA SOCIALIST PARTY

A party's potentialities for winning political power need to be gauged in terms of both its electoral strength and appeals and its organizational strength. We shall deal with both of these briefly.

Electoral Strength

The Socialist Party in the 1952 general elections contested 1,799 seats for the state legislature and won 124, compared with 2,248 won by Congress, 147 by the Communists and allies, and 77 by the KMPP. The Socialists did best in Bihar, Orissa, Uttar Pradesh, and Vindhya Pradesh in the North and Hyderabad, Madras, and Travancore-Cochin in the South. The KMPP won most of its seats in two states, Madras and West Bengal, and a few in Mysore. After the merger of the Socialist Party and the KMPP in 1952, the new Praja Socialist Party emerged in six states as the major opposition party to Congress: Assam, Madhya Pradesh, Mysore, Saurashtra, Uttar Pradesh, and Vindhya Pradesh. After surveying the areas of Socialist electoral strength, several conclusions can be drawn:

1. The Praja Socialist Party is the most national of all the opposition parties in its appeal. While the Communist Party and the Jan Sangh are also recognized by the Election Commission as national parties, neither of these parties reaches into as many areas of India as does the PSP. The more than 17 million votes which the constituent elements in the present PSP received in the 1952 elections were scattered throughout the

country. In fact their wide distribution prevented the Socialist Party, the Kisan Mazdoor Praja Party, and the Subhasist Forward Bloc from winning legislative seats in proportion to their votes.

2. Although the Party has some appeal in nearly all sections of the country, its hold is greatest in the northern states stretching from Assam on the east to Saurashtra on the west. Interestingly enough, it is in some of these same areas that the appeal of Gandhi was greatest.

3. In the South a three-way fight has developed in a number of states among Congress, the Communists, and the Socialists. This has happened in Travancore-Cochin, Madras, Andhra, and Hyderabad. In each of these states the Socialists are the third party. If situations develop where no one party is capable of forming a government, the attitude of the Socialists toward coalitions and toward other parties may be crucial.

4. In other states the fight between national parties is confused by the existence of strong regional parties. In Orissa, Bihar, and Bombay, regional parties place second, in between Congress and the Socialists.[20]

5. In general the Socialist strength is greatest in politically stable states. In areas where communal parties have their greatest influence—Central India and the former princely states—the Socialists are weak. Likewise, where the Communists are a major force, as in South India, the Socialists are in a third position.

Where the Socialists are the major opposition party, it is virtually a straight fight between the Socialists and Congress. This suggests that the communal and Communist parties are as much an obstacle to the Socialists as they are to Congress. In the long run it appears that the weakening of communal and

[20] In Orissa the Ganatantra Parishad, a party formed by several rulers of the former princely states which now comprise Orissa, won 31 seats, compared with the Socialists' 10 and Congress's 67. In Bihar the Jharkhand Party, a tribal party, has 32 seats, compared with 24 for the PSP and 240 for Congress. And, finally, in Bombay, where Congress holds 269 seats, the Socialist's 9 are surpassed by the 14 seats of the Peasants and Workers Party, a Marxist left party and anti-Brahman overtones.

anti-democratic forces is essential to the growth of democratic socialism in India.

6. The results of the by-elections have generally shown that the individual parties which merged to form the Praja Socialist Party have been able to maintain their strength. In fact they increased the number of their seats in Parliament and the legislatures of Travancore-Cochin and Andhra during the special elections held in those states in February 1954 and February 1955, although the popular vote of the PSP remained relatively constant.

Organizational Strength

One of the major organizational problems of the Socialist Party since it was formed in 1934 and now a major problem for the Praja Socialist Party has been the defection of party leaders. Minoo Masani, Sampurnanand (now Chief Minister of U.P.), Achyut Patwardhan, and Kamaladevi Chattopadhyaya are among the early leaders of the movement who subsequently resigned either from the Party or from positions of responsibility in the Party. A number of defections occurred in the 1930's when the Socialists continued their Popular Front program with the Communists. And still more defections occurred when the Socialists broke from Congress in 1948. Shortly after, a pro-Communist section of the Party led by Mrs. Aruna Asaf Ali broke away to form the Left Socialist Party. This soon merged with the Communist Party. There were, however, surprisingly few defections when the merger of the Socialist Party and the KMPP took place.

Since the creation of the Praja Socialist Party, an incident of major importance has been the defection of Prakasam, the leader of the PSP in Andhra State. Prakasam accepted an invitation from the Congress Party to become Chief Minister of Andhra in violation of the decision of the PSP National Executive. Prakasam then resigned from the Party and took with him a number of his followers, thereby causing a split in the state's Party organization.

The PSP has been further disrupted by a number of disputes inside the Party which we have mentioned. In particular, confusion over the Party's role as an opposition party and its relations with other groups has badly hurt the morale of the Party rank and file. Two special conventions of the Party were held to resolve some of the disputes—one at Betul (in Madhya Pradesh) in June 1953 and another at Nagpur (also in Madhya Pradesh) in November 1954—but neither of these prevented the Lohia group from breaking with the PSP at the end of 1955.

Party leaders have also complained of widespread indiscipline inside the Party. This was a major theme in the report of the General Secretary at the first PSP conference in December 1953 and again in the resignation speech of Chairman Kripalani at the Nagpur conference. According to the General Secretary, "there were occasions when work [of the National Executive] had to wait because there was no quorum," when members publicly made known their own points of view even before the National Executive had the opportunity to discuss such questions, and when Party journals freely printed articles criticizing directives of the National Executive.[21] "Resistance to discipline has adversely affected the organizational ties between the centre and the state units. In many states . . . the parliamentary section instead of working as a limb of the party is working as if it was an independent organization. . . . The parliamentary section thus going its own way, the other sections, like the labour section, the students' section, the peasant section very naturally tend to follow in its footsteps, with the result that the provincial offices, bereft of all contacts, initiative and authority are reduced to the status of mere postoffices."[22]

But in spite of these organizational difficulties, the membership of the Party has increased considerably since independence. From a party membership of 12,360 (and another 6,200 on probation) in 1949 before the Constitution was changed to open membership and to allow group affiliations, the membership jumped to 151,972 in 1950 and then to 295,554 in 1951.[23] After

---

[21] N. G. Goray, *Report Presented to the First Conference of the Praja Socialist Party* (Bombay: Praja Socialist Party, 1953), p. 10.

[22] *Ibid.*, p. 11.

[23] Figures from "Organizational Report," *Report of the Seventh Annual Conference of the Socialist Party* (Patna, 1949), p. 161, and *Concerning Organization* (Bombay: issued by the Central Office, Socialist Party, 1952).

the widespread dissension in the Party during 1954 and 1955, however, membership dropped to 189,000. According to the report of the General Secretary to the PSP national convention in December 1955, there had been a decrease of 71,000.[24] Lohia's defection had apparently led to the exodus of a substantial number of Party members.

The Socialists have a considerable hold in the trade union movement. The Hind Mazdoor Subha, the second largest national trade union federation, is sponsored by the PSP. According to a statement in 1953 by the Deputy Labor Minister,[25] the HMS had 804,000 members, compared with 1,548,000 in the Congress-sponsored Indian National Trade Union Congress, 758,000 in the Communist-sponsored All India Trade Union Congress, and 384,000 in the Marxist-leftist United Trades Union Congress.

On the peasant front, the Socialist-sponsored Kisan Panchayat has some influence, but in general the level of Socialist organization among the peasantry does not equal that among the working class. However, the Socialists have been active in a number of peasant *satyagrahas* (civil disobedience movements) in Bombay and Uttar Pradesh, which presumably have strengthened their hold in those areas. In theory, the Socialists are dedicated to a dual policy of constructive and agitational work among the peasants, but neither in the organizational reports of the PSP's General Secretaries nor in the election results has there been an indication of any overwhelming successes among the peasantry.

A final word might be said about the Socialist approach to organizational questions. The PSP, like other leftist parties, has been acutely aware of the need for developing a strong and efficient party organization.[26] The Socialists, especially the Party leaders, have been very much aware of the fact that democratic

[24] *Statesman*, December 28, 1955.

[25] Quoted by Oscar Ornati, "Indian Trade Unions since Independence," *Far Eastern Survey*, XXII (August 1954), p. 1.

[26] As an aside, it might be mentioned here that concern for organizational questions does not play such a major role among the Hindu communal parties.

socialism, as distinct from Marxist-Leninist socialism, involves not only a different attitude as to the kind of society envisaged, but a different theory of methods and organization as well.

Prior to 1949, before the Socialists had fully accepted democratic socialism, the Socialist Party was organized more or less along revolutionary lines, with a small but relatively disciplined organization. With the Socialist shift in ideology came a change in the kind of party organization. This has obviously raised new problems, especially with regard to party discipline, that have not yet been solved. The Socialists are torn between the need for greater discipline, which would make the Party more unified and presumably more effective, and the need for maintaining a maximum of freedom inside the Party and a variety of points of view. Although the Party has outlined rules for the conduct of its members which aim to balance democracy with discipline,[27] in practice these rules have not always been followed.

Another question that has been raised in the PSP and not settled—and it is a major question in the Congress Party as well—deals with precisely what role the Party organization itself can play in nation-building activities. Although it is a widely accepted notion in Western democratic theory that the party organization must be subordinate to the elected parliamentary representatives in the making of government decisions, it may still be possible for the party organization to serve a useful function in constructive work beyond the narrowly political sphere. Shortly before his death Gandhi proposed that the Congress Party be reorganized as a social service organization but this was rejected by the Congress High Command, although Congress leaders have in principle felt that Party workers ought to be involved in village and city constructive activities. Jayaprakash Narayan, Asoka Mehta, and other Socialist leaders have urged that their Party increasingly turn toward constructive activities, but no large-scale program along these lines has been developed.

[27] See, for example, "Bangalore Rules Regarding Code of Conduct," in *Concerning Organization, op.cit.,* pp. 17-18.

3. The Socialist Break from Congress

How does a revolutionary organization under a colonial regime adapt itself to the position of a political party functioning within the rules of an independent democracy? Before independence, the Congress Socialist Party had operated as an organized group within the Indian National Congress; its enemy was the British, and its organization, its ideology, and its relations with Congress centered around the removal of this enemy from Indian life. On August 15, 1947 the enemy was gone. The first and most basic problem of the Socialists at the time of independence was the question of their relations with the Indian National Congress. Upon this depended their organizational form, the kind of techniques they employed, and even the ideology they propagated.

This chapter deals with relations between the Socialists and Congress in the months shortly before and after independence, which led to a decisive break between the two parties. In order to understand why the Socialists left Congress one must first understand what their formal relationship to Congress had been.

The Congress Socialist Party had been formed in 1934. Its leaders felt that they could be most effective as an organized group within Congress. Rather than operate as individuals within Congress or establish a separate party, they organized as a party within a party with their own machinery, discipline, and thesis.

The Socialist decision to organize within Congress meant that no one could become a member of the Congress Socialist Party without first becoming a member of the Indian National Congress. It also meant that Congress Socialists could take an active part in Congress affairs, present their point of view to other Congressmen, take part in Congress national conventions, and even become Congress office bearers.[1]

[1] Several Congress Socialists became members of the All India Congress Committee and even of the Congress Working Committee, the highest body in Congress.

SOCIALIST-CONGRESS DIFFERENCES

From the time of its formation, the Congress Socialist Party had major differences with the National Congress. First, the Socialists wanted to make Marxian socialism as well as independence India's goal, and, second, they objected to the Gandhian emphasis on non-violence as the technique for winning freedom. More specifically, the Socialists opposed the Congress's decision to take part in the 1936-1937 elections under British rule, and they opposed the Congress's decision to form governments in those provinces where it had won a majority of provincial Assembly seats. Before the war they supported the demand by Subhas Chandra Bose that an immediate struggle be launched against the British, and although during the war they accepted the Congress-sponsored Quit India movement, they advocated methods of their own which were not acceptable to the dominant Congress leadership.

When the Congress leaders and the Congress Socialists returned to public life in 1945, some coming out of jail and others coming from the underground, the earlier struggles between the Socialists and the Congress leadership continued and intensified. Let us first see what some of their differences were, and then we shall examine the factors which made these differences so intense as to result in an organizational break between the Socialists and Congress.

Post-war differences with Congress centered primarily around the strategy to be pursued toward the British. The Congress leadership was willing to negotiate with the British Cabinet Mission sent to India by the Labour government, but the Socialists were not. Only a week after his release from jail in April 1946, Jayaprakash Narayan, the leader of the Congress Socialists, declared: "I refuse to accept that the Cabinet Mission now in Delhi is out to concede full Independence to India. It is just possible that the negotiations going on in Delhi may break at any moment at any stage."[2]

In early July when the All India Congress Committee met

[2] *Amrita Bazar Patrika,* April 23, 1946.

in Bombay to ratify the Congress Working Committee resolution accepting the Cabinet Mission's proposals, the opposition was led by Jayaprakash Narayan, who said: "The Quit India Movement of 1942 had been launched to rid India of British imperial power, but that struggle did not achieve its end though it released new forces which have taken the country far toward its goal. The question today before the country was not whether to accept the so-called Constituent Assembly scheme sponsored by British imperialism, but how to utilize the new forces to drive the British out of India."[3] Although Jayaprakash had the support of the left wing, the vote to endorse the Congress Working Committee's decision to enter the Constituent Assembly was 204 to 51.

The attitude of the Congress Socialists and the left wing was thus quite different from that of the Congress leadership. Nehru, Patel, and the other Congress leaders believed that the Labour government sincerely intended to transfer power, and that the British Cabinet Mission had been sent for this purpose. While there were elements in the proposals with which they were dissatisfied, the sincerity of the British was on the whole not doubted. For this reason Congress leaders decided to take part in the elections to the Constituent Assembly and were prepared to form an interim government prior to the actual transference of power. The Socialists believed, in accordance with traditional Marxist theory, that power would not and could not be transferred by the will of the British, that the negotiations that were now going on were the product of the mass action of the '42 movement (discussed below), and that the British were stalling and had no intention of transferring power peacefully. Under these circumstances the Socialists considered it necessary to urge the masses to prepare for a mass struggle. As late as December 1946 Jayaprakash, speaking at Benaras, proposed a program for revolution in a few months if the Constitution framed by the Constituent Assembly was not accepted by the British government.[4] Jayaprakash apparently believed that this would happen.

---

[3] *Hindu*, July 8, 1946.
[4] *Leader*, December 19, 1946.

Differences with the Congress Party continued to grow in the following months. The Socialists not only refused to take part in the Constituent Assembly, but also refused to accept the Mountbatten Plan for the partition of India. At the All India Congress Committee debate over the partition proposal in June 1947, the Socialists and leftist members strongly expressed their opposition, while Nehru, Pant, and Patel gave their support. The final vote was 157 to 20.[5]

Still other issues divided the Socialists from the Congress Party. Differences had developed over economic policy. The specific issues on which such differences existed were never publicly debated, except that the Socialists expressed their opposition to the Congress proposal for compulsory arbitration between management and labor. In general, however, it was well known that the Socialists looked upon private industry less kindly than did the Congress leadership. The Socialists declared that complete *swaraj* (freedom) meant not only the attainment of independence from the British, but the development of a socialist state. A large section of the Congress Party could not agree with this point of view.

The issues of policy, then, which divided the Congress Socialists from their parent organization were, first, differences over the manner in which independence could be achieved, and, second, differences in their conception of the future Indian state. Although these differences grew and became more intense between 1946 and 1948, it is important to note that they were essentially the same as those which the Congress Socialists had had with the Congress Party since 1934. As a matter of fact, the differences between 1938 and 1940 which resulted in the withdrawal from Congress of Subhas Chandra Bose and a substantial portion of the left wing were perhaps as intense as, if not more intense than, those existing from 1946 to 1948. Furthermore, by 1948 when the split between the two organizations finally oc-

[5] *Pioneer*, June 16, 1947. Although the Socialists spoke against the partition plan, when the voting occurred they decided to abstain since they felt that no purpose would be served at that stage by voting against the resolution.

curred, independence had already been achieved and differences over tactics and strategy were no longer an issue.

SOCIALIST-CONGRESS LINKS

The variable, "differences in ideology and issues," between Congress and the Socialists inside Congress was more or less constant between 1934 and 1948. What were the links, then, which bound the Socialists to Congress during this period?

First, when the Socialists decided to organize within rather than outside Congress, they looked upon Congress as the main organization of the nationalist movement, an organization with a long history of struggle against the British.

Second, the Socialists recognized that Congress was not only the prime organization working for independence, but also the only mass organization. No other organization could hope to rival Congress in building mass support, and if another organization were established it might severely injure the national anti-imperialist movement, a movement which was faced on the one hand with the challenge of British might and on the other with the communalism of the Muslim League.

Third, and this should not be underestimated, was the personal appeal of Gandhi. Although many of the Socialists rejected Gandhi's philosophy of non-violence and what to them appeared to be a "feudal" economic outlook, they were attracted to him as a personality, and as a man who commanded confidence and support from the masses. While one might disagree with Gandhi, no one could question his sincerity, his willingness to listen to various points of view, and his efforts to arrive at compromises which would maintain the unity of the national movement.

Fourth, perhaps most crucial of all, was the tolerance of the Congress for various points of view, and a willingness to allow those who held differing points of view to organize themselves within the Party. Such organized groups were a characteristic feature of Congress. Not only were the Socialists, the Communists, Marxist leftists, and others allowed to organize their own parties within the Party, with their own programs, leadership, party conventions, etc., but they were given complete freedom of expression and permitted even to have their spokesmen participate as office bearers of the Congress. This toleration for organized parties within Congress, incidentally, declined considerably after independence was achieved.

Fifth, once having become members of Congress, the Congress Socialists soon developed a dual allegiance, first to their own leaders and organization, and second to the Congress Party and its leaders. Not only Gandhi, but other leaders of Congress, such as Sarojini Naidu, Jawaharlal Nehru, and Maulana Azad, were respected by many Socialists.

What were the factors which led to the breakdown of these links? They were several: the failure of the younger Congress Socialists who joined at the time of the '42 movement to develop loyalties toward the parent Congress Party; the threat to the Socialists from Congress activity in the trade unions; the campaign of the Congress leadership to force the dissolution of the Congress Socialist Party; the growing strain in relations between Gandhi and the Congress and the subsequent death of Gandhi; the enormous self-confidence of the Socialists as a result of the popularity which grew out of their participation in the '42 movement; and, finally, the achievement of independence, which eliminated the British threat that had helped to unify the nationalist movement. Let us examine some of these factors in detail.

THE '42ERS: THE BREAKDOWN IN LOYALTIES

When the Quit India movement was launched, its leadership soon fell largely into the hands of the Socialists, partly because the top Congress leadership had been hastily incarcerated by the British and partly because the Congressmen who had taken part in the civil disobedience movements of the '20's and '30's were now too old for active participation in a militant movement. Furthermore, while the Congress leadership reluctantly approved of the civil disobedience program after the failure of negotiations with the British, the Socialists and the non-communist left enthusiastically welcomed it.[6] The Socialists were therefore psychologically prepared to lead the struggle and thereby attracted younger militant elements from schools and colleges throughout the country.

While working in the name of Congress, many of the Socialists, especially the younger and newer members, developed their own techniques. While one wing of the Socialists claimed to stress Gandhian techniques, others concentrated on underground activity and sabotage, as opposed to the traditional Gandhian methods of *satyagraha* (non-violent civil disobedience) and negotiations. "The essence of the underground," wrote the Socialist leader Asoka Mehta, "lies in building up parallel authority . . . to deny and destroy the authority of the occupying enemy and to that end project its own power."[7] With the disruption of the Congress organization and the arrest of most of the Congress leadership during the war, the Socialist-dominated underground paralleled not only British authority, *but also the Congress organization*. This meant first of all that the younger newcomers had rejected the efficacy of Gandhism and non-violence, and, secondly, that the Socialists had developed confidence in their own ability to win mass support. While all sections of the Congress Socialist Party emphasized their loyalty to Congress during the war, the consequence of the '42 movement and the creation of an underground organization which virtually operated outside the Congress Party structure was the development of a new group of Socialists whose feeling of loyalty to the parent Congress body was not as strong as that of the older Socialists who had joined the CSP in the 1930's.

With the close of the war, the Socialists, confident of their new strength, called for a reorganization of Congress that would organizationally absorb those who had joined the '42 movement.

But the Congress Party failed to do this to the satisfaction of the Socialists. Jayaprakash complained that only here and there had those who had participated in the '42 movement been placed

---

[6] One major exception was M. N. Roy's non-communist socialist group, which did support the war.

[7] Asoka Mehta, "The Underground," *Janata*, I (February 10, 1946), p. 2.

on Congress Committees. Thus the failure of Congress to accord recognition to the newcomers inevitably led to conflict. In Bihar, Orissa, Bombay, and other states where the Socialists were strong, conflicts soon developed between the Socialist rank and file and the Congress state leadership.

BOMBAY AND THE TRADE UNION QUESTION

The most serious point of conflict between the Socialists and orthodox Congressmen occurred in the city of Bombay in 1947. It was in fact the Bombay Socialists, led by Asoka Mehta, who spearheaded the drive to bring about the secession of the Socialists from the Congress.[8]

For many years the Socialists had been highly active in the city of Bombay. Their early national leaders, Minoo Masani (who had been mayor of Bombay), Asoka Mehta, Achyut Patwardhan, and Aruna Asaf Ali, were all active in Bombay. As one of the biggest industrial centers in India, Bombay with its large working class has been a major source of strength for the Congress Socialists. Because of the city's importance the national office of the Congress Socialist Party was established there. Asoka Mehta, the best-known trade unionist in the Party, worked and lived in the city and was the leader of the Socialists there.

[8] Bombay State is actually made up of three linguistic areas or provinces, Maharashtra, Gujerat, and Kanara, each with its own Pradesh Congress Committee. The city of Bombay, being a meeting place for all three linguistic groups, has a Congress Committee of its own, led by S. K. Patil, well known as the "strong man" of the city's politics.

With regard to the word province, it should be pointed out that it has two meanings. Before independence those parts of India which were under direct British control, and after independence but prior to the 1950 Constitution those parts which had been under such control, were referred to as provinces; and in both periods those parts which were under the Indian princes were called states. After 1950 the princely states were grouped together into larger states, and then both the old provinces and the new states were referred to as states. For the sake of simplicity, the word state has usually been used in this work, even when we are speaking of non-princely areas before 1950.

Province is also often used in India, as it is in the first paragraph of this footnote, to refer to a linguistic area.

To add to the confusion, the word *pradesh* is generally translated as province or state, although the Pradesh Congress Committees do not always coincide with state boundaries, e.g. in the case of the PCC of Maharashtra or of Bombay (city).

It was primarily over the trade union question that the conflict grew so intense in Bombay. Until 1947 the trade union movement had been united in the All India Trade Union Congress
(AITUC), but in that year, as a result of Communist domination
of the AITUC, the Congress Party decided to withdraw its support and form its own trade union organization. The movement
on the part of Congress for the formation of a new trade union
organization was particularly active in Bombay, where Gulzarilal
Nanda, Minister of Labor and Housing of Bombay State and
Secretary of the Hindustan Mazdoor Sevak Sangh (a Congress-
sponsored workers' organization), urged Congress trade unionists
to break away from the Communist-dominated AITUC. Nanda
had the active support of S. K. Patil, the leader of the Congress
Party in the city of Bombay. He argued that the Hindustan Mazdoor Sevak Sangh should be the medium through which the
Congress could work. In reply to Nanda, Asoka Mehta admitted
that the AITUC was Communist-dominated, but he opposed
the creation of a new organization since, as he said, "the AITUC
has built up a considerable loyalty in the working classes." He
concluded that it would be better to make certain that the
AITUC becomes the "real organ of the working class by passing
Government legislation that would require trade unions to submit to Government audits, to hold regular elections under impartial tribunals and so on than to create a new organization."[9]

In May 1947, however, Congress decided to withdraw from
the AITUC and to form its own trade union organization called
the Indian National Trade Union Congress (INTUC). The
fight for control of the labor movement was now in full swing.
For many years nearly all the political parties—Communists,
Congress, Socialists, and left Marxists—had operated within the
AITUC. For the most part, it had been the Socialists among the
Congressmen (apart from the Communists) who had been particularly active on the trade union front. The Socialists generally
looked upon the trade union front as their domain, and viewed
Congress work in this area with suspicion.

[9] Asoka Mehta and Rohit Dave, "Congress in Crisis—New Problems, New
Methods," *Janata*, ii (May 4, 1947), p. 7.

With the formation of the INTUC, Asoka Mehta, who in large measure formulated the trade union policy of the Socialist Party, argued that inasmuch as Congress had withdrawn from the AITUC it was no longer possible for Socialists to support that body, since by themselves it would not be possible to wrest control from the Communists. As for the INTUC, Mehta rejected Socialist participation on the ground that "the keystone of the arch of the INTUC is arbitration in industrial disputes . . . I am a believer in arbitration in industrial disputes. But I cannot accept it as the sheet anchor of trade unionism."[10] Mehta further declared that "so long as the Congress remains what it is, there must inevitably develop an estrangement between it and the organised working class. The deadlock will be avoided either by the Congress becoming in place of the Indian National Congress—the Indian Socialist Congress, or the TUC forfeiting its independence and integrity. The Socialists should therefore keep away from both the organisations and build up a workers' movement that will have in it the vitality and the vision to realize a powerful Socialist Party capable of reshaping, along democratic lines, the destinies of Free India."[11]

Soon after, the Socialist Party National Executive decided to withdraw from the AITUC and, instead of joining the INTUC, to build a trade union movement apart from both organizations. The National Executive stressed the need for developing a trade union movement impregnated with democratic socialist ideas as necessary for the establishment of a democratic socialist society.

In order to rally the masses around the Congress Socialists and thus gain control of the Congress party machinery, the Socialist leadership had, since the end of the war, stressed the importance of mass organization.[12] The Socialist emphasis was not to be on parliamentary work but on constructive work and trade union and peasant organization. Only in this way, they felt, could the Congress Socialist Party make effective use of the popularity it

10 Asoka Mehta, "Objectives of Labour—Can the INTUC Help to Achieve Them," *Janata*, II (May 25, 1947), p. 7.

11 *Ibid.*, p. 7.

12 Jayaprakash Narayan, "To All Fighters for Freedom," *Janata*, I (July 28, 1946), p. 6.

had won during the '42 movement, and express that strength by organized power within the Congress Party.

The work of the Congress Party on the trade union front thus came as a serious blow to the Congress Socialists, especially in the city of Bombay, where the Socialists' strength largely grew out of their trade union following. Relations grew so strained that in January 1948 the Socialists resigned from the city's Pradesh Congress Committee (PCC) and decided to oppose Congress in the municipal elections. They decided, however, to continue as members of Congress in the city, pending a decision of the Socialist Party national conference in February. This decision to compete against Congress in the municipal elections was strongly and bitterly denounced by Sardar Patel, then the Deputy Prime Minister, and by S. K. Patil, the Bombay Congress leader. Toward the end of January the Executive Committee of the city's Pradesh Congress Committee decided to expel seventeen Congress Socialists for three years. They were cast out for indiscipline, that is, for standing in the municipal elections without the approval of the Bombay PCC.[13] For all intents and purposes, the break between the Socialists and the Congress Party in the city of Bombay was by this time complete.

CONGRESS AGAINST THE SOCIALISTS

We have already described how, after 1946, the Socialists rejected the main line of the Congress Party policy toward the British Cabinet Mission and then toward the Mountbatten Plan and how in 1947 the Socialists rejected the Congress decision to break from the AITUC and create their own trade union organization. Throughout these two years both the Socialists and the Congressmen were involved in efforts either to stabilize or to terminate their relationship within the Congress. From 1946 to 1948 a complicated series of maneuvers took place on the part of the leadership of both parties in which the Socialist minority was at a great disadvantage. In order to understand what the maneuvers involved and why the Socialists were a minority in the organization, we must first briefly discuss the conflict between

[13] *Nation*, January 23, 1948.

the Socialists and the Party organization during the previous decade.

The Socialists, ever since the formation of the Congress Socialist Party in 1934, had sought to influence Congress policy in two respects: the way in which the national struggle should be carried on and future economic policy. These attempts at influencing the Party necessarily involved a conflict with the dominant conservative leadership, which accepted Gandhi's principles of non-violence and on economic questions rejected the socialist approach. Because of this the Socialists along with the left wing sought to constitute themselves as a force within Congress which would be ultimately capable of changing Congress policy, and presumably of assuming positions of power and leadership in the national movement. These efforts, which were relentless throughout and after the war, proved dismal failures, failures which resulted primarily from three major events.

The first involved the respective attitudes of the Socialists and Congressmen toward the 1936 elections. The Socialists, on the one hand, first opposed Congress participation in the elections and then objected to the decision of Congress to take office in the provinces. The Congress leadership, on the other hand, after a long and arduous debate agreed both to participate in the elections and to form Congress Ministries in those states where Congress held a clear majority in the legislature. The CSP-sponsored "anti-ministry" movement had failed. In seven provinces Congress assumed office. Having gained power, its prestige and influence increased. As a result the conservative leadership further strengthened its control of the Congress organizational machinery.

But in the years that followed, from 1938 to 1940, as a result of the war situation, the left wing demand for the launching of an immediate struggle won considerable support. The growth of the left wing culminated in the triumphant election of Subhas Bose as Congress President in 1939 over the objections of Gandhi. In conflict with Gandhi, Bose subsequently left Congress. But by their unwillingness to join Bose in his move to leave Congress, the Socialists by 1940 had lost control and influence within the left wing. Having broken with Bose and the left, the Socialists found themselves in a weak position inside Congress. Had the entire left wing remained in Congress, it might have been possible to dislodge the conservative leadership. But in large measure the break was unavoidably precipitated by the passage of the famous Pant Resolution at the 1939 Congress convention. This resolution required that the Congress President (Bose) appoint his powerful working committee after consultation with Gandhi. Gandhi's refusal to work with Bose and his endorsement of the conservative leadership soon forced Bose and a sizable section of the left wing to leave Congress. The Socialists, however, were not prepared to leave the main organization of the national movement.

With the exodus of the left wing and the refusal of the Socialists to leave Congress with Bose, the Socialists were left without strength either among the left wing or in the Congress Party. But once again the Socialists rebuilt themselves, this time as a result of the war and the "Quit India" resolution of the Congress. Their leadership in the anti-British underground and the heroic acts performed by Jayaprakash Narayan and other Socialists during that struggle gave them considerable mass strength at the close of the war. But again the Socialists were badly weakened, this time by their wrong appraisal of the intentions of the Cabinet Mission. Had the Cabinet Mission failed and a mass struggle begun at this time, the Socialists might have come to dominate the national movement, but the achievement of independence through negotiations seriously hurt the Socialists and conversely strengthened the conservative Congress leadership. While the Socialists called for a militant struggle which never came, the conservative leadership took part in the 1946 elections, gained control of the Constituent Assembly, and formed the interim government. Political power—and all that implies—had fallen into the hands of the Congress Party leadership, while the Socialists, by refusing to enter the Constituent Assembly, the interim government, or the provincial governments, shared none of that power or the prestige which ultimately accompanied it.

Thus the reluctance of the Socialists to participate in the Congress provincial Ministries; their ambivalence in the struggle between Bose and Congress, which resulted in their failure to win strength either inside Congress or outside in the left wing; and ultimately, most crucial of all, their refusal to take part in the 1946 elections, join the Constituent Assembly, and share power— all left the Socialists in a weak minority position inside Congress from 1946 onward and the conservative leadership in firm control of the Party organization.

With this background in mind one can understand why the Socialists were in a minority in their conflict with Congress from 1946 to 1948. What had changed after 1946 in the relationship between the two groups was neither their differences nor the fact that the Socialists were a minority, but rather the level of tolerance of the Congress leadership, or at least a large and influential section of the leadership, which now wanted the Congress Socialist Party either to disband, with its members merging into the Congress organization, or to get out.

An attempt was made in 1946 to place a substantial number of Congress Socialists on Acharya Kripalani's Working Committee. At the Meerut convention, where Kripalani had been elected Congress President following Nehru's resignation to become the Prime Minister of the interim government, discussions were held between Jayaprakash Narayan and a number of Congressmen, including both Sardar Patel and Kripalani. Jayaprakash had hoped that the General Secretary of the Congress would be a Congress Socialist, and that several people whose names he proposed would be included on the Working Committee. But he was considerably disappointed later upon seeing the list of names for the Congress Working Committee, and he was especially unhappy that Shankar Rao Deo, rather than a Congress Socialist, was selected as General Secretary. Jayaprakash felt that this was a rejection on the part of the Congress leadership of Socialist cooperation. Shortly after, he submitted his own resignation from the Working Committee.

The attacks against the Socialists by the conservative Congressmen were led by Sardar Patel.[14] Precisely what Patel's motives were in attempting to bring about the dissolution of the Congress Socialist Party as an organized group inside Congress, it is difficult to say. The fact is that organized groups had existed in Congress for some time. If Patel genuinely felt that with independence there was no longer any room for such organized groups, this happily coincided with his own opposition to the Socialists, who were then the only organized group within Congress.

Patel made quite clear that he had fundamental ideological disagreements with the Socialists. He wrote: "It is far from me to suggest that there is no room for implementation of social or economic theories in this country. My only concern is to ensure that before this country becomes a field of economic or social experiments its foundations are well and truly laid and economic and social structure is sufficiently strong to withstand the stress of those experiments. If we fail to consolidate the country or to exploit its industrial potentials by pooling all available resources, i.e. those of the state and private enterprise—disaster undoubtedly faces the country so that neither socialism nor any other ism would find any healthy growth."[15]

What is important in understanding Patel's role in forcing the Socialists out of Congress is not that he had differences with them—for such differences he had had for many years—but that he now felt that the Socialists either had to disband their organization within Congress or get out. What is also important is that the Socialists keenly felt that Patel and the Congress leadership were systematically attempting to push them out of the Party. Ultimately the Congress Party did take steps to make the Socialist position inside Congress untenable.

The Congress leadership first demanded of the Socialists that,

[14] Sardar Patel had been very influential in selecting the Working Committee and the General Secretary in 1946 when Kripalani was President. Kripalani later made quite clear that he had had little voice in selecting his own Working Committee. While Kripalani had his differences with the Socialists, he was also at odds with Patel. See Chapter 4 below on KMPP-Congress split.

[15] *Nation*, June 27, 1948.

considering their differences with Congress, they drop "Congress" from their name so as not to exploit the title. The Socialists agreed to do this at the Cawnpore conference of the Congress Socialist Party in early 1947.[16] And at the same convention it was decided to open the Party to non-Congressmen. This was decided on the grounds that the Socialist Party could then admit members from the princely states, who were not allowed to join the Congress Party because the Congress Constitution did not yet recognize branches in those states.[17]

After the Cawnpore convention of the Socialist Party, the Congress campaign to get the Socialists out intensified. A committee of Congress had been meeting for some time to consider amending the Congress constitution to prohibit organized groups within the Party. In the latter part of February, shortly after the assassination of Gandhi, the All India Congress Committee voted in favor of adding a clause to the Congress Constitution barring membership in the Congress to those who are members of political parties having separate creeds and constitutions.

The Congress ruling severed the remaining links with the Socialists and, at the Socialist Party Convention at Nasik in March 1948, the Socialists decided to dissolve their connections with Congress. But this decision was made only after considerable effort on the part of a group of both Congress and Socialist leaders to heal the breach between the opposing sections of both parties. Gandhi, particularly, took steps, before the Congress ruling was passed, to keep the Congress sections together. As one Socialist wrote: "A few leaders of the Socialist Party met Gandhiji. He was of the opinion that time was not ripe for Socialists to leave Congress. He wished that for some time the Congress should carry on with the cooperation of all sections and face the difficult problems of the country. . . . He believed that in the existing conditions cooperation of the Socialists with the Congress was essential."[18]

[16] "Socialist Party New Orientation," *Janata*, II (March 9, 1947), p. 1.
[17] *Ibid.*, p. 2.
[18] Acharya Narendra Deva, "Congress and the Social Change," *Janata*, VIII (August 30, 1953), p. 5.

From 1946 until his death in early 1948, Gandhi made considerable effort to keep the Socialists within the Congress. When Acharya Kripalani resigned as Congress President in 1946, Gandhi proposed to the Working Committee that Jayaprakash Narayan be elected to replace him. When the Working Committee rejected this, Acharya Narendra Deva's name was proposed, but he too was turned down, and Sardar Patel's influence prevailed as opposed to Gandhi and Nehru.

GANDHI AND THE SOCIALISTS

No examination of the factors and events leading up to the Socialist break from Congress can be complete without further mention of Gandhi's relationship with the Socialists. Over the years Gandhi has been variously characterized as an "economic reactionary with a feudal outlook," a spokesman for the "bourgeoisie," a "socialist," and even as a "pro-communist." It is not our intent here to explore Gandhi's political personality, as fascinating as that might be, but to point up his role in keeping the Socialists within Congress.

It was Gandhi more than any other man in the Congress who sought to keep the Socialists inside the national movement. It was his request that a Socialist—Acharya Narendra Deva or Jayaprakash Narayan—be made Congress President in 1946. And it was he who had frequent consultations with both Socialist and Congress leaders. Gandhi and the Socialists were particularly drawn together as a result of the partition of India, which they both deeply regretted. Neither Gandhi nor the Socialists observed Independence Day as a day of celebration. Again, Gandhi and the Socialists were drawn together by their agreement on the future of Congress. Gandhi submitted to the Congress Working Committee a draft constitution (which was completed on the day of his assassination), in which he urged that the Congress be disbanded as a political party and be made instead a "Lok Sevak Sangh" or social service constructive working organization. This proposal for the dissolution of Congress as a party was eagerly welcomed by the Socialists.

But the relationship between Gandhi and the Socialists extended beyond their agreement on these specific issues. As Acharya Kripalani wrote some years later: ". . . Gandhiji had great affection for the young leaders of the Socialist Party of India and in many subtle and psychological ways he affected their views and their opinions about the essentials of his basic principles and philosophy of life and the many schemes of reconstruction which he placed before the country. It is no wonder, therefore, that though the Socialist leaders have perhaps slender faith in the economic value of the 'charka' [spinning wheel], they continue to wear khadi [homespun cotton cloth], while the younger members of the party who never came in contact with Gandhiji are indifferent to it. The older members, however, recognise the value of khadi as a mark of identification with the masses of India."[19] Gandhi's attitude toward the Socialist leadership was further explained by Kripalani when he wrote: "Gandhiji expected the young socialist leaders who had come in close contact with him to be the second line of leadership, when we of the Gandhian age were too old to bear the strenuous burdens of the freedom fight which was not expected to end so suddenly and prosaically. . . . He gave expression to these ideas often."[20]

Among the older Socialists—especially Acharya Narendra Deva and Jayaprakash Narayan—Gandhi's personal influence was a major factor in keeping them in Congress. But among the younger members who joined during the '42 movement, Gandhi's influence was not so great. In spite of Gandhi's efforts, the attempts at reconciliation failed, and the pressures to withdraw grew. With the passage of the amendment to the Congress Constitution (over Gandhi's objections), even the most reluctant members of the Socialist Party agreed to leave. A day before Gandhi's assassination in late January 1948, Jayaprakash told him of their intention to leave. Gandhi said he was sorry and thought that it would be a difficult task for them, but made no effort at that late date to prevent them from carrying through

[19] Acharya J. B. Kripalani, "The Merger," *Vigil*, III (October 4, 1952), p. 6.
[20] *Ibid.*, p. 6.

their decision.[21] Gandhi's death dissolved whatever emotional barrier to a break might have remained.

THE SOCIALIST ATTITUDE

While an influential section of Congress sought to get the Socialists out, a large section of the Congress Socialist Party was eager to leave. There can be little doubt that the bulk of the Socialist rank and file, especially those who came in during the '42 movement, wanted an independent party.[22] Its noisiest spokesman was Mrs. Aruna Asaf Ali, a member of the Congress Socialist National Executive but a newcomer to the Party. It was she, along with Achyut Patwardhan, who led the rank and file in their opposition to the Cabinet Mission and the Constituent Assembly.[23] She wrote a series of articles in *Janata*, the official Socialist organ, urging a break with Congress. When the Congress Constitution was amended to bar organized groups, she welcomed it and urged the Socialists to leave.[24]

In Bombay, rank-and-file feeling toward the Congress was especially bitter, as we have already noted, over the Congress trade union policy. In other states too, conflict between the rank and file of the Socialists and the Congress leadership was intense. Frequent rank-and-file letters and articles in *Janata* described discriminatory practices on the local level.

Large-scale opposition inside the Congress Socialist Party to a break came only from the state of Uttar Pradesh. There, Hariharnath Shastri, a member of the National Executive, a former

[21] From an interview by the author with Jayaprakash Narayan in Nagpur on November 27, 1954.

[22] From an interview by the author with Mrs. Kamaladevi Chattopadhyaya, a former Socialist leader, in New Delhi on December 1, 1954.

[23] It is interesting that in Burma the Communists also refused to accept the settlement with the British because it resulted from negotiations rather than a mass struggle. This view was held in spite of the fact that in Burma, unlike India, it was a leftist socialist group which carried on the negotiations. It appears that in both India and Burma there were groups who had become so committed to the particular *techniques* of achieving freedom that alternative methods were unacceptable. It can probably be argued that the Burmese Communists and the Indian Socialists (in fact, the entire left wing in India) were psychologically pre-disposed toward a revolutionary course.

[24] Aruna Asaf Ali, "Time to Decide," *Janata*, III (February 29, 1948), p. 3.

President of the AITUC, and perhaps the leading Socialist trade unionist in North India, strongly opposed the Socialist trade union policy and the growing urge of the Socialists to break with Congress.[25] When the Socialist Party decided not to take part in the Congress-sponsored INTUC, Shastri resigned from the Socialist Party saying that "the unfinished task of national revolution demands the full-fledged allegiance of all sections of the people and every progressive group in the country, including the Socialists and the Congress."[26]

Other leaders of the Socialist Party in U.P. also opposed a break with Congress or were reluctant to go ahead with it. Among them were Acharya Narendra Deva, an elder statesman and a former President of the Congress Socialist Party.

The reasons for the opposition to such a break in U.P. are clear. The Socialists were stronger in the Congress Party organization there than in any other state. While the Socialists elsewhere had as their objective the gaining of control of the Congress Party organization, the Socialists in U.P. in large part already had such control. Damodar Swarup Seth was President of the U.P. Pradesh Congress Committee, and Acharya Narendra Deva was its Vice Chairman. The Socialists in U.P. felt, therefore, that little could be gained by breaking with Congress and leaving the popular Congress Party name to conservative elements within the Party. On the other hand, in the city of Bombay, where the Socialists had considerable strength and popularity, control of the Congress Party was in the hands of S. K. Patil and a conservative anti-socialist leadership. When the break with Congress finally came, the greatest number of defections from the Socialist Party were in U.P., where a sizable element decided to remain within the Congress Party.[27]

25 Hariharnath Shastri, "Should Socialists Support the INTUC?" *Janata,* II (May 18, 1947), p. 3.

26 *Hindustan Times,* July 27, 1947.

27 In an interview with the author in Bombay on February 14, 1954, Asoka Mehta said that in general wherever the Socialists were in a minority inside Congress as in Bombay they were eager to leave, but where they commanded a majority, as in U.P., they wanted to remain inside Congress.

SOCIALIST OPTIMISM

A major element in the willingness of the Socialists to terminate their relations with Congress was their growing confidence in themselves after and even shortly before 1946. Their major role in the '42 movement led many Socialists to believe, especially the younger ones, that independence and social change could come through the efforts of a Socialist Party apart from the Congress. They soon became aware of their own ability to arouse mass feelings and were especially pleased at the rousing receptions given to Jayaprakash, Lohia, and other Socialist leaders in April 1946.

These feelings of optimism were reinforced by the Bombay municipal elections in early 1948, in which the Socialists won 26 seats to the Congress's 47, an impressive number for a new opposition party.

Since the formation of the Party in 1934, the Congress Socialists had been organized more or less on Leninist lines with a limited but select membership. Admission to membership depended upon the fulfillment of work quotas and followed a probationary period.[28] The size of the Socialist membership, therefore, was no indication of its exact strength. In June 1947, shortly before the break, the Socialists estimated their membership at 8,000 and claimed the allegiance of about 100,000 workers.[29] Thus the growing confidence of the Socialists was further suggested by the fact that by the end of 1948, not long after the split, serious discussions were under way to open the Party to mass membership.

CONCLUSION: REASONS FOR THE BREAK

We have described in some detail the circumstances leading to the break between the Socialists and Congress in 1948. We have also described some of the links between the two groups before the break occurred: that Congress was the recognized

[28] Jayaprakash Narayan, "The Structure of the Socialist Party," *Janata*, III (November 21, 1948), p. 3.
[29] *Hindustan Times*, June 14, 1947.

leader of the national struggle and that it commanded mass support, that Gandhi served to reconcile groups within the movement, that there was considerable tolerance within Congress for divergent groups, and, finally, that the Socialists had developed considerable loyalty to the Congress organization and sections of the Congress leadership. With the close of the war and the advent of independence these links between the Socialists and Congress were soon broken.

We have described how the '42 movement resulted in the growth of a Socialist rank and file which had few loyalties to the Congress Party and which had developed confidence and optimism in its own capacity to be victorious through its own efforts. The subsequent attempt by the Socialists to expand their power to a point commensurate with the mass influence they felt they held was frustrated by the Congress leadership on the trade union front and by the Congress's unwillingness to give high-ranking positions to the Socialists or to give recognition to the younger elements by placing them on local committees. The Socialist rank and file grew intensely bitter toward Congress and with the arrival of independence the unity resulting from the presence of a common enemy broke down still further.

The attempt by the conservative Congress leadership and by local Congress officials to force the dissolution of the Congress Socialist Party contributed to the Socialist feeling of being unwanted. Gandhi's influence delayed the break, but his failure to convince the Congress leaders to give recognition to the Socialists destroyed the only remaining possibility of a settlement. Gandhi's death finally terminated the last link between the parties.

That ideological differences existed between the two parties, there can be little doubt. Such differences had existed for many years. Sardar Patel and other Congress conservatives were particularly intent on getting out of their way elements with which they had basic disagreements and which were increasingly threatening to their position. On the other hand, the Socialists were growing increasingly confident of their own strength and became less anxious to achieve a settlement which would allow them to remain in Congress—even if the Congress leaders should be willing to agree to a settlement.

Many of the older Socialist leaders were hopeful that they could remain inside Congress, but they were under enormous pressure from their own rank and file to lead the Socialists out of Congress. Some of the Socialist leaders recognized that the alternative existed of working as a loose group inside Congress with no particular label or organization, much as the conservative elements did. But the strong identifications of Congress Socialist members with their own Party made such an alternative impossible. The fact is that it was never seriously considered by the rank and file.[30]

In this case study we have placed our emphasis on the non-ideological elements involved in the Socialist break from Congress. The fact is that major differences between the two parties existed from the time of the formation of the Congress Socialist Party, and, as we have already noted, the differences which existed after the war were no greater than and perhaps not nearly so great as those which existed before 1940. New elements in the situation were the increased mass prestige of the Socialists, attempts by the Congress leadership to prevent the Socialists from increasing their power inside Congress followed by a campaign by Congress leaders to get the Socialists out, and a growing breakdown in the allegiance of the Socialists to their parent organization.

Ideological differences may have been frequently referred to by Socialist leaders and the Socialist rank and file, but they appear to be marginal in comparison with the other factors which ultimately led to the break.

[30] The only serious discussion one can find of this alternative is in a speech by Jayaprakash Narayan at a summer camp of the Congress Socialist Party at Dehradun in May 1946. See Jayaprakash Narayan, *The Socialist Way* (Lucknow: Dulabeylal Bhargava, 1946), pp. 4-5.

4. The Kisan Mazdoor Praja Party Break from Congress

In September 1952, after the general elections, the Socialist Party and the Kisan Mazdoor Praja Party (KMPP) successfully merged to form the Praja Socialist Party (PSP). Together they constituted India's largest opposition party. The KMPP had been a new party, formed shortly before the 1952 elections by Acharya Kripalani and other former Congressmen. The circumstances which led to the formation of the KMPP are the subject of this chapter; the next chapter considers the KMPP's successful merger with the Socialist Party.

Since independence the Congress Party has been ridden with factional disputes that have threatened to destroy the Party organization. Before the general elections a number of major defections occurred which changed the character of Congress as a national movement. The Communists, the Socialists, the Marxist left, and finally the Kisan Mazdoor Praja Party group all severed their ties with Congress. Since the 1952 elections, factional disputes inside Congress have continued but defections from the Party have thus far ceased. The major successes of Congress in the elections cautioned those who thought power could be won outside the Congress fold.

The groups and individuals that made up the Kisan Mazdoor Praja Party broke from Congress in 1950 and 1951. They were largely individuals who at one time held important positions in the Congress Party or in Congress governments. This case study will describe how the factional dispute between these groups and the Congress organization began and grew until a split finally occurred. In the last chapter on the Socialists we described the behavior of a group which did not have power but wanted it. In this chapter we shall describe the behavior of groups and individuals who wielded power but lost it.

ACHARYA KRIPALANI

The break from Congress was led by Acharya Kripalani, at one time the Congress General Secretary and later the President of Congress. Acharya Jiwant Ram Bhagwandas Kripalani was born in 1888 at Hyderabad, Sind (now in Pakistan), received his M.A. at Bombay University, and then returned to the Sind, where he became a school teacher and later a Professor of History at Muzzaffarpore College in Bihar. When Gandhi came to Bihar in 1917, Kripalani left his college position to join the Mahatma and from then on remained a close disciple. In 1918 Kripalani was chosen as personal assistant to Pandit Madan Mohan Malaviya, then President of the Indian National Congress, and a few years later at the request of Gandhi he became Principal of Gujerat Vidyapith, a national university founded by Gandhi at Ahmedabad. For five years Kripalani taught at the University and was soon dubbed Acharya (teacher). In 1930 he took an active part in the Salt Satyagraha movement (in which salt was extracted from sea water under Gandhi's leadership, in violation of the government salt monopoly), and was sentenced to one year's imprisonment. At the end of 1934 he was elected Congress General Secretary, a post he held for twelve years, and in November 1946 at the Meerut session he was elected the fifty-fourth President of Congress.[1]

Kripalani was elected Congress President to replace Jawaharlal Nehru, who had resigned to become the head of the new interim government. Although the election to the office of Party President was a great honor to Kripalani, the next year, 1947, was a year of great personal frustration for him.

With the formation of the interim government, the leading Congressmen—Prasad, Nehru, Sardar Patel, Rajagopalachari, and others—all colleagues of Kripalani, assumed responsible positions in it. Soon after the formation of the government, relations between Patel and Kripalani became exceedingly strained, for Patel did not consult Kripalani on government policy. Other members of the government also came into conflict with Kripalani.

In principle the conflicts were over the extent to which members of the government ought to consult with Party leaders on

---

[1] J. S. Bright, *President Kripalani and His Ideas* (Lahore: Indian Printing Works, 1947), pp. 17-35.

matters of state policy. Patel pointed out that in a democracy the government could be responsible only to the elected legislature and not to the Party, but Kripalani felt that the Party had to be a "link between the government and the people" and that the views of the Congress President had to be considered on important matters.

These conflicts grew out of Kripalani's conception of the role of the Congress President in pre-independence India. The position of Congress President had held a unique place in Indian life. To some extent the Indian National Congress had become a government paralleling the British authority. Its national conference became a national assembly; its resolutions had the moral authority of law; and its leaders were the spokesmen for the nation. The Congress President was thus second only to Gandhi and later to Nehru as the leader of the national movement. A set of expectations had been built into the role of Congress President. These expectations were shared by Kripalani, who had worked with Congress Presidents as General Secretary for twelve years.

Kripalani was further frustrated by his own lack of influence even inside the Congress organization. While only a few months before he was selected Party President, Kripalani had written of the importance of the role of the Working Committee as the President's cabinet within the Party, his freedom to select his own Working Committee was severely limited.[2] In a statement to the press announcing the names of the Congress Working Committee, Kripalani said: "If my distinguished predecessors found the task of selecting their colleagues difficult, I have found it much more so. They had in this unenviable task the advice and guidance of Gandhiji of which his absence has deprived me. My difficulties were further enhanced by the fact that my predecessor in office, Sri Jawaharlal Nehru, had infused considerable new blood in the committee. Jawaharlalji is a great leader. He can instruct and guide. With his personality and prestige, he can shoulder the responsibility of his colleagues and, if need be, stand

[2] Acharya J. B. Kripalani, *The Indian National Congress* (Bombay: Vora and Co., Ltd., 1946), pp. 55-56.

alone. I have not all these advantages. *I can feel secure only with old and tried colleagues. Yet I was loath to undo what my predecessors had done so recently. Therefore, in selecting names I have made the fewest possible changes.*"[3]

Of the fourteen-member Working Committee appointed by Kripalani, all but four members had been on the previous Committee, and Sardar Vallabhbhai Patel, with whom relations had become exceedingly strained, was to continue as Treasurer. Kripalani privately told friends that he felt that Patel, not himself, dominated the Committee.

There was no one issue over which Kripalani decided to resign as Congress President. His inability to control his own Working Committee, the failure of the interim government to consult with him on various measures, the minor role he played in the negotiations with the British, all these combined to increase Kripalani's frustration. The shift of emphasis from organizational to government work had left Kripalani isolated. There were frequent private complaints to Gandhi, who soon became aware of the growing differences between the government leaders and Kripalani. At Gandhi's request, Kripalani in November 1947 submitted his resignation and, also at Gandhi's request, made it irrevocable. Gandhi saw to it that the resignation was quiet, without incident, and final. Describing Kripalani's resignation to the All India Congress Committee, the Congress General Secretaries wrote:

". . . The Congress President briefly indicated the circumstances which obliged him to resign from the office of the President. He said that ever since his election as President of the Congress, the question that perturbed his mind had been 'what should be the relation of the Congress Executive or the Working Committee to the Government at the Center.' This is a matter which is bound to effect for good or ill not only the character of the Central Government in the new set-up but also the position of the Congress in the country. The indefiniteness of the relation has already caused confusion in the minds of Congress and the general public who do not know and cannot yet

[3] Quoted by Bright, *op.cit.*, pp. 139-140. Italics mine.

understand where the responsibility for any particular decision or the want of it lies.

" 'How is the Congress,' the President further explained, 'to give the Government its active and enlightened cooperation unless its highest executive or its popularly chosen head is taken into full confidence, on important matters that affect the nation.' The Congress cannot 'serve as a living and effective link between the government and the people unless the leadership in the government and in the Congress work in the closest harmony. Any action which weakens the organization of the party or lowers its prestige in the eyes of the people must sooner or later undermine the position of the Government.' The President therefore felt that if the present confusion was not checked in time 'the Congress as an organization will speedily disintegrate and its place in the national life will be captured by some other organization, maybe militant communism or by the Communist Party.' Acharya Kripalani said that he discussed this problem both with Gandhiji and his colleagues in the Working Committee. The need for this cooperation was recognized in theory but he found it missing in practice. 'It may be,' he said, 'due to the fact that all of us are not united on basic policies or it may be that this cooperation is lacking because I who happen to be President of the organization do not enjoy the confidence of my colleagues in the Central Government. If that is so then I should be the last person to stand in the way of what is necessary in the interests of this nation,' and hence his resignation.

"The A.I.C.C. would have liked to discuss the resignation of the President before accepting or rejecting it. But the President made his decision to resign irrevocable. He further advised the A.I.C.C. that there should be no discussion on his resignation. Gandhiji in his opening speech tendered similar advice to the A.I.C.C. The A.I.C.C. therefore had no option but regretfully to accept the resignation of Acharya Kripalani. They elected unanimously Dr. Rajendra Prasad to be the President of the Congress."[4]

4 *Indian National Congress Report of the General Secretaries, November 1946–December 1948* (New Delhi: All India Congress Committee, 1949), pp. 31-34.

Kripalani's resignation was thus quiet and effective. It was clear from what he said that the differences had less to do with basic policies than with his failure to win the confidence of the government leaders.

TANDON-KRIPALANI ELECTION

The decisive turning point in Kripalani's relations with Congress occurred three years later when he again ran for Congress President but was defeated by Purushottamdas Tandon in the election of September 1950. This election involved not just a conflict between two leading Congress personalities but a struggle between groups inside the Congress organization as well. For an understanding of the significance of this contest, one must understand the nature of the conflict inside Congress.

The year 1950 was one of great turmoil in India. Serious communal tensions had arisen in East Pakistan and resulted in a mass exodus of Hindus from there to West Bengal. Relations between Pakistan and India became exceedingly strained and violent conflict between the two nations seemed imminent. It was in this setting that conflicts arose inside both Congress and the government over policy toward Pakistan and more generally over the government's secular policies.

Sardar Patel, who was then Home Minister and perhaps the most powerful force inside the Congress, not only was the darling of a Hindu-conscious group within the Party but also wielded great influence among leaders of commerce and industry who disliked Nehru's socialist views. Nehru's preoccupation with international questions and Sardar Patel's concentration on home affairs generally prevented any conflict between the two men. With Patel's keen organizational sense and Nehru's command of mass support, the two men constituted a complementary team. But in 1950, differences between Patel and Nehru widened, especially as both home and foreign affairs centered around relations with Pakistan. Neither man openly attacked the other or the other's policies, but it was soon clear to the general public and to Congress leaders that differences existed and that around each of these men there clustered a number of national and regional supporters.

During the fifty-sixth session of Congress, at Nasik, Patel gave his support for the election of Congress President to Purushot-tamdas Tandon, who opposed Kripalani. Tandon, who had lost the contest for Congress President the year before, is a Congress-man from Uttar Pradesh, a strong advocate of Hindi as the national language, a frequent quoter of Sanskrit, and a promoter of Hindu culture. In his home state of U.P., Tandon belonged to a group of conservative Hindu-minded Congress leaders who dominated both the Party and the state government.

Opposition to this U.P. group and support for Acharya Kri-palani centered around the late Rafi Ahmed Kidwai, a leading U.P. Muslim nationalist, a member of the Congress Working Committee, and a close associate and supporter of the Prime Minister. Until August 15, 1947 Kidwai had been Home Minister in the U.P. government; then he entered Nehru's Cabinet as Communications Minister. From that time on, at Nehru's re-quest, Kidwai refrained from openly participating in U.P. affairs.[5]

The Nasik contest for Congress President, therefore, involved more than a struggle between two men, for Tandon had the open support of Patel and his supporters while Kripalani was backed by Kidwai and his colleagues. Kidwai and Kripalani had hoped to get the open backing of Nehru, whose lack of sym-pathy for Mr. Tandon's viewpoint was well known. The Kidwai-Kripalani group felt that were Nehru openly to support them, Kripalani's victory over Tandon would be assured. But Nehru, perhaps because he hesitated to come into open conflict with Sardar Patel, did not take part in the election. The result: Tan-don, 1,306 votes; Acharya Kripalani, 1,092. Sardar Patel sub-sequently assured Nehru that there could be no question but that he, Nehru, would receive complete support in whatever policies he pursued. Nonetheless the Tandon-Patel victory was widely interpreted as a defeat not only for Kripalani but for

[5] From an interview by the author with Rafi Ahmed Kidwai in New Delhi in May 1954.

Nehru as well. In any event, there could be little doubt that, even assuming a large number of persons voted for Tandon not because of his policies but because of his personality, a large section if not a majority of the Congress Party showed great sympathy for a more Hinduized outlook in politics.

THE CONGRESS DEMOCRATIC FRONT

On September 20, 1950, a little more than two weeks after Tandon's victory, a Kidwai-Kripalani group of about fifty Congressmen from various states decided to form a "Democratic Front" within the Congress Party. With the approval of the group, Kripalani released a statement in which he said that at his invitation fifty of his friends, including Rafi Ahmed Kidwai, Dr. P. C. Ghosh, Mr. T. Prakasam, and Mr. K. Kelappan, had met twice at Nasik and had decided to form a bloc within Congress "to energize the organization and rid it of the corrupting influence of power politics and make it more democratic and serviceable."[6] The statement went on to say that thus far Congress governments had failed to fulfill the minimum expectations of the people, and that Congress itself is "threatened by irresponsible authoritarian forces." "The group that we propose to organize shall be called Congress Democratic Front. Its basic policies and programme are the same as laid down at the Jaipur Congress in its resolution on Fundamental Rights and Economic Programme. . . . As far as possible [the work of the Congress Democratic Front would] . . . be done in cooperation with the existing Congress Committees."[7]

Soon after, at a press conference, Kripalani denied that he had decided to form the Front after the results of the Congress Presidential election and added that, even before the election, friends within and without Parliament had been asking him to form such a group.[8]

---

[6] *Hindustan Times*, November 3, 1950.
[7] *Ibid.*, November 3, 1950.   [8] *Ibid.*, November 4, 1950.

THE FORMATION OF THE
KISAN MAZDOOR PRAJA PARTY

We have already described the circumstances leading up to the creation of the Congress Democratic Front: Kripalani's resignation as Congress President in 1947; the defeat of Kripalani in the election for Congress President by Tandon, who was supported by Patel, in 1950; the differences between Tandon and Kidwai; and, finally, the formation of the Front by Kripalani and Kidwai.

From September 21, 1950 until May of the following year considerable effort was made on the part of the Congress leadership to dissolve the Congress Democratic Front. Early in December the Congress Working Committee met to decide whether any disciplinary action ought to be taken against the Front. The majority of the Committee disapproved of the creation of the Front while a minority, in support of the Front, denied that any breach of the Congress Constitution was involved. Nonetheless the majority of the Committee felt that any disciplinary action might only help to strengthen the Front.[9] Although no disciplinary action was taken, in the months that followed relations between the dissidents and Congress grew increasingly strained. In November 1950, dissidents in West Bengal resigned from Congress to form their own Party, and in April 1951 dissidents in Andhra likewise broke from Congress to create the Praja Party. By the latter part of April the leaders of the Congress Democratic Front were openly talking of severing relations with Congress.

Finally, on May 3, 1951, forty representatives of the Democratic Front met at Kripalani's home in New Delhi to discuss the question of breaking away from Congress and forming a separate party. On the following day, the members of the Front listened to addresses by Nehru and Maulana Azad urging the Front to dissolve itself. The representatives agreed to disband the Front but resolved to hold a convention at Patna in a month.[10]

On May 17th Kripalani in a public statement announced his resignation from Congress, ending his thirty-year-old association

[9] *Hindu*, December 5, 1950.   [10] *Hindustan Times*, May 4, 1951.

with the organization which he once headed as President and served as General Secretary for twelve years. Others followed suit and submitted their resignations to the Congress office.

The convention of dissident Congressmen was scheduled for June 16th and 17th at Patna. During the few weeks preceding the convention frantic efforts were made by all sides to effect some sort of compromise. A number of Congressmen made attempts to call a special All India Congress Committee session to reach a compromise with the Kripalani group that would allow the dissidents to remain inside Congress, but failed to convince Kripalani to postpone the Patna convention.[11]

KIDWAI AND THE KMPP

The Patna convention met as scheduled on June 16, 1951. An Executive Committee was formed consisting of Kripalani, Kidwai, Prakasam (from Andhra), P. C. Ghosh (from Bengal), and Kelappan (from Malabar). The Kisan Mazdoor Praja Party was officially brought into being, and Acharya J. B. Kripalani was elected as its first President. The convention approved the Party's Constitution, passed resolutions, and approved a manifesto. The manifesto presented as the key plank of the Party's program the overhauling of the administrative machinery, which "lacks efficiency, integrity and a spirit of service."[12] The manifesto called for decentralization of authority, aid to backward classes, an austerity drive to create the necessary capital to increase production, land to the tiller, more reclamation projects, encouragement to cottage and decentralised industries, an equitable distribution of wealth, basic education programs, greater aid to displaced persons, and an independent foreign policy.[13]

Although Kidwai had been one of the founders of the Congress Democratic Front and one of those who had prodded Kripalani most, his relations with the new Kisan Mazdoor Praja Party were somewhat unclear. Although he was placed on the Central Council of the new party, he did not address the Patna

[11] *Hindu*, May 30, 1951.
[12] *Kisan Mazdoor Praja Party Bulletin*, July 31, 1951, p. 25.
[13] *Ibid.*, pp. 24-31.

convention and, while reports about the impending resignations of both Kripalani and Kidwai had been circulating for several months, Kidwai did not submit his resignation to Congress when Kripalani did. Kripalani explained that since Kidwai was a member of the central government Cabinet, he and Kidwai wanted to give the Prime Minister time to find a substitute.[14]

The fact is, however, that the delay in Kidwai's resignation had little to do with giving the Prime Minister time to replace him. Kidwai's delay was due to his unwillingness to sever his ties with Congress and, more important, with the Prime Minister. Unlike Kripalani, Kidwai was not isolated in Congress politics, for although his relations with the U.P. government and the U.P. Congress were unsatisfactory, he had close relations and influence with the Prime Minister. Kidwai was resentful that neither he nor any of his supporters were placed on the Congress Working Committee by President Tandon, and he felt that the Prime Minister might yet intervene and force changes in the Working Committee which would be satisfactory to him. At Patna, Kidwai told the press that he had not resigned from Congress because he understood that the coming Bangalore session of the AICC was going to consider ways and means of reforming Congress. "I look to that meeting with hope," he said. "If the attempts that are being made by the Prime Minister and others to reform the Congress succeed, not only will I remain in the Congress, but also many of those who have resigned will like to go back and rejoin it."[15]

At the Bangalore session of the All India Congress Committee in July, a final attempt was made, this time by the Prime Minister, to effect a reunion of the dissident forces with Congress. In the hope that Nehru would not attempt to reconstitute the high command (i.e. the Working Committee), the AICC and the Working Committee gave him a free hand to draft the election manifesto and the resolutions.[16] "It was an open secret," wrote the *Times of India* correspondent, "that the Congress President and a majority of members of the Working Committee had little

[14] *Hindu*, June 16, 1951.   [15] *Ibid.*, June 16, 1951.
[16] *Times of India*, July 20, 1951.

desire to facilitate any change of their own accord, unless it became inevitable, for they thought all along that no such organization change was necessary as they truly and fully reflect the
present-day Congress opinion in the country. . . . As for recon-
stituting the Working Committee, Mr. Tandon and his supporters were believed to have asked Mr. Nehru in what manner
they had failed him when the fact of the matter was that they
agree in whatever he did."[17]

But Nehru did ask the Congress President to reconstitute the
Working Committee and the Central Election Committee,[18]
presumably to include Kidwai and some of his supporters. Tandon, however, told Nehru that as Congress President he was
responsible for appointing his own Working Committee. If the
Prime Minister was not satisfied, he was prepared to step down
and the Prime Minister could have a new Working Committee
with himself as President if he wished.[19]

What had led to this breach between Nehru and the Congress
President? Nehru's differences with the Congress leadership had
existed for many years, reaching back into the '30's when he became the spokesman for the socialist point of view inside Congress. When independence came, a conservative leadership was
in control of both the Congress organization and the central
and state governments. Nehru became the Prime Minister and
continued in office partly because his position among the Indian
masses was so strong, partly because of his popularity inside Congress even among those who disagreed with him, and partly because Nehru as Prime Minister, while speaking in terms which
repelled the business community and the more Hindu-minded,
took few steps which could antagonize those groups. So long as
Sardar Patel, the leader of the conservatives, was alive, open
conflicts between Nehru and the Congress organization were
avoided. But with the death of Sardar Patel, conflict became
inevitable.

Throughout 1950 there was considerable criticism of Nehru
from the Congress conservatives who wanted a "get tough" policy

[17] *Ibid.*, July 20, 1951.   [18] *Hindu*, August 8, 1951.
[19] *Times of India*, July 20, 1951.

with Pakistan over the Kashmir dispute and over the problem
of refugees from East Pakistan. Relations between Nehru and
the Hindu-minded Congress leaders were further strained by
Nehru's support for the Hindu Code Bill, which would have
brought reforms in the Hindu social system. Nehru felt that
many Congress leaders did not sufficiently recognize that India
was a secular state. "I am laying stress on this," said Nehru at
the Bangalore AICC session, "because there has been some flab-
biness on this matter even in Congress circles. I feel that on this
subject there can be no compromise of any kind. Unfortunately
there are some communal groups in our country which challenge this secular aspect of the State and which nourish narrow
and reactionary ideals."[20]

Kidwai played a particularly prominent part in persuading
Nehru that the Congress leadership was a threat to his secular
policies. Nehru became convinced that the attacks against Kidwai
by the U.P. group were directed not so much against Kidwai
personally as against the government's policies. Nehru apparently
also became convinced that the group behind Tandon might
dominate the 1952 general election campaign by dominating the
selection of Congress candidates for the various legislatures. He
thus went to the Bangalore session with the intention of
shaping the Congress election program and of bringing about
changes on the Working Committee and the Central Election
Committee.[21]

But in spite of their differences, the Congress leaders were
unwilling to antagonize Nehru. The *Times of India* correspondent wrote from Bangalore: "It is a strange phenomenon of present-day Congress politics that while the rank and file do not see
eye to eye with the Prime Minister on such vital issues as controls, linguistic provinces and prohibition, they idolize him and
applaud his speeches even when he gets rough with them as he
did at Bangalore. They want him at all costs because he alone
comes nearest to the Father of the Nation in his personal and

[20] Jawaharlal Nehru, *Report to the All India Congress Committee* (New
Delhi: All India Congress Committee, 1951), p. 9.
[21] *Hindu*, August 12, 1951.

political conduct, and has attained an international stature unique in the history of modern India."[22]

Events moved rapidly after the Bangalore AICC session and Nehru's failure to persuade Tandon to reconstitute the Working Committee. On July 17th Rafi Ahmad Kidwai submitted his resignation from the Cabinet. On July 21st, in response to the Prime Minister's request, he withdrew his resignation. On July 22nd Tandon criticized Nehru's decision to allow Kidwai to remain in the Cabinet while he was in opposition to Congress. It was reported that, in deference to the wishes of the U.P. People's Congress workers (the name taken by the KMPP group in U.P.), Kidwai had resubmitted his resignation from the Cabinet to the Prime Minister.[23] Shortly after, it was announced that the resignation was accepted. On August 3rd Kidwai issued a statement saying that he was resigning from Congress and joining the new party.[24] A few days later, on August 11th, Nehru in a surprise statement announced his resignation from the Congress Working Committee. This was followed on the 19th by an announcement by Tandon that he was willing to resign as Congress President.

This Congress Party crisis was greeted with considerable cynicism by Kripalani and his intimate followers. The AICC had not yet met to deal with the new situation, but the Kripalani group was confident that no basic changes would occur.

The AICC met on the 8th and 9th of September in Delhi. Tandon submitted his resignation as Congress President and, as was expected, Nehru was elected to replace him. Nehru then appointed a new Working Committee—but one which, surprisingly enough, excluded Kidwai (who had not been on Tandon's Working Committee) but included Tandon.

A week after his selection as President, Nehru issued an invitation "with all the warmth" at his command to all those who had

[22] *Times of India,* July 20, 1951.

[23] *Hindu,* August 1, 1951. The U.P. People's Congress expressed its views at a conference in Lucknow. In an interview with the author in New Delhi in May 1954, Kidwai said that he had submitted his resignation to Nehru under pressure from many of his supporters.

[24] *Hindustan Times,* August 3, 1951.

left the Congress to come back to it.[25] A few days later Kidwai issued a statement saying that most of those who joined the KMPP were anxious to strengthen the Prime Minister's hands "if they are allowed to function effectively in the State Congress Organizations." He added that "most of those who had joined the KMPP were in agreement with the Prime Minister's policy, but had to leave the Congress because they were not allowed to function and to pursue those policies."[26]

In the following ten days Kidwai made a considerable effort to bring about the dissolution of the KMPP and the return of its members to Congress. He requested that a special meeting of the Executive Committee of the KMPP be called. The Committee met in Calcutta on September 28th, but in spite of Kidwai's efforts and optimism Kripalani and other KMPP leaders were unwilling to dissolve the new party.[27]

On October 4th in Lucknow Kidwai announced that he had decided to rejoin Congress, a decision he said he made when Nehru reconstituted the Working Committee.[28]

Kidwai's role in the formation of the KMPP and his subsequent resignation from the new party were hotly debated during this period. There are many Indians who felt that Kidwai played an opportunistic role, that from the very first he had no intention of leaving the Congress but was using Kripalani and the KMPP as a means of improving his own position in Congress. Kidwai's explanation is that when he had resigned from Congress and from the Cabinet he had made clear to the Prime Minister that he would not return unless the Working Committee were reconstituted. Kidwai felt that his resignation from Congress precipitated Nehru's resignation from the Working Committee. According to Kidwai, if he had not resigned from the Cabinet and from Congress, the Nehru-Tandon crisis would not have arisen. When Pandit Nehru became President and reconstituted the Working Committee he felt that he was under

25 *Ibid.*, September 15, 1951.
26 *Hindustan Times*, September 17, 1951.
27 *Hindu*, September 29, 1951.
28 *Ibid.*, October 5, 1951.

obligation to return to Congress even though the changes were not all that he wanted.[29]

It is, of course, difficult to assess motivation for any person. A complex of conscious and unconscious variables enter into the making of a man's behavior, political or otherwise. There are, however, some limited conclusions about Kidwai's motivation which can be drawn from existing evidence.

First, it is fairly certain that at no time was Kidwai eager to leave Congress. He was active in the Congress Democratic Front only so long as it remained inside Congress. He attended the Patna convention but there neither spoke nor expressed his willingness to resign from Congress. When he finally submitted his resignation to the Prime Minister it was clearly under pressure from the U.P. dissident group, who saw an anomaly in their leader's remaining in Congress while they went into opposition.

Second, if Kidwai was not eager to leave Congress, the question arises, Why? We have already pointed out that Kidwai's position vis-à-vis Congress was considerably different from that of Kripalani and others. While Kidwai was in a minority in the Congress organization, he was far from isolated within the government. He held an important portfolio in the Cabinet and, what is more important, was very close to the Prime Minister.

Third, why did Kidwai ultimately return to Congress after he had resigned? To answer this question we must first understand what Kidwai's differences with Congress were and what demands he was making. We have already pointed out that these differences were primarily with the U.P. state government and Congress organization, rather than with the national Party or government. But the local differences came to have national overtones when Tandon, a U.P. leader, received the support of Sardar Patel and was thereby elected Congress President.

It is difficult to say to what extent Kidwai's differences with Tandon and Patel were based on personal ambitions or on dissimilar outlooks. No doubt both were involved. Differences in outlook there certainly were, for Kidwai, a nationalist Muslim,

[29] From an interview by the author with Rafi Ahmed Kidwai in New Delhi in May 1954.

held views which were closer to those of the Prime Minister
than to those of the more conservative, more Hindu-minded
Patel and Tandon. On the other hand it is also clear that Kidwai's defeat by the Tandon group, first in U.P. and then in the
national Congress organization, was a great personal blow.

But so long as Nehru was in a dominant position and so long
as Kidwai retained some influence on the Prime Minister, Kidwai
saw little point in leaving Congress. The position of Prakasam,
Ghosh, Kripalani, and other dissidents was considerably different; since they did not share this access to the Prime Minister,
few pressures existed for them to remain in Congress. For Kidwai
it was always a question of finding ways and means to remain
in the Party, that is, how to achieve some sort of triumph over
Tandon and his group which would give him sufficient prestige
among his supporters and the general public to allow him to
leave the Democratic Front.

It must be remembered that when the Democratic Front was
created, its objective was to reform Congress from within. The
Front left Congress only at the request of the Congress leaders
and when it appeared to the Front leaders that little hope remained of getting the changes they sought. Having joined with
Kripalani in creating the Front and having brought his supporters into it, Kidwai had little choice but to remain with it
even when its members planned to leave Congress and start a
new opposition party. At this point Kidwai launched an attack
against Tandon before the Prime Minister. When Nehru there-
after defeated Tandon, it was then possible for Kidwai to return to Congress with some prestige and with some of his U.P.
followers. It appears likely, then, that Nehru's victory and the
appointment of a new Working Committee did not *force* Kidwai
to return; the more likely explanation is that he wanted to rejoin Congress but needed an opportunity to do so. Such an opportunity was provided by the change in Congress leadership.

A problem for any political leader is how to retain the allegiance of his supporters. For a politician to sever his mass
support without finding a substitute is to destroy his power.
Individuals may hold important positions without having mass

support, but, once there has been mass support, to lose it is to invite defeat. Kidwai's political position in the government and his future political career rested not only on his relations with the Prime Minister but on those with his U.P. supporters as well. How to retain the support of both was the crucial problem.

A combination of circumstances thus affected Kidwai's behavior: his personal defeats by the Tandon group combined with the differences in outlook between him and them; the pressure from his supporters in U.P. whose differences with the state Party had grown to the point where they were ultimately forced to leave the Party; the failure of Tandon to give due recognition to Kidwai by placing him on the Working Committee; and, finally, Kidwai's close association with the Prime Minister.

NEHRU, KIDWAI, AND THE KMPP

We have already described the pulls upon Kidwai from his U.P. supporters. A few words need to be said about his relationship with Nehru, and the relationships of both these men with the KMPP. Apart from his well-known abilities as an organizer and administrator, Kidwai was brought into the government by Nehru to maintain parity between the pro-Nehru and pro-Patel forces within the Cabinet. In the conflict between Nehru and Patel, Patel's organizational abilities and his hold upon the Congress organization were his greatest asset. Kidwai had demonstrated similar skills in UP and nationally in his work during the 1937 elections.

Kidwai's position in the Cabinet was therefore more than just that of a capable administrator. He became the pro-Nehru member of the Cabinet who, with his organizational abilities, was capable of doing things which Nehru often could not or was not willing to do.

A crisis developed within the Congress Party and the government between 1947 and 1950. That Patel, as Home Minister, held dominant positions in the government and Party disturbed Nehru. In the Tandon-Kripalani election, Nehru's political dislike for Tandon was well known, and in spite of the hopes of Kripalani, Kidwai, and their supporters that Nehru would openly support them, Nehru confided his support for Kripalani to only a few top leaders. This sympathy for Kripalani's candidature was never translated into political action, and many of the delegates were unaware of the Prime Minister's views. Had Nehru acted more positively, the election results might have been different.

Similarly, the Kripalani group believed that Nehru might join the Congress Democratic Front and might conceivably even break with Congress and join the new party. Kripalani and the other KMPPers have admitted that there was no commitment at any time from the Prime Minister, but his sympathy for their work was well known. One can also surmise that Kidwai, who was so close to Nehru, may have encouraged these beliefs, or at least made no effort to discourage them.

It was not until the death of Sardar Patel (a death which followed a period of prolonged serious illness and which therefore came as no surprise) that Nehru seemed prepared to make an effort to wrest control of Congress from the pro-Patel group, whose power was made manifest by Tandon's holding the office of Congress President. Kidwai's resignation from Congress and his attacks against the Tandon leadership were presumably discussed with the Prime Minister beforehand. Considering Nehru's close personal and political relationship with Kidwai, it is rather unlikely that such a momentous step should have been taken without prior consultation. Almost immediately afterward Nehru submitted his resignation to the Working Committee, and this was followed by the events we have already described: Tandon's resignation as Congress President (a resignation, incidentally, which was done with much grace and no public recrimination), Nehru's subsequent election as President, the reconstitution of the Working Committee, and Kidwai's return to the Congress Party.

Some observers have expressed the view that Kidwai's act of resignation was done on behalf of Nehru: while Nehru was incapable of making a decision with regard to his relationship with the KMPP and Congress and in particular over what he should do about the Tandon group, Kidwai was prepared to take action and did so. It is pointed out that Kidwai recognized that Nehru was not prepared to make a decision in the matter[30] while, on the other hand, Kidwai's entire political background is that of a decisive figure, capable of making decisions and implementing them. As a man of action, Kidwai was something of an alter ego for Nehru, a man who could act when Nehru could not. According to this interpretation, Kidwai resigned as a means of forcing Nehru to do what he knew Nehru wanted to do but could not do by himself.[31]

Kidwai's role in this case study can therefore be viewed in at least two ways: as a study in the Prime Minister's behavior, with Kidwai in the role of the man of action; or as a study of Kidwai's own behavior as an independent political figure influenced in part by the Prime Minister and in part by his relationship with his U.P. supporters and his attitude toward Tandon's group.

THE BENGAL KRISHAK PRAJA MAZDOOR PARTY

Along with the Kidwai and Kripalani groups, two other large Congress groups, one from Madras and the other from Bengal, took part in the Congress Democratic Front. These two groups provided the largest mass support to the Front and ultimately to the KMPP. No examination of the schism between Congress and the KMPP would be complete without considering some of the local factors which contributed to that schism.

[30] In an interview with the author in New Delhi in May 1954, Kidwai said he felt that Nehru's weakness is his inability to act decisively in carrying out his idealism.

[31] Further evidence for the argument that Kidwai acted on behalf of a reluctant Prime Minister is offered by pointing to Kidwai's role in the Kashmir crisis of 1953. At that time Sheikh Abdullah's Cabinet was replaced and Sheikh Abdullah himself, the Chief Minister of Kashmir, was arrested at the instance of Kidwai, who maneuvered these changes in the Kashmir government. (This has never been documented but was widely believed in government circles in New Delhi at the time.) It is pointed out that Nehru's personal friendship for Sheikh Abdullah prevented him from acting decisively even when it was realized that Sheikh Abdullah's references to an independent Kashmir state were contrary to Indian interests. Kidwai therefore took it upon himself (presumably with Nehru's tacit approval) to replace Sheikh Abdullah. Here again, Kidwai is viewed as a man who does those things the Prime Minister wants done but is himself incapable of doing.

Prafulla Ghosh and Suresh Banerjee, like Kripalani, had also been in positions of authority before the break. Prafulla Ghosh had been the Chief Minister of Bengal and Suresh Banerjee had been the Bengal Pradesh Congress Committee President. But their power had been tenuously held and easily lost.

The Ghosh-Banerjee group, known as the Gandhians, was only one of several groups inside the Congress Party. The national movement had first started in Bengal, and that province's factionalism was perhaps the greatest.[32] Two events shattered the strength of the Congress organization in Bengal: the expulsion of Subhas Chandra Bose in 1939, and the partition of Bengal in 1947. The first event led to the withdrawal from Congress of the Anushilan, the group then dominating the Congress organization in Bengal, following which the Congress high command called upon Suren Ghosh, the leader of the Jugantar group, to form a new Bengal PCC. At the close of the war the Jugantar group therefore dominated the Bengal Congress organization. Suren Ghosh was the PCC President, and Kiron Shankar Roy, a Jugantar supporter, was the leader of the Bengal Assembly Congress Party.

But partition virtually destroyed the Jugantar group. Its membership had come primarily from East and North Bengal, areas which were absorbed into East Pakistan. Kiron Shankar Roy himself initially opted for East Pakistan, thus weakening the Jugantar position in the Assembly.

With no single group in control of either the Assembly or the Bengal PCC, the Congress high command stepped in and gave their support to Prafulla Ghosh of the Gandhian group. Although Prafulla Ghosh had never been a force within Bengal, he was a member of the Congress Working Committee and an ardent supporter of Gandhism. Except for a brief period in the early 1920's when Ghosh was Secretary of the Bengal PCC, the control of the Bengal Congress had been in the hands of those who were not sympathetic to Gandhi's approach. The creeds of non-violence, of the charka (spinning wheel), and of cottage industries had never been widely acceptable in Bengal.

[32] See Chapter 6 below on the left wing in Bengal.

What was to be the Gandhian group was begun in about 1910 and was then called the Brotherhood. The Brotherhood, before the advent of Gandhi, was primarily a student group devoted to terrorism. But at Gandhi's call the group turned to non-violence. In 1921 the group formed the Abhoy Ashram at Comilla, in what is now East Pakistan. The ashram (a kind of retreat), which was started with Gandhi's support, was modeled after Gandhi's own ashram at Sevagram. The members of the Brotherhood, including Ghosh, Banerjee, and, in the beginning, Netaji Subhas Chandra Bose, agreed to remain unmarried so as not to have any ties. (Neither Ghosh nor Banerjee has ever married, although Netaji did.) The ashrams—some 45 branches grew up in Bengal—had two functions: to fight for freedom with Gandhi and to do constructive work along Gandhian lines. Whenever a civil disobedience movement began the members left the ashram to take part, and when things grew quiet they returned to the ashram to do constructive work.[33]

When Prafulla Ghosh became the first Chief Minister of Bengal in an independent India, there were three major constellations in the Assembly: the Gandhians, the Jugantar group, and the Hooghly group. The Jugantar was an old and famous secret terrorist organization started in 1906-1907. Like the Brotherhood or Gandhian group, the Jugantar also abandoned its terrorist tactics to join the national movement under Gandhi's leadership. The Hooghly group, last of the three, was started in 1921 and like the Gandhian group had its own ashram. It derived its strength from areas along the Hooghly River in West Bengal.

Although the Gandhian group had the support of the Congress high command, it had little support in the legislature. P. C. Ghosh built up some mass support by employing vigorous measures against blackmarketeers, but, as one of his opponents explained,[34] the Assembly Party did not support him for it did not feel as if it had its *own* men as leaders. During the early months

[33] This description of the Brotherhood was given to the author by Suresh Banerjee in an interview in Calcutta in January 1954.
[34] Surendra Mohan Ghosh, the Jugantar leader, in an interview with the author in New Delhi on September 17, 1954.

of the new government Ghosh became increasingly critical of some of his ministers who were in the Hooghly group. The Congress members of the Assembly soon started agitating for a new leader. Ghosh felt that Sardar Patel was giving support to the opposition, although Patel denied it. Pressure was subsequently put on Ghosh to appoint Mr. N. R. Sarkar, a leading industrialist, as his Finance Minister, but Ghosh refused.[35] It now became apparent that the Hooghly group, led by Prafulla Sen, and the Jugantar group, headed by Surendra Mohan Ghosh, had combined to overthrow the P. C. Ghosh Ministry.

Soon after Prafulla Ghosh realized that he did not have the support of the Congress members of the Legislative Assembly, he submitted his resignation as Chief Minister. The Hooghly group won over B. C. Roy, a powerful figure in Bengal, and elected him as Chief Minister with the support of the Jugantar group. Although the Jugantar group, like the Gandhians, derived most of its strength from people who had left East Bengal (which had become East Pakistan), it was prepared to join with the West Bengal Hooghly group in anticipation that the change in government would improve its own position, if not give it a dominant voice in the new ministry. It seems that the Jugantar group hoped that, by working with the West Bengal Hooghly group, it might regain some of the support which it had lost as a result of partition.

But in the months following the election of B. C. Roy in January 1948, the Hooghly group successfully consolidated the West Bengal forces, much to the chagrin not only of the Ghosh-Banerjee Gandhians but of the Jugantar group as well. The Hooghly group gradually squeezed both the Gandhian and the Jugantar group out of the Bengal PCC.

From January 1948 onward Prafulla Ghosh, Suresh Banerjee, and the Gandhian group were isolated from Bengal politics. The morale of the Gandhian group dropped as its ministry was overthrown, and as it lost control over the Bengal PCC. Prafulla Ghosh's relations with Sardar Patel worsened after the collapse

[35] Prafulla Chand Ghosh in an interview with the author in Calcutta in January 1954.

of his ministry, but he remained a close associate of Kripalani, with whom he had always been on good terms. From 1948 on Ghosh seriously considered breaking with Congress, but at the request of his friend Shankar Rao Deo, then Congress General Secretary, he decided to remain until the Nasik Congress in 1950.[36] Kripalani's defeat destroyed any hope that interference from the Congress high command could restore the position of the Gandhian group. At this point Ghosh decided to leave Congress. For several months he carried on talks with other Congress dissidents in Bengal. At a conference in November 1950, 100 West Bengal Congressmen decided to leave Congress to form the Krishak Praja Mazdoor Party (Peasants, People's and Workers Party), which, they said, had the same objective as Kripalani's Congress Democratic Front but which would operate outside of Congress. Suresh Banerjee was elected President and Prafulla Ghosh as Secretary.

At a press conference Banerjee outlined a four-point program for the new party: abolition of the zamindar (landholding) system, and making the tiller of the soil its owner; nationalization of all essential and key industries; nationalization of institutions like banks, insurance companies, etc.; and taking over by government of the export and import business of the country.[37] The new party adopted a resolution which said: "We have no differences with the objectives of the newly formed Congress Democratic Front. Only, we think that it would be better to go outside the official Congress to achieve the declared ideals. The activities of this party will, for the present, be confined to West Bengal, but when such other parties inspired by the selfsame ideals are formed outside the Congress in other provinces we shall strive to work together."[38]

What were the reasons for the Gandhian break from Congress in Bengal? By 1950 the Ghosh-Banerjee group felt the futility of staying within Congress. Not only Ghosh and Banerjee but the entire Gandhian group recognized the impossibility of improving its position inside Congress and therefore felt badly demoral-

---

[36] *Ibid.*   [37] *Hindustan Times*, November 17, 1950.
[38] *Hindu*, November 14, 1950.

ized. Before 1947 the problem could not have arisen in this form. Whatever group and personal differences existed could be submerged in a common struggle. Furthermore, while the Bengal Gandhian group had nearly always been in a minority inside the Bengal Congress, it received considerable moral support and recognition from the Congress high command, including both Gandhi and Patel. Gandhi was now dead. By 1950 Patel had turned toward the B. C. Roy group, and in that same year Kripalani, the Bengal Gandhians' last remaining associate among the top leaders, was defeated in the election to the Congress Presidency. If the Gandhian group had never won power, the split might not have occurred. But having had power and then having lost it so completely, the feeling of isolation was all the more intense.

What were the differences between the three groups that precipitated the defeat of the Gandhians? While at one time or another there had been differences between these groups, at the time of independence no issues of state policy, or any other issues for that matter, divided them. The desire for office on the part of the various groups and their leaders seems to have been decisive in their motivation. The Hooghly members and the Jugantar members were dissatisfied with the positions given to them in the Gandhian Cabinet, and when the Hooghly group gained control the Jugantar group was dissatisfied with its position. Rivalry between East and West Bengalis seems to have been another factor, especially in the relations between the Gandhian and Hooghly groups, but that East-West rivalry was not decisive is indicated by the fact that the Jugantar group, which comes mainly from East Bengal, was at various points prepared to join with either group. P. C. Ghosh attributed his overthrow to the machinations of Bengal capitalists who did not consider him sufficiently sympathetic to their cause,[39] while Surendra Mohan Ghosh pointed out that the Birla industrial interests were giving financial support to the B. C. Roy group.[40] While it is true that

[39] From an interview by the author with P. C. Ghosh in Calcutta in January 1954.
[40] From an interview by the author with Surendra Mohan Ghosh in New Delhi in November 1954.

the Roy Ministry has had support from Bengal businessmen, business support seems to have been just one element contributing to the strength of the Hooghly group. Perhaps even more decisive was the fact that, of the three groups, only the Hooghly group derived its strength from West Bengal while the others had been active primarily in areas that had been absorbed into East Pakistan.

The shifts may not have involved any differences in policies, but it became necessary to garb differences in an ideological dress. The statement of policy of the Ghosh-Banerjee group on the formation of the new party seems remote from the differences which they actually had with the ruling Congress faction. The planks for nationalization of industries, banks, etc., and the proposal that export and import business be operated by the government are demands with can be dealt with only by the central government and not by any state government. The remoteness of these demands and the absence of any specific grievances against the Bengal Ministry in the Party's statement further suggests that the differences were not over specific issues of state policy.

The differences that existed had more to do with allegiances within the various groups than any differences in policy. It is important to note that the shifts which occurred were not based on agreements between one or two personalities, but represented understandings between the various groups. Throughout the shifts each group was able to maintain its own solidarity; at no point did any major break occur within any of the groups, perhaps because none of the three groups was formed during the shifts; each group had a long history, with its own group allegiances, leaders, traditions, and the like. It was this group cohesion which made it possible for the Bengal Gandhian group to leave the Congress more or less intact, and do so long before Kripalani and his scattered followers made their break.

THE CONGRESS DEMOCRATIC FRONT IN ANDHRA

As in Bengal, the break that occurred within the Andhra Congress organization centered primarily around local differences rather than differences with the national leadership or with national policy.

Until 1953 Andhra was a Telugu-speaking area in Madras State. In that year the Telugu-speaking districts of Madras were cut out to form an independent state in the Indian Union.

Congress politics in Andhra has long been dominated by three personalities, Mr. Pattabhi Sitaramayya, Mr. T. Prakasam, and his close associate Professor N. G. Ranga. With the elevation of Pattabhi to the Governorship of Madhya Pradesh, Prakasam and, to a lesser extent, Ranga occupied the center of the political stage in Andhra. Shortly after independence Prakasam became the Chief Minister of Madras State while Ranga became the President of the Andhra Pradesh Congress Committee.

Prakasam was a long-time leader of the Congress movement in Andhra, and a supporter of Gandhi's 1920 non-cooperation movement. Soon after the selection of Prakasam as Chief Minister conflict arose between the Andhra supporters of Prakasam and the Tamilnad supporters of Kamraj Nadar, a Congress leader in the Tamil-speaking area of Madras. The Tamil-speaking group, which formed a majority of Madras State, replaced Prakasam as Chief Minister with the help of some discontented Andhra politicians. After ceasing to be Chief Minister, Prakasam supported Professor Ranga for reelection as Andhra PCC President against Sanjeeva Reddi, but Ranga lost by a narrow margin. Ranga protested that the inability of twenty-six delegates to participate in the election because of an injunction was responsible for his narrow defeat. He demanded an inquiry from the Congress President into the elections and also called for an investigation of the "misdealings" of the Madras Ministry. But "Tandon is understood to have pleaded his inability to interfere in the Ministerial affairs of Madras."[41]

Even before the PCC elections, however, the Prakasam-Ranga group had closely associated itself with Kripalani's Congress Democratic Front. As early as November 1950, after Prakasam had been deposed as Chief Minister but before the Andhra PCC

[41] *Hindu*, June 11, 1951.

elections, Prakasam announced that Kripalani had appointed him as the agent and organizer for the Front in Andhra.[42]

But the break between the Prakasam-Ranga group and Congress did not finally occur until some five months later, in April 1951, after the Andhra PCC elections. In the intervening period Prakasam issued a number of statements criticizing the Madras Ministry and calling for the appointment of a committee by the Madras Legislative Assembly to investigate charges against certain Ministers.[43]

The defeat of Professor Ranga in the Andhra PCC presidential election on April 11, 1951 precipitated the withdrawal of the Ranga-Prakasam group from Congress.[44] Following its resignation, the group organized a new political party called the Praja Party (People's Party) with Prakasam as its chairman.

As soon as the new Praja Party was under way, differences developed between Ranga and Prakasam which resulted in a split within the newly formed party. Ranga demanded that the Praja Party be an autonomous body that would cooperate with the Kripalani Kisan Mazdoor Praja Party only in the central Parliamentary work. The Party would maintain its individuality in all other matters including the selection and election of candidates to the state and central legislatures. Prakasam rejected this proposal and protested against Ranga's "impossible demands on the central body."[45] Finally, in August, Professor Ranga broke completely with Prakasam and the KMPP, and announced the formation of a new party, called the Krishikar Lok Party (Peasants and People's Party) with himself as chairman.

Speaking at a press conference Ranga said that his differences with the KMPP were "in respect of organization and character of the party leadership." He did not agree with the KMPP's centralized control. And while the leadership of the KMPP was predominantly middle class, he declared that his party's leadership would be rural. In his new party the provincial branches

---

[42] *Ibid.*, November 17, 1950.   [43] *Hindu*, December 16, 1950.

[44] Professor Ranga in an interview with the author in New Delhi on December 9, 1953 affirmed that his withdrawal from Congress was the result of his election defeat.

[45] *Hindustan Times*, July 4, 1951.

would be autonomous and might even have different names.[46]

On August 25 and 26, 1951 about 400 delegates of the new party held their first convention in Delhi, under the chairmanship of Professor Ranga.[47] Out of the Congress dissensions in Andhra, then, had grown two new parties: one, led by Prakasam, became part of Kripalani's Kisan Mazdoor Praja Party, and the other, led by Ranga, became an independent party primarily confined to Andhra.[48]

The similarity in developments in Andhra to those in Bengal are striking, as are some of the differences. As in Bengal, the Congress dissidents were led by a deposed Chief Minister, and, as in Bengal, the differences between the dissidents and Congress were personal rather than ideological. To an even greater extent than in Bengal, regional differences, especially between the Tamil and Telugu groups, played a substantial part. And, as in Bengal, the dissidents ultimately broke from Congress to form parties of their own.

Unlike Bengal, however, the dissident groups in Andhra tended to center more around leading personalities than group allegiances. In Bengal the dissident Gandhian group had a history and tradition of its own. The leaders had strong attachments both to one another and to their group. They were thus able to leave Congress earlier than did the dissidents in Andhra, and they were able to leave with their group intact. In Andhra, however, the discontented individuals centered around two distinct personalities. While Ranga was a close associate of Prakasam, he had followers of his own. The two groups around Ranga and Prakasam were separate: their relations were based largely on the relations which existed between their two leaders, so that when Prakasam and Ranga fell apart their groups fell with with them. A veteran Andhra journalist and a close friend and associate of Prakasam has clearly summarized the circumstances which led to the creation of these two new Andhra parties:

" . . . Mr. Prakasam's departure from the Congress was due to no intellectual disagreement with the principles and policies of

---

[46] Hindustan Times, August 23, 1951.   [47] Ibid., August 26, 1951.
[48] In March 1955 Professor Ranga led his party back into Congress.

the Congress. Avowedly it was caused by Congress ministerial
degeneracy in the matter of implementing the high standards of
Gandhian preaching in the actual administration, but its real
provocation lay in the circumstances that had brought about the
termination of Mr. Prakasam's Chief Ministership. The Praja
Party would never have been formed if Mr. Prakasam had continued to be at the helm of affairs in the Congress party and
government. The new party had no impersonal foundation in
irreconcilable differences with the Congress in outlook and endeavour on the part of its founders. Mr. Prakasam was in fact
a better Congressman than most others, and, if still he left, it
was because of the stature he had reached, which excluded the
possibility of his being in any party except at the top level of
leadership. . . . The formation of the Praja Party was the inevitable result.

". . . Mr. N. G. Ranga soon left the Praja Party for the same
reason that impelled Mr. Prakasam to leave the Congress, his
domineering nature disqualifying him for any but the first place
in any organisation. A party had to be found for Mr. Ranga to
lead and so the Krishikar Lok Party was carved out of the
Praja Party, though there was precious little of divergence in
politics between the Praja Party and the Krishikar Lok Party."[49]

THE CREATION OF THE KMPP:
THE MEN AND THEIR MOTIVATIONS

Four major figures took part in the creation of the Kisan
Mazdoor Praja Party: Acharya Kripalani, T. Prakasam, Prafulla
Chand Ghosh, and Rafi Ahmad Kidwai. Of these, only the latter
failed to break with Congress. The three who left shared the
same motivations and left under somewhat similar circumstances.
Kripalani, Ghosh, and Prakasam were all men who had been
wielders of power either in the Congress Party or in provincial
governments. Their defeats did not arise out of ideological conflicts but resulted from the fact that they were not personally
acceptable to other groups and individuals who wielded greater

---

[49] Khasa Subba Rao, "Spotlight on Men and Politics," *Hindu* (Andhra
State Supplement), October 1, 1953.

power: Prakasam was not acceptable to the Tamils; Prafulla Ghosh was not acceptable to the West Bengal Hooghly group; and Kripalani was not acceptable to Patel and his group. As a result of their defeats and following their unsuccessful attempts at regaining power, each of these men was politically isolated. None were given government or Congress Party positions. And whatever efforts they or their followers made to regain position met with defeat. Prakasam supported Professor Ranga, who was defeated for Andhra PCC President; Ghosh was forced to resign as Chief Minister of Bengal; and Kripalani was defeated in his attempt to be reelected Congress President.

Each of these men had a concept of his own importance which was not always shared by others. Kripalani, for example, is highly conscious of the prestige that ought to accompany age and experience, expects such recognition from others, and is highly frustrated when he fails to receive it.[50] Both Prakasam and Prafulla Ghosh maximized not only their importance to their respective states but the strength of the public support they had. Each felt that his failure to receive recognition within the Congress Party could be compensated for by launching a new party which would give him the support he felt was due. Prakasam's sense of importance went so far that he felt that nothing less than the Chief Ministership would be acceptable. This feeling was so strong that in 1953 he resigned from his Party to become

[50] Seven years after Kripalani resigned as Congress President protesting that he was not consulted on government policy, he resigned as Chairman of the Praja Socialist Party. The writer observed Kripalani publicly submit his resignation at the Socialist convention in Nagpur in November 1954. In his resignation speech Kripalani complained that he received almost no respect from either the leaders or the rank and file of the Party; so long as his judgments were not being listened to he felt that he could no longer continue as Party Chairman. In part, Kripalani found himself in this isolated position in both Congress and the Praja Socialist Party because he lacks the support of any major group or faction in the country. As Congress General Secretary for twelve years, he did not have the opportunity to build any local support the way other Congress leaders did. Then too, the fact that Kripalani comes from an area which is now part of Pakistan (the Sind) also precluded his having any local support. Without the continuous support of any single group of followers, Kripalani's position in any organization he has been in— Congress and the Praja Socialists—has always been personally very frustrating.

the Chief Minister of a Congress government in the new Andhra State.[51]

It is important to note that none of these men are leaders or spokesmen for any economic interest group. Kripalani, as we have observed, had no large organized following and those behind Prakasam and Prafulla Ghosh had no economic differences with others in the Congress Party. They defected only because they felt that they had not received sufficient recognition within Congress.

In general, the rank and file supporters of both Prakasam and Ghosh felt as strongly as, if not more strongly than, their leaders did about leaving Congress. Kidwai's supporters even exerted considerable pressure on him to submit his resignation to Congress; and many refused to return to Congress after their leader did. The groups behind Prakasam in Andhra and Prafulla Ghosh and Suresh Banerjee in Bengal remained intact when they left Congress; the faction which did not remain with Prakasam was the supporter of Professor Ranga, and when he chose to break with both Congress and Prakasam to create his own party his supporters remained loyal to him. None of the factions therefore broke with their leaders in their decision to break from Congress; to the contrary, the loss of recognition to their leaders was felt equally by them.

In describing the circumstances leading first to Kripalani's resignation as Congress President and then his resignation from Congress following his defeat by Tandon, and the circumstances involved in the formation of the Krishak Praja Mazdoor Party in Bengal and the Congress Democratic Front in Andhra, we have seen in each instance what effect the loss of power had upon these groups and individuals. We do not mean to imply here that these men do not have a sense of public dedication. Since they have spent their lives working for the nationalist cause and dedicating themselves in the Indian tradition of self-sacrifice,

[51] In 1953 Prakasam was the leader of the Praja Socialist Party in Andhra; when he resigned from the PSP to become Chief Minister, most of his supporters joined him in forming a new party—the Praja Party.

it would be unfair to say that they are not motivated by a concern for the "common weal."

None of these men nor their supporters would have considered breaking from Congress before independence, when to do so not only would have been injurious to the national movement but would have been looked upon by masses and leaders alike as being a "betrayal." These men were in fact among the strongest supporters Congress had. But with the coming of independence, there was an enormous decline in Congress prestige as a result of the increase in corruption, the unsatisfactory economic situation, and the disillusionment which accompanied these factors. Now that unity in the national movement seemed unnecessary and the prestige of Congress had declined, it seemed possible for a dissident group to defeat Congress in the coming elections, and, failing that, the dissidents were confident of their ultimate victory. But victory or not, they could not see themselves as minor powerless figures inside Congress; and being thrust into such a role would have been a blow to their own prestige and to that of their followers.

5. The Merger of the Kisan Mazdoor Praja Party and the Socialist Party

In just the five short years from 1947 to 1952, the Indian people had to adjust themselves to the change from the role of natives under foreign rule to that of citizens under self-rule. Although the new constitution was approved in January 1950, consciousness of what it means to live under a democratic constitution was not felt until the 1952 general elections.

In these five years Indian political leaders and their followers had to adjust to a new set of rules. They had to learn to measure their strength by votes rather than militant demonstrations: they had to change their goals and they had to develop new assessments about enemies and friends. The adjustment to a new set of rules was not the same for each of the parties, nor was it uniform within a party.

PRE-ELECTION RELATIONS

By 1951 the leaders of the Socialist Party recognized that if they were to be victorious in the coming elections they would have to admit into their party the dissidents who had just recently broken with Congress, or, as an alternative, arrange an electoral alliance with them. The Socialists had already taken part in a large number of by-elections in the various provinces and had more experience with the new set of rules than some of the other groups.

Asoka Mehta, the Socialist Party's General Secretary, analyzed the twenty-eight by-elections held between January 1950 and March 1951 for the provincial legislatures. Mehta concluded that the Socialist Party was the second largest party in India, enjoying more support than all other opposition parties put together.[1] Mehta further noted that Congress, with a little over 50% of the popular vote in the by-elections, had won 71.4% of the seats because the small parties had split the opposition vote and

[1] Asoka Mehta, "Straws in the Wind—An Analysis of Recent By-elections," *Janata*, VI (June 3, 1951), pp. 6-7.

thereby prevented the Socialists from gaining seats. Mehta concluded that if the other opposition parties heeded "the clearly expressed wishes of the people" and did not contest those seats for which the Socialist Party had put up candidates, then the Congress Party "would be routed at the polls."[2]

In accordance with this analysis the Socialist Party during the pre-election period carried on negotiations with a number of the opposition parties so as to avoid triangular fights. Such arrangements were made with the Jharkhand Party (in Bihar), the Revolutionary Communist Party of India (in Bengal), the Scheduled Caste Federation, and the Subhasist Forward Bloc.

The emergence of the Kisan Mazdoor Praja Party on the national scene with a potential that could rival that of the Socialist Party appeared as a threat to the Socialist Party's election plans. Such a party, felt the Socialist leaders, could split the opposition vote and assure a Congress victory. The Socialists, therefore, were particularly eager to induce the Congress dissidents either to join the Socialist Party or to agree not to compete in the same areas.

As early as November 1950, the Socialist Party showed considerable friendliness toward the Congress dissidents. At that time, discussions were held between Jayaprakash Narayan and Acharya Kripalani to explore the extent to which the newly formed Congress Democratic Front and the Socialist Party could cooperate to combat such things as blackmarketeering and corruption. Jayaprakash again met with the Front leaders in April 1951. He appealed to them to join the Socialist Party, if the Front should leave Congress, or at least to cooperate in the elections.[3]

The Socialist Party was apparently eager to see the dissident Congressmen join with them rather than form their own party. When it seemed likely that the Democratic Front was going to secede from Congress, Jayaprakash repeated his appeal.[4]

A few days later, at a meeting of the Democratic Front to discuss the question of breaking away from Congress, Kripalani

[2] *Ibid.*, p. 8.   [3] *Hindustan Times*, April 29, 1951.
[4] *Ibid.*, May 1, 1951.

told the press that Jayaprakash's invitation would be considered when and if the Front left Congress.

But it was soon evident that Kripalani and the KMPP leaders did not intend to merge with the Socialist Party. Following the dissolution of the Front on May 4, 1951, Kripalani and the dissidents proceeded instead to prepare for a national convention at Patna, in Bihar. Kripalani made it clear that there would be no merger. He said that in the coming elections the Praja Party would work in cooperation with the Socialist Party, but there was no question of merging the two parties.[5]

A few days later Jayaprakash announced that the KMPP and the SP had agreed to an election alliance so that the fight against Congress could be straightforward. He explained that the details of the alliance would be worked out by the state organizations of both parties. There were no plans for the establishment of a Joint Parliamentary Board to select candidates. Selection would be made by mutual adjustment.[6]

But in spite of earlier hopes, the electoral alliances in the various states did not always materialize between the KMPP and the Socialist Party. In Madras the two parties failed to arrive at a consensus; elsewhere district and provincial committees often failed to agree upon candidates. The Madras KMPP Executive Committee rejected an alliance with the Socialists in response to a statement Jayaprakash was alleged to have made in Calcutta, that other political parties should merge with the Socialist Party as a condition for electoral cooperation.[7]

If the Socialists were prepared to merge or cooperate more closely, why were not the KMPPers? KMPP leaders argued that for a variety of reasons none of the other opposition parties could offer the kind of opposition which was needed in a democracy. The Hindu communal parties had no possibility of success. As for the Socialist Party, wrote Kripalani, ". . . it has failed to capture the imagination of the people. . . . The chief reason for this is that as soon as Gandhiji became an active force in Indian politics, his personality and political philosophy were the major

---

[5] *Hindu*, August 22, 1951.   [6] *Times of India*, September 17, 1951.
[7] *Hindustan Times*, October 20, 1951.

deciding factors in the country's public life. . . . The psychological atmosphere created in favour of his philosophy is so great
that it has made it difficult for the nation to accept the Socialist
Party's outlook. . . . The average man in India . . . gets confused
about what actually the Indian Socialists stand for. The Socialists
are still, more or less, a party of intellectuals. . . . Often their
learned theses, full of technical words and phrases in vogue in the
West, when translated in provincial languages, have little meaning for the unlettered masses. . . . The Socialist Party as at present cannot by itself succeed in forming a strong opposition party
to the Congress within the legislature and in the country."[8]

The new party, in answer to its critics, attempted to develop
an ideology of its own as a justification for its existence. While
at first Kripalani denied that the Party had an ideology, and
aimed instead at implementing the Congress program, as the
elections grew closer he emphasized that the Party was based
on the "Gandhian way." By the time of the elections, the new
party claimed for itself the heritage of Gandhi. And since Kripalani, Ghosh, and Prakasam had all been staunch followers
and associates of Gandhi, their claim gained some credence.

What is important to note, however, is that this ideological
"development" was no obstacle to closer collaboration or even
merger with the Socialist Party, which had itself endorsed the
Sarvodaya Plan written by the Gandhian constructive workers.
In its own way the Socialist Party, and especially Jayaprakash
Narayan, had grown closer to the Gandhian ideals professed by
the KMPP. The barriers between the KMPP and the Socialists
were thus not ideological ones.

FORCES OF REPULSION

What, then, were the barriers? We have already noted that
the Socialists, on the one hand, recognized that without some
kind of arrangement the KMPP would split the opposition vote.
The KMPP leaders, on the other hand, showed no such awareness.

The primary barrier to close relations was the high expecta-

[8] Acharya Kripalani, *Towards Sarvodaya* (New Delhi: KMPP, 1951), pp. 5-6.

tions which the KMPP leaders held that their party would be a great success in the elections, emerge as a powerful opposition, and in some states even be in a position to form governments. While the Socialists were equally optimistic, their past experiences in the by-elections warned them of the effects of splitting the opposition vote.

The extent to which both the KMPP and the Socialist Party optimistically miscalculated their electoral prospects was brought out by the contrast between the large number of candidates each entered in the general elections and the large number of deposits each lost. (See Table 3 below.) The fact is that all the parties, with the exception of Congress, overestimated their strength and underestimated the strength of Congress. It was this miscalculation which in great part helps to explain the multiplication of parties which took place before the elections and the eagerness of some of them, including the KMPP, to stand alone.

Not only was the KMPP's national voting average poor, but even in its supposed strongholds of Madras and Bengal its showing was disappointing. In Madras, where the KMPP has hopes of becoming the majority party, it won only 35 seats in an Assembly of 375. The Communists, with 62 seats, did far better. In West Bengal the KMPP won only 15 seats in an Assembly of 238. In the House of the People in New Delhi the KMPP won only 9 seats, compared with 362 for Congress, 12 for the Socialists, and 23 for the Communists.

What were the reasons for such gross miscalculations by the KMPP, and for that matter by most of the other parties? To understand them, we must first refer back to the events which occurred between 1947 and 1952.

While much had been accomplished during these five years—the assumption of power by a nationalist government, the integration of the princely states, the inauguration of the Five Year Plan shortly before the election, the maintenance of some degree of law and order—a number of things also happened which many expected to affect the Congress Party adversely, including the following: partition, which left not only the Social-

TABLE 1

Popular Votes for the House of the People

	Votes Polled	Percentage of Total	Seats Won
Congress	47,665,875	45.0%	362
Socialists	11,216,779	10.6	12
KMPP	6,156,558	5.8	9
Communists[a]	3,484,401	3.3	23
Jan Sangh	3,246,288	3.1	3
Scheduled Caste Federation	2,501,964	2.3	2
Ram Rajya Parishad	2,151,603	2.0	3
Krishikar Lok	1,489,615	1.4	1
Hindu Mahasabha	1,003,034	.9	4
Independents	16,778,749	15.8	41
Other parties	10,249,629	9.8	29
Totals	105,944,495	100.0	489

[a] The unofficial CPI vote, which includes CPI allies, was 5,723,000, or 5.4% of the total vote, and the unofficial total of CPI and allied seats in the House of the People was 27. See Richard L. Park, "Indian Election Results," *Far Eastern Survey*, XXI (May 27, 1952).

Source: Votes Polled and Percentage of Total: Election Commission, *Report on the First General Elections in India 1951-52*, Vol. II (Statistical) (Delhi: Manager of Publications, 1955), pp. 11-12. Seats Won: Ministry of Information and Broadcasting, Government of India, *India, A Reference Annual 1953* (Delhi: Publications Division, Government of India, 1953), p. 28.

ists but a sizable conservative group unhappy; the failure of the government to reach a settlement with Pakistan on the Kashmir dispute; the enormous refugee problem in the Punjab and especially in Bengal; the violent activities of the Communists in the states of Hyderabad and Madras; corruption in the government and in the Congress Party; and widespread dissensions inside the Congress organization.

It was the last, perhaps, which more than anything else gave hope to the opposition groups. The KMPP Congress dissidents saw what appeared to be an endless stream of defectors entering their party. They believed that the country was growing dissatisfied with the Congress and would turn toward those who not only accepted Congress ideals but promised to carry them out. They were convinced that their own leaders—Kripalani, Prakasam, and Ghosh—were of such national and provincial stature, even as compared with the Socialist leaders, that those who were dissatisfied with Congress would turn toward them.

TABLE 2

General Election Results for the Legislative Assemblies

	Congress	Social-ists	KMPP	Hindu[a]	CPI and Allies	Other Parties	Inde-pendents	Total
Assam	76	4	1	—	1	9	14	105
Bihar	240	23	1	1	—	52	13	330
Bombay	269	9	—	—	—	19	18	315
M. Pradesh	194	2	8	3	—	2	23	232
Madras	152	13	35	—	62	51	62	375
Orissa	67	10	—	—	7	35	21	140
Punjab	97	1	—	—	4	20	4	126
U.P.	390	18	1	3	—	3	14	429
W. Bengal	151	—	15	13	28	16	15	238
Hyderabad	93	11	—	—	42	15	14	175
M. Bharat	75	4	—	17	—	—	3	99
Mysore	74	3	8	—	1	2	11	99
PEPSU	26	—	1	2	2	21	8	60
Rajasthan	82	1	1	34	—	7	35	160
Saurashtra	55	2	—	—	—	1	2	60
T-Cochin	43	11	—	—	—	16	38[b]	108
Ajmer	20	—	—	3	—	3	4	30
Bhopal	25	—	—	1	—	—	4	30
Coorg	15	—	—	—	—	—	9	24
Delhi	39	2	—	4	—	—	3	48
H. Pradesh	24	—	3	—	—	—	8	36
V. Pradesh	41	10	3	4	—	—	2	60
Totals	2248	124	77	85	147	273	325	3279

a Hindu parties include Jan Sangh, Hindu Mahasabha, and Ram Rajya Parishad.
b 32 of these were won by a Communist-dominated alliance.
Source: Ministry of Information and Broadcasting, Government of India, *India*, *A Reference Annual 1953* (Delhi: Publications Division, Government of India, 1953), p. 98.

POST-ELECTION RELATIONS

In the months following the 1952 general elections, steps were taken by the KMPP and the Socialist Party to merge. In late September 1952 the merger was completed and the joint party named the Praja Socialist Party.

The official point of view as to how and why the merger took place is presented in several Party Documents.[9] According to this official line the initial step toward merger was taken with the passage of a resolution by the National Executive of the

9 *The Merger: How and Why* (Bombay: Praja Socialist Party, 1952); see also Asoka Mehta, "The Why and How of the Merger," *Janata*, vii (August 31, 1952), p. 1.

TABLE 3

Index of Expectations and Consequences

	Aspirations[a]	Defeats[b]	Victories[c]
Congress	3,153	2.7%	70.0%
CPI	465	42.4	22.8
Socialists	1,799	57.8	6.8
KMPP	1,005	65.0	7.7
Jan Sangh	717	67.6	4.7
Other parties and independents	8,171	72.2	8.4

a Number of seats contested.
b Percentage of deposits lost. Each candidate for state legislative assemblies obtaining less than one-sixth of the total valid votes forfeited his deposit of Rs. 250 (about $50).
c Percentage of seats won of those contested.
Source: Election Commission, *Report on the First General Elections in India 1951-52*, Vol. II (Statistical) (Delhi: Manager of Publications, 1955), pp. 186-187.

Socialist Party in February 1952 which urged all parties "linked by deep-rooted allegiance to nationalism, devotion to the liberties and rights of the people and burning anxiety for social change to come together and build up the vital leadership the people need to fight and end the reactionary rule of the Congress."[10]

A few months later, in May 1952, the Socialist Party in a special convention at Pachmarhi reaffirmed this point of view.[11] From Pachmarhi, representatives of the Party proceeded to Delhi to meet with spokesmen of the KMPP. On June 1, 1952 the two parties, following meetings between Kripalani, Jayaprakash Narayan, and Asoka Mehta, issued a joint statement. They agreed to form a single parliamentary party to function with "a common leader and a common discipline." They also concluded that "every effort is to be made to bring about a merger of the two parties. . . ."[12]

The representatives of the two parties agreed to a common program for the parliamentary party, which called for an egalitarian social order, local initiative and village democracy, land to the tiller, decentralization of industry, nationalization of key

10 Mehta, "The Why and How of the Merger," *op.cit.*, p. 1.
11 *Ibid.*, p. 1.
12 *The Merger: How and Why, op.cit.*, Appendix A, p. 35.

industries, a free trade union movement, civil liberties, the spirit of austerity and *swadeshi* (buying home-made, i.e. native-made, goods), economic equality and social mobility, and a policy of neutrality and non-involvement of India in foreign affairs. Asoka Mehta, the Socialist Party General Secretary, concluded that "the basic programme of the legislative party that was drawn up in May showed that on no material points did the two parties differ."[13]

At a meeting in Lucknow, which ended on August 25, 1952, the two parties agreed to merge. Acharya Kripalani, on behalf of the KMPP, met with Acharya Narendra Deva, Rammanohar Lohia, and Asoka Mehta of the Socialist Party. They approved the basic program drawn for the Parliamentary Party, agreed upon a name, accepted the constitution of the Socialist Party until a plenary conference of the unity party could be held, and decided to hold a meeting of representatives of the two parties in Bombay during the following month to complete the merger.

As scheduled, the joint meeting of the representatives of the two parties took place in Bombay on the 26th and 27th of September 1952. Kripalani was elected Chairman of the meeting. He described the great similarity in outlook between the two groups and talked of their attempts at cooperation before the elections and the effect of the failure to cooperate upon the outcome of the elections.[14] Kripalani told the meeting that the multiplicity of the parties opposing Congress was responsible for the Congress victory by a plurality vote. After the elections both groups felt that the radical parties in the opposition should unite.

Kripalani further pointed out that as far as basic principles go there is complete identity between the two parties. "We both want a classless and casteless society free from social, political and economic exploitation. The Socialists call it the Socialist society. We call it the Sarvodaya society."[15]

After Kripalani concluded his speech, Jayaprakash Narayan spoke a few words. He said that "It was good that ideological

[13] Mehta, "The Why and How of the Merger," *op.cit.*, p. 1.
[14] *The Merger: How and Why, op.cit.*, pp. 15-16.
[15] *Ibid.*, p. 20.

issues were kept out when we agreed to merge. This tided over a number of difficulties. There have been no doubt misunderstandings and other difficulties, but, I am sure, mutual trust, faith and forbearance will help us to get over these difficulties and this party will become the builder of a new India."[16]

The merger resolution was moved and adopted without discussion. The joint meeting then agreed to call the party the Praja Socialist Party and elected a twenty-two-member National Executive.

The Socialist and KMPP leaders greeted the merger with much enthusiasm. Asoka Mehta called it ". . . the major political event not merely after the General Elections but after the achievement of freedom. . . . [Furthermore] The KMPP-Socialist merger has isolated the Communists and opened up the prospects of weaning away the people from them. . . . The dangerous polarisation between the Congress and Communist ends."[17]

Kripalani called it a great event after independence. "In India, wherever there is a Sangam,[18] the place is holy. I hope that soon this happy 'Sangam' will be joined by other groups."[19]

According to the official account it appears that the merger occurred very quickly and with few difficulties; whatever difficulties there may have been were easily overcome. On the basis of this official description and on the basis of other accounts and statements made by the leaders and rank and file of the two parties we can try to assess why this merger was so easily concluded. (In a later chapter, when we deal with the communal organizations and their unsuccessful attempt to merge, we shall point up some of the differences in behavior and suggest some reasons for those differences.)

The merger did not take place after the elections solely because the Socialists willed it. We have already pointed out that for a variety of reasons, even before the elections, the Socialists offered to admit the Congress dissidents into their party and in lieu of this were prepared to negotiate an electoral agreement on the

16 *Ibid.*, p. 24.
17 "The Momentous Merger," *Janata*, VII (August 31, 1952), p. 1.
18 The confluence of rivers, considered holy by Hindus.
19 "The Momentous Merger," *op.cit.*, p. 2.

national level. The decision to carry out the electoral agreement
on a provincial rather than national level was a disappointment
to the Socialist leaders. The point is that what the elections
changed was not so much the Socialist attitude as the attitude
of the KMPP leaders.

After the elections the Socialists were more intent upon merger
than ever before. In their assessment of the electoral results, Socialist leaders pointed out that a disastrous polarization was taking place between Congress and the Communists. Although the
Socialists received more votes for the House of the People than
the Communists and their allies (11,216,779 to 5,723,000), the
Communists and their allies, by concentrating their efforts in a
few districts, received more than twice as many seats (27 to 12).
Similarly, in the state Assemblies the Communists and their
allies outnumbered the Socialists by 147 to 124 seats. Furthermore, while the electoral results were uniformly considered a
great blow to the Socialist Party, especially after the high expectations and predictions of the Socialist leaders, the returns were
generally viewed as a great victory for the Communists, especially since the Communists had just emerged from a ban and in
some states were still under a ban. Also, the Socialist seats were
thinly scattered among a number of states with no impressive
hold in any one state, whereas the Communists were heavily concentrated in West Bengal, Madras, Hyderabad, and Travancore-
Cochin. In the latter three states the Communist position was
particularly enhanced by the failure of Congress to win a clear
majority of the seats. The Communists had won a stronghold in
South India. The election results thus elated the Communists
but disheartened the Socialists. This was evident from the speeches
delivered at the special convention of the Socialist Party at Pachmarhi which was called for the purpose of evaluating the elections. The need for consolidating the non-Communist, non-Congress forces was the major theme of speakers at the convention.
The Socialist leaders at Pachmarhi were especially distressed by
the success of the Communist united front policy, which in
Madras had even won over the KMPP.

Concluding his report as General Secretary, Asoka Mehta told the delegates that "Polarisation of the country between the Congress Party and the Communist Party would mean not merely the end of democratic processes and of the freedom of the people to question and to change, but an invitation to internal strife. . . . It suits the Congress and the Communists to belittle us, because each hopes to gather adventitious support by showing the other as the sole alternative."[20] This fear of polarization is evident in nearly all the statements of Socialist Party leaders during the period.

While the election results *reinforced* the Socialist desire for greater consolidation of the opposition forces, the results brought about a *change* in attitude on the part of Kripalani. Whereas before the elections Kripalani was unwilling to consider a merger, he was now eager to bring it about. In his post-election writings he ceased to stress the ideological differences between Gandhism and Marxism. In fact, in his meetings with Jayaprakash Narayan to discuss merger, Kripalani was unwilling to discuss ideological questions although Jayaprakash was prepared to raise them.[21] Kripalani's eagerness for a merger was further indicated by his willingness to reach an amicable settlement with the Socialists on the KMPP-Communist alliance in Madras. While Kripalani, unlike the Socialists, has always been willing to work with the Communists in the state legislatures,[22] he was prepared to terminate his party's coalition with the Communists in Madras, if this were an obstacle to a merger with the Socialists.

Had Kripalani been unwilling to make such a concession to the Socialists, the situation in Madras could have been a fatal obstacle to merger. Briefly, events in Madras leading up to the KMPP-Communist alliance were as follows:

As a result of the elections in Madras State no one party won a clear majority of the Assembly seats. In a legislature of 375, Congress secured 152, the Communists 62, the KMPP 35, and

---

[20] *Report of the Special Convention Held at Pachmarhi, Madhya Pradesh, May 1952* (Bombay: Socialist Party, 1952), p. 65.
[21] From an interview by the author with Acharya Kripalani in New Delhi in January 1954.
[22] *Ibid.*

the Socialists 13. The remaining seats were scattered among independents and the Tamilnad Toilers, the Krishikar Lok Party, the Commonweal Party, the Muslim League, the Forward Bloc, the Scheduled Caste Federation, and the Justice Party. The non-Congress legislators thus numbered 223 as compared with 152 for Congress. In February 1952 a convention of non-Congress Assemblymen met in Madras to explore the possibility of creating a non-Congress coalition government. The convention elected T. Prakasam, who was then the KMPP leader in Madras State, as chairman and issued a program, which the legislators, who called themselves the United Democratic Front, said they would carry out if they formed a government.[23] The United Democratic Front (UDF) contained 164 members: 70 from the CPI and its fellow travelers, 36 from the KMPP, 19 Tamilnad Toilers, 5 from the Commonweal Party, 2 from the Forward Bloc, 1 from the Scheduled Caste Federation, 1 from the Justice Party, and 30 independents.

The Socialist Party strongly opposed the Front and made clear that it would join neither with the UDF nor with Congress. When the national Socialist leaders spoke of the polarization between the Communists and Congress, they referred not only to the electoral successes of the Communists but the tendency of the Communist Party to draw other parties toward its united fronts. The Socialists, whose hatred for the Communists extends back to the popular front days of the late 1930's, looked upon the merger with the KMPP as one means of drawing the non-Communist democratic forces away from such fronts.

For a brief period after the merger it appeared as if Kripalani and Prakasam wanted to continue the alliance with the Communists on the grounds that it was a "previous commitment" of the KMPP.[24] But both Asoka Mehta and Jayaprakash Narayan publicly condemned the alliance as being an anomaly for a Socialist Party whose policy with regard to cooperation with the Communists has never been ambiguous. ". . . it would be a

[23] For a Democratic Government in Madras State (Bombay: People's Publishing House, Ltd., 1952), p. x.
[24] Free Press Journal, September 2, 1952.

fantastic situation in which the PSP would be fighting the communists everywhere and a wing of it would be cooperating with them in the Madras legislature. . . . Either KMPP-SP merger is looked at in the larger perspective and a consistent policy is followed, or the merger would defeat itself from the very start. If the merger is desirable in the higher interest, sacrifice will have to be made."[25]

The fact is that most KMPP leaders were prepared to make such a sacrifice in the interests of a merger with the Socialists. While many KMPP leaders in Madras State were openly threatening to leave their party if the PSP demanded that they withdraw from the UDF,[26] Prakasam himself remained silent. This may have been partly because he recognized that a hostile attitude might involve an open break between himself and the new party, a break which he was not yet prepared to make, and partly because he realized that the reason for the original formation of the UDF—that a non-Congress coalition government could be formed in Madras State—no longer was valid since the Congress with some independents and minor groups had successfully formed a government there. Thus the fundamental *raison d'être* for the UDF no longer existed, from Prakasam's point of view, now that the possibility of forming a non-Congress government had disappeared. Prakasam diplomatically told the joint meeting of the Socialist Party and the KMPP in Bombay that "the situation will have to be reviewed,"[27] and privately Kripalani assured the Socialists that the Madras coalition would end in due course.[28] On the basis of these comments, Socialist leaders felt assured that the Madras alliance would end.[29]

If the KMPP leaders were prepared to make concessions to the

[25] Jayaprakash Narayan, "KMPP and UDF," *Janata*, VII (September 7, 1952), p. 12; see also Asoka Mehta, "Smash UDF Says Asoka—KMPP Should Terminate Its Old 'Commitment' to the Reds," *Janata*, VII (September 7, 1952), p. 1.

[26] *National Herald*, September 7, 1952.

[27] *The Merger: How and Why, op.cit.*, p. 31.

[28] From an interview by the author with Acharya Kripalani in New Delhi in January 1954.

[29] *Free Press Journal*, September 23, 1952; the KMPP-Communist alliance in Madras was actually terminated within a few months after the completion of the merger in September.

Socialists, the Socialists were likewise prepared to be diplomatic in their dealings with the KMPP leaders. The Socialists never proposed that the KMPP dissolve; they urged that the two parties should merge on equal terms.[30] In the formation of *ad hoc* State Committees for the merged party, both parties were to have equal voice irrespective of their strength. The Socialists also agreed that ideological questions would not be considered during the merger talks. Finally, when the negotiations took place, the Socialists agreed to make Kripalani the Chairman of the new party, and to make the KMPP leaders the Chairmen of their respective state parties in U.P., Madras, Malabar, Vindhya Pradesh, West Bengal, and Madhya Pradesh. However, Socialists were to be the Party Secretaries in most of the states and Asoka Mehta the General Secretary. Thus while the Party machinery was to be in the hands of the Socialists, the prestige of being party Chairmen was given to the KMPPers.

CONCLUSION: REASONS FOR THE MERGER

The merger of the Socialist Party and the Kisan Mazdoor Praja Party was the first major party merger in independent India. The merger resulted in a consolidation of the two largest opposition parties and created a single party whose total strength in the 1952 general elections was 17 million votes or 16.3% of the popular vote. And shortly after the merger, the new Praja Socialist Party was joined by the smaller Subhasist Forward Bloc, a party in West Bengal.

Since 1952 other parties have attempted to merge but none with as much ease or success as the Socialists and the KMPP. One other major attempt, that at bringing about a merger of all the major Hindu communal organizations, was completely unsuccessful.[31] Why then was it possible for the Socialists and the KMPP to join together?

First, there was a basic consensus in outlook on the part of the two groups. They had common experiences in the national movement; they had both experienced frustration with Congress;

---

[30] From an interview by the author with Acharya Kripalani, *op.cit.*
[31] See Chapter 10 on the Jan Sangh–Hindu Mahasabha merger attempt.

they had both been disappointed in their election defeat. Furthermore, since the death of Gandhi, the Socialists had drawn increasingly closer to the Gandhian outlook, and the KMPP had absorbed a good deal of Socialist economic thinking, so that there were no ideological barriers to merger.[32] But while it is true that without such a basic harmony in outlook a merger would probably not have been possible, both sides, during the merger discussions, deliberately minimized whatever differences they had. But as we shall see later, when we discuss the attempted merger of the Hindu communal parties, an agreement on basic principles need not result in a merger.

What made a merger possible was the eagerness with which both sides welcomed the proposal and their willingness to compromise. The pre-election belief of the Socialists that the smaller parties would split the opposition vote and thus take seats from them was reinforced by the election returns. Polarization between the Congress and the Communists made them even more eager to merge with similarly minded groups than ever before.

Furthermore, the elections brought about a fundamental change in the thinking of the KMPP leaders. Even more than the Socialists, they had miscalculated their electoral strength. Considering their large expectations before the elections, they felt then that to merge with the Socialists would have constituted a step down. Rather than be submerged in another organization they were prepared to "go it alone." Their subsequent election defeat and the enormous disillusionment which Kripalani and his colleagues experienced led them to recognize that they were leaders with little mass appeal.[33]

A confidant of Kripalani told the writer that shortly after the elections Kripalani privately talked of liquidating the KMPP or retiring from active politics. In the sense that Kripalani was eager to dissolve the Party in one way or another, this description of Kripalani's motives seems accurate. The available evidence

[32] The Socialists now spoke of non-violence and ends and means. Their economics had shifted from Marxism to Gandhism with an emphasis on cottage industries, village self-sufficiency, and the importance of decentralization. The Socialist leader, Jayaprakash Narayan, became a confirmed Gandhian.

[33] Kripalani himself had been defeated as a candidate for Parliament.

suggests that Kripalani viewed the merger less as a means of strengthening his own position and more as a means of terminating an organization whose position seemed hopeless. Inspired as he was less by ideological considerations and more by an exaggerated sense of his and his colleagues' mass appeal, there was little point in continuing an organization which had demonstrated its inability to win mass support. Merger with the largest opposition party seemed the only alternative to either remaining a minor third party or dissolving.

Once the leadership of both parties became convinced that a merger was desirable, the major problem became how to overcome whatever objections might arise from the rank and file. *In general it might be said that whenever attempts at a merger are made, the rank and file of the parties involved are more opposed than the leadership, and conversely, whenever the prospects of a split within a party occur, it is again the rank and file rather than the leadership which generally favors the move.*

In this merger attempt, however, there was relatively little opposition from the rank and file of the KMPP. Organizational and party allegiances were not strong since the Party was relatively new. And while there were a number of groups in the KMPP which were well knit, especially in Bengal and to a lesser extent in Madras State, in those areas the KMPP was the larger of the two and had little fear of being submerged by the Socialists. In U.P., however, where the Socialists were stronger, many of the KMPPers were reluctant to see a merger.[34] But elsewhere the KMPP rank and file showed little opposition.

On the other hand, there was considerable objection from some of the Socialist rank and file. In U.P., for example, there was much opposition from the student and ex-student members of the Party who joined during the '42 movement.[35] Rank and filers from U.P. and West Bengal, especially, criticized the merger as marking a step further away from Marxism. Earlier, delegates

[34] The *Hindu*, June 23, 1952, reported that at a conference of the KMPP in U.P. only five out of forty-two speakers gave complete support to the merger proposals presented to them by Kripalani, while twenty-nine spoke against the merger.

[35] *Hindu*, June 23, 1952.

from these areas to the Socialist convention at Pachmarhi were critical of the speech by Lohia in which as Party President he called for a modification of the Party's acceptance of Socialist theory so as to bring the Party closer to the Gandhian as opposed to the Marxist position. And when the merger took place a small group of Socialist Marxists led by Sheela Perera of West Bengal refused to join the new Praja Socialist Party and continued to work in the name of the old Socialist Party.

Many Socialist rank and filers criticized their leadership for the haste in which the merger took place and for failing to place the merger proposal before the entire Party. Jayaprakash Narayan and Asoka Mehta went to some effort to prove that the decision was democratically made. They pointed out that the political resolution of the Pachmarhi convention approved a consolidation of like-minded political parties and their eventual merger; furthermore, the Delhi and Lucknow agreements with the KMPP had been ratified by the Socialist General Council.[36]

A number of Socialist rank and filers privately told the author that in voting for the Pachmarhi political resolution calling for the consolidation of parties they were thinking in terms of other groups joining with the Socialist Party and not in terms of a merger on an equal basis, a merger which involved a reorganization of the Party, the leadership, and ultimately the program.

Many of the Socialists pointed out that by merging with the KMPP they were not gaining an influx of party workers, except from a few local areas, but were only adding a few leaders with some national and regional reputations. The KMPP, they claimed, had almost no organization as did the Socialist Party; it was a party of leaders with few followers. It was grossly unfair, they argued, to merge with the KMPP on an equal basis. Furthermore, many of the Socialists remembered vividly the role which Kripalani had played in 1947 in opposition to the Congress Socialist Party.

But of all the reasons for opposing the merger, the most frequently heard was that the merger would result in "diluting"

---

[36] *The Merger; How and Why, op.cit.*, p. 8; see also Mehta, Asoka, "Is Merger Decision Undemocratic?" *Janata*, VIII (September 14, 1952).

the Party; by which was meant, first, that the Marxist ideology would be toned down still further, and, second, that the Party would now be joined by a group of older Congressmen who had not participated in the '42 movement in the way the younger Socialists had, and who did not share the same experiences and outlook. While the Socialist leadership felt that much would be gained, a large part of the rank and file felt that something of their group spirit and ideology would be lost.

But however widespread the opposition from the Socialist rank and file may have been, there was little opportunity for it to be expressed. The Pachmarhi conference concluded in the last week of May 1952. On June 1st the Delhi Agreement for the establishment of a unified parliamentary party was signed. On August 25th at Lucknow the agreement to merge was drawn, and it was approved in Bombay a month later. Within the space of a few months the merger was complete. Had there been a national convention of the Socialist Party to approve the merger, it is difficult to say whether it would have been approved, but it is certain that there would have been much opposition to it.

6. Marxist Left Parties in Bengal

For several decades Bengal has been the center of left wing Marxist activity in India. Marxist left parties can be found in other states, but there are few which cannot trace their origins to Bengal. Most of the Marxist left parties have their national headquarters in Calcutta, Bengal's capital city, and with few exceptions the nationally known Marxist left leaders have been Bengalis.[1] By Marxist left parties we are referring here to those Indian parties which claim to be Marxist or socialist but which are organizationally separate from the Communist and Socialist parties. In popular writing in the West, these parties would probably be called Trotskyite, but in the strict technical sense of being supporters of Trotsky and/or the Fourth International that term cannot accurately be used here.

REVOLUTIONARY ANTECEDENTS

As elsewhere in Asia, groups dedicated to Marxism sprang up in India after the Russian revolution. But the antecedents of these groups appeared in Bengal at least a decade or two earlier with the rise of terrorist and revolutionary nationalist organizations. Two early revolutionary organizations especially, the Jugantar and the Anushilan Samiti, laid the groundwork for the later left wing parties.[2] Among the early revolutionaries were

[1] In the elections for the House of the People the Marxist left parties captured approximately 2,766,000 votes in the 1952 elections. Of these, the only major Marxist left party outside of West Bengal was the Peasants and Workers Party, which is in the Marathi-speaking areas of Bombay State, Madhya Pradesh, and Hyderabad. In West Bengal six Marxist left parties participated in the 1952 elections: the Marxist Forward Bloc (which received a national vote for the House of the People of 911,096), the Revolutionary Socialist Party (393,984), the Subhasist Forward Bloc (115,875), the Revolutionary Communist Party of India (26,245), the Bolshevik Party of India (25,792), and the Socialist Republican Party (which did not stand for the House of the People). This compares with a vote of 11,216,779 for the Socialist Party and 5,723,000 for the Communists and their allies. In West Bengal itself, the Marxist left parties won 586,889 votes for the House of the People out of 7,615,932, as compared with 720,304 for the Communists and 831,448 for the Socialists and KMPP combined. Figures from Election Commission, *Report on the First General Elections in India 1951-52*, Vol. II (Statistical), (Delhi: Manager of Publications, 1955).

[2] The most authoritative work on the early revolutionary organizations is

writers and publishers of large numbers of newspapers and books which had considerable impact upon rising young nationalist sentiment.[3]

After the partition of Bengal by Lord Curzon in 1905, terrorist and revolutionary activities expanded suddenly. The revolutionaries boycotted British goods, and they attempted to blow up a train in 1907, to take the life of the Mayor of Chandernagore in 1908, and—the most famous incident of all—to kill a district judge in 1908. This last resulted in the accidental death of two English ladies, and led to the Alipore Bomb trial and the arrest of many revolutionary leaders.[4]

With the advent of Gandhi's first non-cooperation movement in 1921-1922, most of the Bengal revolutionaries joined Congress. They were deeply impressed with Gandhi's hold upon the masses, and recognized the necessity of converting the nationalist movement from that of a small elite to a widespread mass organization. Although the revolutionaries joined Congress, they did not accept the principle of non-violence which guided Gandhi's program.[5] While the revolutionaries remained inside Congress, some until Subhas Bose's break from it shortly after the beginning of the war, their activities continued alongside the non-violent work of the Congress organization.

There was thus a nationalist movement operating parallel to Congress which was prepared to use violence, and did, a movement which broadly accepted the leadership of Gandhi and the Congress Party but which was prepared to use its own methods. This movement continued to prod Gandhi and the Congress

---

the *Sedition Committee 1918 Report* (Calcutta: Superintendent of Government Printing, India, 1918). This is an official Government of India report and is often referred to as the Rowlett Committee Report.

[3] James Campbell Ker, *Political Trouble in India 1907-1917* (Calcutta: Government Printing Office, 1917). Chapter II gives a useful account of the literature of the Bengal revolutionaries, and Chapter III lists the leading revolutionary newspapers.

[4] Bejoy Krishna Bose, *The Alipore Bomb Trial* (Calcutta: Butterworth and Co., Ltd., 1922).

[5] In general, Bengalis did not readily accept Gandhi's principles although many joined in his movement. It is more than a coincidence that the two greatest challenges which Gandhi faced within Congress were from C. R. Das and Subhas Chandra Bose, both Bengalis.

Party to move faster and to intensify its activities. It urged complete independence even while the Congress leadership was prepared to accept Dominion status; and it urged civil disobedience movements when the Congress leadership still hoped that further negotiations would bring concessions from the British rulers.

In the 1930's, members of these revolutionary groups, as well as individuals heavily influenced by them, formed Marxist left parties inside Congress.

THE PARTIES

The Revolutionary Socialist Party (RSP) is among the largest of the Marxist non-communist, or rather non-Stalinist, parties in India. Its strength is largely confined to Bengal and Travancore-Cochin. It is the largest political group inside the United Trade Union Congress, one of the four national trade union federations. The RSP arose out of the Anushilan revolutionary group. In about 1930, the Anushilan changed its name to the Hindustan Republican Army, then to the Hindustan Republican Socialist Army; thus signifying its acceptance of socialist ideas.

As a result of the nationalist agitation in 1930 (which included the famous Chittagong Armory raid, when revolutionaries led an armed insurrection in the town of Chittagong, near Burma), a large number of revolutionaries were placed in jail, where they remained until 1937 and 1938. So long as these revolutionaries did not disturb the British prison authorities they were allowed to keep in touch with one another in jail, read books, do research, and study, as well as have their own football, volleyball, and cricket tournaments. During this period a large number of the revolutionaries were completely won over to socialism and were imbued with Marxist ideas.[6]

Several of the Anushilan revolutionaries prepared a thesis while in jail which they issued upon their release. With the adoption of this thesis by the Central Committee of their newly founded party in September 1938, the RSP became a distinct political group on the national scene.

[6] From an interview by the author with Tridib Chaudhuri in New Delhi in December 1953.

The thesis called for "communism and classless society," with the overthrow of foreign imperialist domination as the first task. The proletariat was viewed as the "only consistently revolutionary class"[7] and was conceived as being allied with the peasantry and the lower middle classes. In opposition to the Gandhian outlook, the RSP declared that final victory will "assume the form of a dictatorship, i.e. it is inevitably bound to rely on military force, on the arming of the masses and not on institutions established by 'lawful' and 'peaceful' means."[8] Self-determination, a constituent assembly, the annulment of foreign debts, agrarian reform, abolition of princely states, liquidation of rural indebtedness, nationalization of key industries and foreign concerns, the eight-hour day and social insurance—these were the slogans of the new party.

The thesis further declared that the Party "recognizes the USSR as the base of the coming Socialist World Revolution and seeks to defend it from external attacks," but that it believes internationalism to mean working wholeheartedly for the development of the revolutionary movement in one's own country.[9]

The new party became an organized group within the Congress Socialist Party, just as the CSP was an organized group within the Congress; that is to say, the RSP like the CSP had its own thesis, its own organization, its own propaganda, its own leaders, and above all its own allegiances and loyalties. It is important to note that while the RSP had avowed differences with the Communist Party, there appeared to be no important differences, until somewhat later, between it and the Congress Socialist Party.

The revolutionaries had a history and tradition of their own which they wished to continue. While the Congress Socialist Party was being built in 1934, the revolutionaries were in jail, continuing the associations they had had before. It seemed only right to them, therefore, that they should continue to work to-

---

[7] *The Thesis and Platform of Action of the Revolutionary Socialist Party of India—What Revolutionary Socialism Stands For* (Calcutta: Revolutionary Socialist Party Central Committee, 1946), p. 7. The first edition was published in 1938.

[8] *Ibid.*, p. 9.   [9] *Ibid.*, p. 15.

gether as an organized group. What their subsequent differences were with the Congress Socialist Party we shall discuss later.

The RSP threw its complete support to Subhas Chandra Bose, who for several years had had the support of the Anushilan and Jugantar organizations against the dominant pro-Gandhian national leadership. The RSP supported Bose for President of Congress and supported him in his opposition to the famous Pant Resolution, which required that the President of Congress appoint his Working Committee in consultation with Gandhi. At the Anti-Compromise Conference at Ramgarh, organized against the Congress leadership, the RSP continued to uphold the Bose group. The essential issue in this struggle between Bose and the Congress pro-Gandhian leadership was ostensibly the policy which Congress ought to pursue in the event of war: whether preparations for a mass struggle against the British should begin in anticipation of war or whether a mass struggle should be postponed because of the threat of war. But beyond the conflict over issues was a conflict between two wings of the Congress organization for control of the Party.

In 1940 the RSP described the war as the "Second Imperialist War" and argued that the revolutionary socialists must organize the pro-struggle elements within the Congress into an "Anti-Imperialist Peoples Front."[10] It was at this point, in 1940, that the RSP set itself up as a separate party apart from the Congress Socialists, and declared that the CSP was pseudo-Marxist and had moved away from Marxism-Leninism to "Social-Gandhism."

The Party maintained its anti-war policy even after the German attack upon the Soviet Union. In its thesis adopted by the Central Committee in 1941, the Party declared that the fundamental character of the war had not changed. Only a free and Soviet India, they declared, could help Soviet Russia.[11] In another policy statement the RSP declared that an invasion of India by Japan would be resisted but it would not mean a quali-

10 *War Thesis of the RSPI* (Calcutta: Revolutionary Socialist Party Central Committee, 1940), p. 21.

11 *Thesis of the RSP on the Russo-German War—Intensify National Struggle. On to Revolutionary Defence of USSR* (Calcutta: Revolutionary Socialist Party Central Committee, 1941), p. 18.

tative change in their characterization of the war, which was basically an "imperialist war."[12] Another resolution endorsed the Quit India slogan of the Indian National Congress.[13]

For many years Jogesh Chatterjee was the leader and the General Secretary of the RSP, but after independence and Chatterjee's forced retirement due to age, control of the Party—which is organized along Leninist lines with an all-powerful Central Committee, a Political Committee, and a Secretariat with a General Secretary and three area secretaries—fell into the hands of a younger group: Sreekantan Nair, MP and General Secretary of the Party and its leader in Travancore-Cochin; Tridib Chaudhuri, an MP from Bengal; Makhan Paul, the Bengal Provincial Secretary; and Jatin Chakravarty, the Party's trade union leader and organizer in Bengal.

The Revolutionary Communist Party of India (the RCPI, not to be confused with the CPI) is the party of Saumyen Tagore, the grandnephew of the great poet. Saumyen Tagore was a member of an unofficial communist group of the early '20's and was one of the organizers of the early Peasants and Workers Party in Bengal, Bombay, and Madras. In 1927 Tagore went to Moscow as a representative to the Communist International and was a delegate to the 1928 Moscow conference. For nearly eight years, before 1934, Tagore traveled through the Soviet Union and Europe. He opposed the "soft" policy of the Communists toward fascism in Germany in the early '30's and attacked the Communist Party of India for its "ultra leftism." His opposition to the official Communist Party grew so intense that in 1934 he broke with the Party and formed the Communist League, which later changed its name to the Communist Party, and finally to the Revolutionary Communist Party of India. The RCPI opposed the pre-war united front movement, criticized the war as an imperialist war, supported the Quit India movement, and bitterly attacked both the Russian invasion of Finland and the Stalin-Hitler pact.

[12] *Ibid.*, pp. 19-21.
[13] *On National Struggle of August 1942* (Calcutta: Revolutionary Socialist Party Central Committee, 1942).

Like the RSP and the CPI, the RCPI is organized along Leninist lines which branch up from party cells to a Central Committee at the top. After the war the Communist Party entered its terrorist phase, and in 1948 one wing of the RCPI began terrorist activities and was expelled from the Party after its raid on the Jessup engineering firm in Calcutta, which resulted in the death of several foremen. This group looted the factory, attacked a police station, and attempted to escape the police by fleeing in a jeep, but it was ultimately arrested and jailed.

The RCPI has some influence in Assam tribal areas and among some Calcutta students. It claims a total membership of about 5,000 to 6,000,[14] of which some 500 are claimed to be in Calcutta.

The Bolshevik Party of India had as its predecessor a group called the Bengal Labour Party, created in 1933 by N. Dutt Mazumdar, a young Bengali who had been deeply impressed by Marxist ideas during his stay as a student at the London School of Economics. Dutt Mazumdar and his group became deeply involved in trade union organizing in Bengal, and won some influence among the dock workers.

In about 1936 the Labour Party and the Communist Party for nearly all purposes combined, i.e. the members of the Labour Party, while retaining their organization, became members of the Communist Party. With war approaching, the Labour Party established a group called the Bolshevik Party, which was to be its underground wing when the war, which the Labour Party opposed, broke out. But differences soon developed between the Communist and Labour parties: the Labour Party, led by Mazumdar, broke with the Communists by its declaration that the war was imperialist and in its support for the Quit India movement. Mazumdar and the Labour Party then went underground, but in December 1942 Mazumdar was arrested. After his release from jail he ran on a Congress ticket for the Bengal Assembly in 1946, was victorious, and was soon made a Minister

[14] From an interview by the author with Saumyen Tagore in Calcutta in January 1954.

in the Congress government, a post he held until June 1952 when he lost his seat in the general elections.[15]

But although the Labour Party died with Mazumdar's entrance into Congress, the Bolshevik Party continued. Bishwanath Dubey, an active trade union organizer, is now the leader of the Party. While the Bolshevik Party members broke with the Communists by supporting wholeheartedly the Bose leadership in 1939, the Bolshevik Party soon lined up behind the Communists in their support for the "People's War." During the war some of the Bolshevik Party members joined the Communist Party, but the remainder continued in their own organization. The Bolshevik Party claims a membership of 3,000,[16] primarily in Bengal, but scattered in the states of Assam, U.P., Madhya Pradesh, Bihar, Bombay, and Madhya Bharat.

The Bolshevik Party calls itself "the Party of the Indian Working Class" and claims to be based upon "the correct formulation and implementation of the principles of Marxism-Leninism."[17] The Party condemns the "Anglo-American imperialists" and expresses its support for the "glorious successes achieved by the Soviet Union in the field of post-war reconstruction and the consolidation of the People's Democracy in China through sweeping agrarian reforms."[18]

Like the other leftist parties, the Bolshevik Party calls for abolition of landlordism without compensation and land to the tillers, and for the repeal of the Preventive Detention Act; opposes retrenchment; and supports linguistic redistribution of states, confiscation of foreign capital, nationalization of industry, and quitting the Commonwealth.

The All India Forward Bloc is the largest Marxist left party in Bengal. The Forward Bloc was founded in 1939 by Subhas Chandra Bose as a means of uniting all the leftist groups in Con-

[15] Biography from Dutt Mazumdar in an interview with the author in Delhi in October 1954.

[16] From an interview by the author with Bishwanath Dubey in Calcutta in June 1954.

[17] *Political Statement of the Central Committee Bolshevik Party of India* (Calcutta: Bolshevik Party of India Central Committee, 1952), p. 1.

[18] *Ibid.*, p. 2.

gress in opposition to the then existing Congress Party policy.[19] Bose had demanded that an immediate militant struggle be launched against the British. His new organization was intended as a front for the existing left wing groups but in a short time it became a political party. Early in 1942 the Forward Bloc was banned for advocating armed revolt against the British. By then, Subhas Bose had escaped from India and was organizing the Indian National Army in Southeast Asia.

Several things must be noted about the early Forward Bloc. First, it had had no clear ideology as had the other leftist parties. While Bose talked of Marxism and Socialism, he had never clearly spelled out his ideas except as they pertained to the ways and means by which independence was to be attained. The Party thus had a program, but it could not be said to have had an ideology, in the sense that it had no general outlook, especially for post-independence India. And second, while the Party had been formed by Bose and had been organized around him, it was denied his active leadership almost from the very beginning. His early arrest followed by his escape from India to Germany, Japan, and then Southeast Asia withdrew him from active party politics in India.

From 1942 through '45 and '46, most of the Forward Bloc leaders were underground or in jail, while their party was under ban. On June 10, 1946 the Working Committee of the All India Forward Bloc, at a meeting in Bombay, approved a new manifesto for the Party in which it declared itself to be a socialist party with an ideology and program based upon the concept of a militant class struggle.[20]

Shortly after the manifesto was approved, R. S. Ruikar, Vice President of the Forward Bloc, and Mrs. Lila Roy, a member of the Working Committee, along with several others, were released from jail. They objected to the Marxist orientation of the new thesis and contended that, furthermore, it had been

[19] Subhas Chandra Bose, *The Indian Struggle 1935-1942* (Calcutta: Chuckervertty, Chatterjee and Co., Ltd., 1952) gives a detailed account of the early history of the Forward Bloc.

[20] *Programme of Post-War Revolution, Draft Manifesto of the Forward Bloc* (Bombay: All India Forward Bloc, 1946), p. 65.

written under the influence of Communist infiltrators. From 1946 until 1948, bitter rivalry existed between the pro-Marxist and anti-Marxist sections of the Party.

In December 1948 the anti-Marxist section met at Calcutta, while the pro-Marxist wing met at Chandernagar, the French settlement outside of Calcutta. The Calcutta conference, which elected as its chairman R. S. Ruikar, now the Party's General Secretary, and as the chairman of its Reception Committee Mrs. Lila Roy, expelled the Marxist wing for holding a rival conference under the Party name. It then declared itself a socialist party and appointed a subcommittee to "restate clearly its ideology and philosophical position . . . [in terms of] the ideology and philosophy of Netaji Subhas Chandra Bose."[21]

In the meantime the Marxist section of the Forward Bloc, meeting at Chandernagar, declared that non-Marxist elements had infiltrated the Party and that the Chandernagar meeting was called "to stamp out all lethargy, counter-revolutionary deviation and reformist opportunism from the party."[22]

It is interesting to note that the two parties (by this time they were two distinct political parties) had almost the same political program. Both parties condemned India's continued membership in the British Commonwealth and the corruption which had entered Congress, and both called for socialism. Where they differed was in regard to tactics and strategy. The non-Marxist Subhasist Forward Bloc claimed, on the one hand, to reject the ultra-leftist tactics of the Communist Party, while on the other, unlike the Socialist Party, it did not believe socialism could be realized by stressing parliamentary means or constitutional evolution.[23] The Marxist Forward Bloc, while not commenting on either the CPI or the SP, advocated "the revolutionary seizure of power by the workers and peasants in the factories and in the fields."[24]

---

[21] *Programme and Policy of Netaji's Party—What Forward Bloc Stands For* (Nagpur: All India Forward Bloc, 1949), p. 7.

[22] *From Arrah to Chandernagar—A March Towards Social Revolution* (Calcutta: All India Forward Bloc, undated [1949?]), p. 4.

[23] *Programme and Policy of Netaji's Party, op.cit.*, p. xiii.

[24] *From Arrah to Chandernagar, op.cit.*, p. 11.

As a result, on the trade union front, the Subhasist Forward Bloc entered the Socialist-dominated Hind Mazdoor Sabha while the Marxist group remained in the Communist-dominated All India Trade Union Congress. During the election campaign in 1951-1952, the Marxist group cooperated with the Communists, while the Subhasist group worked with the Socialist Party.

After the election, and after the merger of the Kisan Mazdoor Praja Party and the Socialist Party into the new Praja Socialist Party, the Subhasist Forward Bloc and the PSP merged, with Mrs. Lila Roy and R. S. Ruikar both joining the National Executive of the new party. The Marxist Forward Bloc continued after the elections, although in January 1954 another split occurred within the Party which resulted in the expulsion of Satyapriya Banerjee, the Party's only MP in Delhi, and Amar Bose, a member of the Bengal Assembly. Both were expelled for advocating closer relations with the CPI.[25]

POINTS OF SIMILARITY: FORCES OF ATTRACTION

A favorite pastime of left wing groups, and one which, in a sense, is essential to the very survival of these groups, is to point up the differences between their own organizations and those of other left wing parties. But in order to understand what these differences are, it is first necessary to consider some of the similarities.

First, the leadership and the bulk of the rank and file of most of these Marxist left groups come from Bengal. In spite of their names, the Revolutionary Communist Party of *India*, the *All India* Forward Bloc, the Bolshevik Party of *India*, and so on are not All India parties, but tend to be confined to Bengal and nearby areas. Although some of these groups have organizations in other states, for the most part their strength is in Bengal.

Second, each of these left wing groups has a long history, tradition, and organization of its own. The Socialist Republican Party, among the newest (and smallest) of the groups, was begun

25 Subsequently the expelled members, both of whom have a strong hold among trade unionists in the Marxist Forward Bloc, preferred to form their own party rather than merge into the CPI.

in 1947, but the Forward Bloc dates back to the 1930's, the Bolshevik Party and the Bengal Labour Party to 1933, and the Revolutionary Socialist Party, although officially launched in 1938, to the beginning of the century. These organizations, therefore, are not elusive factions.

Third, the left wing parties, with all their emphasis on ideological questions, have in fact tended to center around individual personalities. Almost all of the parties owe their origin to one key figure. It is difficult to conceive of a Forward Bloc without the leadership of Netaji Subhas Bose. Similarly, the RCPI was founded and built by Saumyen Tagore, the Bengal Labour Party and the Bolshevik Party by Dutt Mazumdar, and the Socialist Republican Party by Sarat Chandra Bose.

Fourth, all these parties claim to be "revolutionary," to reject the principles of parliamentary democracy. They do not, therefore, measure their strength or their prospects by electoral results, but rather by their ability to lead mass demonstrations, rallies, etc. Although they participate in elections, they tend to view them as opportunities for building mass strength and not as a means for bringing about a social transformation.

Fifth, none of these groups, without exception, accept Gandhi's principles of non-violence. Among the leftists in Bengal there has been a certain fascination for militancy and violence. The pages of Bengal newspapers and magazines are filled with tales of martyrs who fell before bullets or lathee charges; with pictures of dead or injured martyrs with bare backs or chests with open wounds. The anniversaries of their deaths are appropriately celebrated with the erection of public statues, and the accounts of their feats are continually retold. The fascination for violence even finds· expression at political conventions. At the Revolutionary Socialist Party convention in 1947, for example, one member of the Party, Professor Girdhari Lal, gave a public demonstration of jujitsu along with a lathee, sword, and dagger display.[26] This positive feeling for militancy and violence may be one of the basic reasons for the frustration experienced by

[26] *Second All National Party Convention of RSPI, 1947* (Muzaffarpur: Hindustan Press, 1947), p. 2.

the left wing in Bengal when independence was achieved peacefully.

Sixth, all the left wing groups are characterized by their adherence to a "thesis." There is an important difference between a party "program" or "platform" and a "thesis," a difference not so much in content, although such differences exist, as in psychological meaning to subscribers. A thesis is, first of all, characterized by its statement of the party's "ideology."[27] The General Secretary of the All India Forward Bloc, R. S. Ruikar, presents a justification for and a definition of "ideology" which would probably, in basic meaning, be accepted by most leftists. "It is necessary that we must have a comprehensive view of life, a clear insight into the forces and factors that lead to progress or regress, into the laws and methods of their working and a precise formulation of our ideals and objectives with due regard to these forces and factors which help or impede us in our march. In simple, a political party to be worth its existence, must have an ideology—a system of thought to guide its actions."[28] An ideology is thus a "comprehensive view of life" and a party thesis is the expression by a political organization of that "comprehensive view." It is therefore more than a program or platform which enumerates the issues on which a party takes a stand, the laws which it advocates or opposes, or the foreign policy it endorses.

The thesis has a different meaning to its members than an ordinary program. The beginnings of a left wing group or party is accompanied by the writing of a thesis which expresses the basic values of the members of the group. When like-minded people join together to form a group, the members want to be assured that their values will not be damaged, that their basic outlook is accepted by the other members of the group and will not be challenged by them. Psychologically, *the manifesto or thesis is primarily for the members, not for the masses*. The

[27] We are not concerned here with defining ideology in any "objective" sense, but only to show the meaning it has to those who employ the term.

[28] *Ideology of Netaji—Thesis of the All-India Forward Bloc* (Calcutta: Leftist Book Club, 1949), p. 2.

manifesto can be characterized as a consensus on basic values, and the group thereby agrees that these values are sacrosanct. Because of their agreement on basic values, which allows them to debate issues within an accepted framework, discussion, not argument, may then take place between members. Once the group has its manifesto, intra-group communication is facilitated, but communication with those outside is made more difficult. Discussion with those who reject one's "comprehensive view of life" is difficult and agitational politics readily replaces discussion.

The manifesto or thesis can thus be distinguished from a political platform partly by the content of the document itself and partly by the attitude of the members toward the document. Individuals in a group can disagree more readily over a platform than over a manifesto. The platform generally assumes an agreement of values and goes on to make specific demands; the manifesto articulates values, reinforces them for its supporters, and provides a kind of value protection for the group. The platform deals with only small segments of attitudes and behavior; the manifesto's view is comprehensive. More concessions and compromises can thereby be made in a platform than in a manifesto, which has less flexibility. In terms of psychological meaning to the members of a group, *the commitment to a manifesto is greater than that to a platform.*

It might also be noted here that while a formal thesis is especially characteristic of the leftist parties, adherence to some kind of "comprehensive view of life" is characteristic of the Hindu communal parties as well. The Hindu parties, however, rely more heavily on the words of the party leaders and of certain classical writings of either present or past *gurus* (teachers). The *guru* is a leader with some miraculously given power. Savarkar fills this charismatic role in the Hindu Mahasabha, and Golwalkar (who is usually called *Guruji* or "Reverend Teacher") does so in the Rashtriya Swayamsevak Sangh. While there is some charisma associated with most Indian leaders, the rightist groups seem to rely more heavily on charismatic leaders as their guides on value questions, while the leftist generally rely on doctrines enunciated in the party thesis, or in the writings of Marx and his disciples.

A seventh characteristic of the left wing parties in Bengal is their general agreement on most issues. They all claim to be socialist; advocate nationalization of industry, confiscation of land without compensation and land to the tillers, withdrawal from the Commonwealth, confiscation of foreign capital, planning, and government welfare programs; and denounce "Anglo-American imperialism" while praising the Soviet Union and the People's Government of China. *Were leftist parties merely groups formed to advocate the adoption by the government of certain legislation and a particular foreign policy, there would be no obstacle to the merger of the various left parties into a single party.*

POINTS OF DISSIMILARITY: FORCES OF REPULSION

A. The Marxist Left and the Socialists

The left parties of Bengal have nearly all looked upon the Socialist Party as the "left maneuvering instrument of the Indian Bourgeoisie."[29] This characterization developed after 1938 as a result of the events which were occurring in the nationalist movement. From 1934 (when the Socialist Party was formed) until 1938, the Party, then the Congress Socialist Party, won considerable respect from the various leftist groups. Even the Forward Bloc, which later became one of its bitterest enemies, wrote some years later that from 1934 to 1938 "the party made considerable headway and virtually assumed the leadership of the left-minded elements within the Congress."[30] The CSP's united front with the Communist Party gave it an aura of revolutionary respectability among leftists. And the sympathy which Nehru frequently expressed publicly for the Socialists was another source of strength for the Party. In addition, some of the former terrorist-revolutionaries drifted into the CSP, including the entire Revolutionary Socialist Party, which, as we have

[29] *Draft Thesis—The All India Forward Bloc* (Ludhiana, East Punjab: Published by General Mohan Singh [1951?]), p. 58.
[30] *Ibid.,* p. 58.

pointed out, formed its own organization within that of the CSP. But the attempt of Subhas Chandra Bose to unite the left movement under his leadership, beginning with his election as Congress President in 1938 and culminating with the formation of the Forward Bloc in 1939 and the meeting of the famous Anti-Compromise Conference at Ramgarh in the same year, resulted in a reshifting of attitudes within the leftist movement.

The Bose-Congress conflict not only involved a struggle within the national movement between "leftist" and "rightist" groups vying for leadership, but also involved a struggle within the leftist movement itself—not so much between personalities, since Bose's leadership of the left was accepted by all, but between organized groups within the leftist fold. The Communist Party and the Congress Socialist Party both sought to shape the tide of leftism in their own way. The fact that Bose never clearly defined his leftism (so that for many years since then the question of the extent to which Bose was committed to Marxism has been debated) and that the Forward Bloc was a loose bloc rather than a tightly knit political organization, meant that a great deal of room existed within the leftist movement for maneuvering.

The reelection of Bose as Congress President at Tripura in 1939 marked a high point for the leftists. The resumption of the national struggle against the British seemed in the process of reaching fulfillment. But following the election of Bose, G. B. Pant offered a resolution at the Tripura conference, with the support of the conservative Congress leadership, that Bose form his Working Committee with the approval of Gandhi. The leftists recognized this as a means of removing Bose's power and prestige as Congress President by denying him a Working Committee of his own choosing. In the bitter controversy over the Pant Resolution, the CSP ultimately decided to remain neutral, in large part so as to maintain unity within Congress. The resolution was passed and shortly after, as expected, Bose was forced to resign as Congress President. He then formed a Left Consolidation Committee made up of the CPI, the CSP, the Royists (followers of M. N. Roy), the Forward Bloc, and the smaller left wing and revolutionary groups which joined either as members of the Forward Bloc or as members of the CSP. Bose organized a day of protest against the "Anti-Struggle Decision of the Working Committee," which prohibited local Congress units from conducting mass struggles without the approval of the AICC. The Congress high command then threatened to expel those who joined the protest. The Royists withdrew immediately and before the end of the year the Socialists, followed by the Communists, both withdrew from the Left Consolidation Committee.[31]

The smaller left wing groups, however, continued their support of Bose and his policy of militant struggle against the British. They became embittered toward both the Socialists and the Communists for their unwillingness to continue behind Bose. The Revolutionary Socialist Party, which until then had operated inside the CSP, severed its connections, declaring that the CSP had moved away from Marxist-Leninism to "Social-Gandhism."[32] The RCPI had always been critical of the CSP because it operated within Congress, and it looked upon the CSP's present "betrayal" as another indication that it was in alliance with the bourgeoisie.

With the isolation of the Communists and the Socialists from the Bose group, leadership of the remaining leftists fell into the hands of the Forward Bloc. They too bitterly denounced the Socialists for their failure to oppose the Pant Resolution at Tripura and their unwillingness to support Bose in his policy of militant struggle. After the war the Forward Bloc condemned the Socialists for their neutrality on partition and for their belief in "the illusion that socialism may be achieved through constitutional means."[33]

The differences between the Marxist left and the Socialist Party which developed between 1938 and 1940 were intensified during the post-war era as the Socialist Party shifted from the role of a revolutionary Marxist organization to that of a Gan-

[31] See Bose, *The Indian Struggle*, *op.cit.*, for a first-hand description of his conflict with Congress during this period.

[32] *War Thesis of the Revolutionary Socialist Party* (Calcutta: Revolutionary Socialist Party Central Committee, 1940), p. 21.

[33] *Draft Thesis—The All India Forward Bloc, op.cit.*, pp. 60-61.

dhian-influenced democratic socialist party. The following circumstances appear to be the reasons for the decline of the Socialist Party in Bengal and their divergence from the Marxist left parties: the failure of the Congress Socialist Party to give complete support to Bose between 1938 and 1940; the fact that the Quit India Movement in Bengal fell under the control of the Forward Bloc and other left parties, rather than the Socialists as in other parts of India; the Socialist Party's growing emphasis on Gandhism, which is viewed as a reactionary outlook by Bengali leftists; the Socialist acceptance of constitutional rather than violent revolutionary change; the non-Bengali leadership of the Socialist Party; the increasing respectability of the Socialist Party, which made it unpalatable to discontented revolutionary leftists.

B. *The Marxist Left and the Communists*

If the split between the Marxist left and the Socialists occurred between 1938 and 1940 over attitudes toward the Bose movement, the split between the left and the Communists occurred even earlier, in the late '20's and early '30's, over their respective attitudes toward the Congress Party.

The Congress Party, or "movement" as its supporters preferred to call it, always had a remarkable hold on its constituent elements. Even though parallel nationalist activities were conducted alongside the Indian National Congress—the revolutionary terrorists, the constitutional-minded liberals, and others—none of these activities ever became a permanent threat to the dominant position of the Congress. The early revolutionary terrorists, who later became imbued with Marxist ideas, were attracted by Gandhi's and the Congress's success at winning mass support and building a mass organization. Although the terrorists continued their activities into the early '30's, they soon developed a dual loyalty, first to their revolutionary organization and second to the Indian National Congress.

The Communists, however, in accordance with international Cominform policy at that time, refused to take part in the Congress and accused it of being a bourgeois organization seeking not genuine independence, but the transference of power from one bourgeois class to another. Communist isolation from the national movement continued through the early 1930's until the era of the international popular front line of the Communist movement. Before the shift, young Indians, and especially Bengali leftists, were alienated from the Communist Party by the Party's rejection of Congress. The reaction of Dutt Mazumdar, the founder of the Bengal Labour Party (later the Bolshevik Party), was rather typical. Mazumdar was studying at the London School of Economics in 1928 when an Indian member of the British Parliament formed the London branch of the Indian National Congress which he joined. In 1932 Mazumdar returned to India a confirmed leftist, like a large number of returning students, but he refused to join the Communists because of their attacks against the national movement. Mazumdar then entered trade union organizing and in 1933 formed the Bengal Labour Party.

Although the Communists later joined the Congress movement, the leftists continued to feel that the Communist Party was guided by the dictates of Soviet policy. As proof, the leftists catalogue a series of "betrayals" beginning with the failure of the CPI to support the national movement in the '20's and early '30's and running through their failure to give complete support to Bose, their support for the war effort and their opposition to the Quit India movement, the "right" deviation of the Communists after the war when they supported the Nehru interim government, and their "left" deviation adventurists policies from 1947 to 1951.[34]

Other criticisms of the CPI have been made by the left groups, involving differences not only in current strategy but in evaluation of the international and domestic situation and of the meaning of the socialist revolution. The Revolutionary Socialist Party in its 1950 thesis upheld the classic "Revolutionary Socialist Way posed by Marx, Engels and Lenin" as opposed to the

[34] See Tridib Chaudhuri, *The Swing Back* (Calcutta: Revolutionary Socialist Party, 1950).

"new fangled China Way of Mao Tse-Tung and Cominform."[35]
More recently the CPI policy of a "Broad Democratic Front"
was condemned as a "class collaborationist programme of action."[36] The CPI is accused of trying to woo the wealthy, capitalist Tata and Birla families by "falsely characterising them
as 'national' bourgeoisie in foolish parrot-like imitation of Chinese phrases."[37]

It is important to note, however, that with all these differences, there is a far wider range of agreement between the leftists
and the Communists than between the leftists and the Socialists.
The Communist Party is still viewed basically as a Marxist revolutionary party, and although on occasion some leftists will publicly deny that the Communists are either revolutionary or
Marxist, they will not characterize the Communists as they do
the Socialists. For the Socialists are viewed as traditional social
democrats and as the second line of defense of the bourgeoisie.
The Communists frequently "deviate" from the correct line,
which is to admit that they may have been correct or that they
are capable of being correct. *But the Socialists do not "deviate,"
any more than any bourgeois group can be said to have "devi-
ated" from the correct revolutionary path.*

C. Differences within the Marxist Left

Once having clarified their views on the Socialist Party and
the Communist Party of India, the leftist parties do not take
great pains to explain their differences with one another. Members of the leftist parties generally look upon other leftist groups
as either being minor or as being close to the Socialists or the
Communists. The Revolutionary Socialist Party leaders, for example, feel that the Bolshevik Party, the Socialist Unity Center
(which broke off from the RSP), and the two wings of the Forward Bloc either have large pro-Communist groups or are actually pro-Stalinist parties. The RCPI, they feel, is a highly sectarian
party and Saumyen Tagore, its leader, a very difficult person to

[35] *The Leninist Way* (Calcutta: Revolutionary Socialist Party, 1950), p. i.
[36] *Draft Thesis—The All India Forward Bloc, op.cit.,* p. 70.
[37] *Bolshevik Party Central Committee Political Statement* (Calcutta: Bolshevik Party, 1952), p. ii.

work with for personal reasons. On the other hand Saumyen Tagore criticizes the RSP and other leftist groups for their willingness to work in united fronts with the Communists. In contrast he justifiably points to his record of unwillingness to collaborate with the Communists. The Bolshevik Party feels that it has "systematically and correctly followed the path of Marx, Engels, Lenin and Stalin by upholding the banner of . . . socialism and by trying to consolidate the leadership of the working class in the Indian political movement."[38] The Bolshevik leaders declare that theirs is a national communist party, and that neither the CPI nor other leftist parties are true working class parties with a working class, trade union composition like that of the Bolshevik Party.[39]

Whatever the similarities between the leftist parties, the forces of repulsion have been so great that unity has not so far been possible. By examining a situation in which an attempt at unity took place, we can better understand the elements which keep the parties divided.

[38] *Ibid.*, p. 10.
[39] From an interview by the author with Bishwanath Dubey in Calcutta in June 1954.

7. An Attempt at Left Wing Unity: The United Socialist Organization

Post-war Bengal was leftist. Demonstrations for the Indian National Army of Subhas Chandra Bose, demands for the immediate launching of a struggle against the British, mass agitation, and the like were daily occurrences. A number of events appear to have provided the immediate stimuli for the rising spirit of leftism. As leader of the anti-British Indian National Army, Bose, the hero of Bengal, had become a national hero. For the first time a national armed force had opposed British power. And for the first time the leadership of the national struggle seemed to shift from Gandhi and his non-violence to Netaji with his emphasis on militant struggle.

In 1946, Bengal leftists, along with leftists throughout India, demanded that an immediate struggle be launched against the British. The Naval Mutiny and the enthusiasm for the Indian National Army indicated to them that the masses were prepared for a final battle for freedom. The negotiations between the Cabinet Mission and the Congress leadership, which followed, were thus a great disappointment to the leftists. The leftists argued that the British were stalling and had no intention of voluntarily relinquishing their empire; but at heart leftist opposition to negotiation was based on the feeling that it would be best if independence came as a result of prolonged struggle rather than prolonged negotiation. The leftists, whose sympathy for the Japanese was no secret, wanted to inflict a defeat upon the victorious British Empire. When independence finally came in 1947 through negotiations and the peaceful transference of power, they felt considerably frustrated.

Other factors contributed to the continuance of leftism in Bengal. The partition of Bengal only reemphasized to Bengalis that independence did not mean a new and happy life, for partition dislocated the life of Bengal, politically, economically, and culturally. Politically, it split the Congress organization between East and West Bengal, resulted in a realignment of forces within the Party, and prevented the establishment of a strong and stable government. Economically, trade between East and West Bengal was severely hurt and the jute industry in particular was badly damaged. By 1950 the shifts in population had disastrously affected the West Bengal economy. And culturally, partition divided an area whose population had been very conscious of its own regionalism and proud of its history, language, and culture.

The advent of independence through negotiation, rather than struggle, and the unwelcomed partition of Bengal, resulted in a wave of anti-British and anti-Congress sentiment that was expressed throughout Bengal by the left wing parties.

THE BEGINNINGS OF LEFTIST UNITY

From 1948 onward a major attempt was made by the left wing parties of Bengal to form a single organization under the leadership of Sarat Chandra Bose, the brother of Subhas Chandra Bose. In the remainder of this chapter we shall describe the circumstances leading up to the formation of this United Socialist Organization, its formation and its development, the obstacles which arose, and the circumstances which led to its failure.

Sarat Chandra Bose was a Bengali lawyer born September 7, 1889 to a renowned advocate from Cuttack, Orissa. He was educated in Cuttack, Calcutta, and England, where he qualified for the bar, and, returning to India, he joined the Calcutta High Court. Upon his return Bose became deeply involved in Congress politics. He first worked under C. R. Das in the Swaraj movement, and then served as President of the Bengal Provincial Congress Committee and as a member of the Congress Working Committee. From 1937 to 1945 he was the leader of the Congress opposition in the Bengal Assembly and in 1946, upon his election to the Central Assembly in New Delhi, became the leader of the Congress Party there. As a close associate and supporter of his brother Subhas, Sarat Bose won considerable popularity in Bengal at the close of the war. With the absence of Subhas, leadership of the left wing probably would have fallen into the hands of Sarat Bose but for the fact that he was called to the Central

Assembly in New Delhi and was from September to November 1946 a member of the interim national government. In November 1946 Bose resigned from the government and the Congress Working Committee, returned to Calcutta, and formed the Socialist Republican Party.[1]

On September 1, 1948 Sarat Chandra Bose started a daily newspaper called *The Nation* which was to be his personal mouthpiece, and the organ of his newly formed Socialist Republican Party. Almost immediately after starting the new paper Bose left for Europe for reasons of health, and while abroad he issued statements to the press calling for the unity of left wing parties in India. "We should like," said Bose, "all the leftist political organizations in India to combine so that the strength of the opposition can properly be measured against the present government."[2]

Bose returned to Calcutta in the latter part of January, 1949, and in April a conference of leftist groups met in Bombay under his chairmanship. Speaking to about seventy-five delegates, he called for the establishment of a coordinating council to facilitate the cohesion of leftist forces. He met with representatives of his own party, of the Forward Bloc, and of the Peasants and Workers Party of Maharashtra. After they had conferred for several days, a Provisional Left Coordination Committee was appointed and resolutions were passed demanding that India declare itself a sovereign republic outside of the Commonwealth, that a new Constituent Assembly be elected on the basis of adult franchise, and that the country be administered on socialistic lines. Other resolutions called for land to the tiller and abolishment of landlordism without compensation; nationalization of key industries; organization of industries on socialistic lines; establishment of linguistic provinces; civil liberties; free education, including university education; the right to food and shelter; and abolition of blackmarketeering, profiteering, corruption, and nepotism.[3]

[1] Biography of Sarat Bose from the *Nation*, February 21, 1950; see also *What We Believe* (Calcutta: Socialist Republican Party, 1948) for the program of the Bose party.

[2] *Nation*, January 5, 1949.   [3] *Ibid.*, April 10, 1949.

The movement for leftist unity received its greatest impetus with the announcement that a special by-election would be held for a vacant seat in the West Bengal Assembly, followed by an announcement on May 6, 1949 that Sarat Bose would contest the seat on behalf of the Socialist Republican Party. Although on May 16th Bose again left for Europe because of his health and was gone during the entire campaign, the movement for left wing unity proceeded on its own momentum.

Later in May the Bengal Provincial Forward Bloc endorsed Bose and called for the establishment of a left front to unite behind him. A few days later the Socialist Party of West Bengal called upon its members to support Bose. The Revolutionary Socialist Party, the Bolshevik Party, the Revolutionary Communist Party of India, the Socialist Unity Center, and both wings of the Forward Bloc, all issued statements on behalf of Bose.[4] Subsequently the leaders of each of these parties toured the South Calcutta Constituency and campaigned in support of Bose.

Although the Congress candidate, Suresh Das, had received the endorsement of both Nehru and Patel, when the votes were in Bose had received 19,030 and Suresh Das 5,780.[5]

ALTERNATIVES

With the victory of Bose the left parties, even more than before, talked seriously of some kind of united organization. In the weeks that followed, Bose's daily, *The Nation*, became the platform for various proposals for leftist unity.

In the June 26, 1949 issue, one unsigned writer called for a united socialist bloc organized along the same lines as Congress and suggested that the Congress Constitution be used as a model.[6] In reply, Shibnath Banerjee, General Secretary of the Bengal Socialist Party, urged *The Nation* to convene representatives of various left parties to find ways and means for bringing about united or common action by socialist parties on specific

---

4 *Ibid.*, May 25, 1949.
5 *Ibid.*, June 15, 1949.
6 "United Socialist Bloc," *Nation*, June 26, 1949.

issues.[7] From London Bose declared that when he returned to India he would make an effort to bring all leftist parties, except the Communists, into a single United Socialist Party.[8]

The difficulties in these various proposals were clearly pointed out by Tridib Chaudhuri, a Revolutionary Socialist Party leader. Two specific suggestions, said Chaudhuri, had so far been made for achieving left unity. "One is that the different left groups should be united on a common platform on the model of the Constitution of the Indian National Congress of the anti-imperialist days. But with several left parties already functioning as independent political organizations outside of the Congress with their own independent programmes and rules of discipline, how can we go back to the position of subsidiary groups within the framework of a common mass organization? Neither would it be very feasible to liquidate immediately all the different left organizations, and then permit the adherents of different groups to somehow mark out their own ideological distinctions without disrupting the common organization. I am afraid none of the existing parties would agree to this procedure. Comrade Shibnath Banerji has suggested a United Left Front of the different parties on specific issues. . . . How does he envisage the United Socialist Front when no specific issues of common struggle are present? . . . It is apparent that such an 'ad hoc' arrangement can hardly provide that united leadership or that sustained and continuous organizational vigour which would be needed to fight the reaction ruling this country today in the name of the Congress, far less could it undertake a Socialist transformation of the entire country."[9]

Chaudhuri then went on to propose the formation of a united left organization "on the basis of a commonly accepted minimum political and economic programme. . . . Every party adhering to the front must ratify the common programme and accept this programme as the minimum programme of its own. There should

[7] Shibnath Banerjee, "Plea for United Socialist Bloc—No Bloc but Platform," *Nation*, July 10, 1949.

[8] *Nation*, July 11, 1949.

[9] Tridib Chaudhuri, "Plea for Socialist Unity," *Nation*, July 17, 1949.

be a Joint Executive adequately representing the constituent parties for the effective campaigning among the masses of the people in favour of the common programme, for the electoral function of the front in coming general elections and for leading the masses in their local and partial struggles for the realisation of the basic demands included in the programme, and last but not least, to assume governmental power when the historical situation would demand that of the left."[10]

According to Chaudhuri's proposal, the executive would arrive at decisions by majority rule; each party would be pledged to carry out the common decisions; each organization would be free to popularize its own ideology and special program before the masses and recruit its own independent membership. But the left front could also accept individual members and give such members a defined but limited status within the front—a detail which would have to be worked out later.

Chaudhuri then suggested a minimum program that would include: breaking from the Commonwealth, abolition of landlordism, land to the tiller, ceilings on landholdings, exclusion of foreign capital, nationalization of key industries, national planning, recognition of Red China, and friendship with the USSR.

Chaudhuri then urged the leaders of three or four of the larger all-India left parties to meet together to work out details. He concluded by saying that at the time it was not likely that the Communists would agree to join such a united left organization, but that a section of the CPI which rejected the Party's present "adventurist-opportunist" policy should be welcomed.[11]

In the end of July 1949 Bose returned to Bombay from the U.K. Speaking before the Leftist Coordination Council which he had formed in Bombay in April, Bose pointed out that both the CPI and the Socialist Party had declined to send representatives to the Council, but that in December there would be a meeting of all other leftist forces in the country.[12] Soon after, Bose

[10] *Ibid.*   [11] *Ibid.*
[12] *Nation,* July 25, 1949.

met with a number of left leaders to discuss ways and means of achieving socialist unity. All were agreed upon the principle of "coordination and consolidation."[13]

It was during this period that relations between the Socialist Party and the various left wing parties reached an acute stage. With the Communists deeply involved in "left adventurist" activities and in most areas under government ban, the possibility of their entering any united front of leftists seemed remote. But relations between the leftists and the Socialists were not so remote. From the beginning it appeared that Sarat Bose and the various leftist leaders were willing to have the Socialist Party enter a leftist front, but the attitude of the Socialist Party toward such a front was unclear.

Ajit Roy Mookerjee, Secretary of the Socialists in Calcutta, and Shibnath Banerjee, the General Secretary of the Bengal Socialist Party, had stated that the Party was in favor of some kind of united action on specific issues rather than in the establishment of a permanent bloc of leftist parties.[14]

The question of left unity had become a major subject on the agenda of the Socialist Party's National Executive meeting in Calcutta. In August Bose had a long talk with Jayaprakash Narayan in Calcutta. Speaking at a public meeting in Calcutta on the following day, Jayaprakash said that his party was prepared on *specific* issues to cooperate with other parties, thus suggesting that he and Bose had not been able to agree on the question of forming a quasi-permanent leftist bloc. This was confirmed by Ajit Roy at a public meeting in Calcutta on August 13, when he announced that his party believed in the formation of one united party rather than a bloc of leftist parties.[15]

By now the position of the Socialist Party was clear. It was prepared to see a single socialist party evolve out of the various left parties, either through the merger of these parties with the Socialist Party or through the creation of an entirely new Socialist Party made up of all these groups. But in the event that such a united Socialist Party could not be created, then the

---

[13] *Nation*, August 5, 1949.   [14] *Nation*, July 10, 1949.
[15] *Nation*, August 13, 1949.

Socialists were not willing to enter a permanent united front of leftists, but would instead support united fronts created for specific issues and for the purposes of the coming general elections.

On this question there was some dispute within the Bengal Socialist Party. The Joint Secretary of the West Bengal Socialist Party, Purnananda Das Gupta, openly opposed the stand taken by his party as ideal but impractical.[16] He resigned from the Socialist Party and joined the newly formed United Socialist Organization of India (USOI).

It was also reported that Shibnath Banerjee, the General Secretary of the West Bengal Socialist Party, had privately agreed with Das Gupta's view and had opposed the decision of the Party's National Executive, but, unlike Das Gupta, had decided to remain within the Party. Banerjee felt that the Socialist Party was overestimating its strength and underestimating the strength of the small leftist parties. He further believed that the United Socialist Organization would isolate the Communists and that the leftist groups would be drawn closer to the Socialist Party since Ruikar of the Forward Bloc, Sarat Chandra Bose, and Jayaprakash, all non-Communists, would dominate the front.

The National Executive rejected the views of Shibnath Banerjee and Purnananda Das Gupta for several reasons. The Socialists felt that the left wing parties did not have a sufficient community of outlook for them to work together for any length of time; that the small left wing parties were breaking up and their workers being pulled into the Communist or Socialist party; that they, the Socialists, were not basically sympathetic to some of these groups, particularly the pro-Stalinist elements of the Bolshevik Party, of the Socialist Unity Center,[17] and of the Forward Bloc; that the USOI was being started by Bose in part so that he could have a party of his own for the coming elections; that it was time to build up their own party strength and not dissipate their energies in any leftist fronts. And finally, Jayaprakash saw the need for a united party with clear principles, based on democratic

---

16 *Nation*, November 12, 1949.

17 The Socialist Unity Center was a very small (even by Bengal standards) leftist party which had split from the Revolutionary Socialist Party.

socialism, but he felt that Bose wanted a political party whose outlook was hazy and which might eventually align itself with the Communists.

Jayaprakash felt that such a leftist front would be external and for the public only, and that such a coalition of divergent parties would be incapable of providing an alternative to government by the Congress. But in spite of all these reservations, if the left wing parties were prepared to merge with the Socialist Party to start a new party, the SP was prepared to take part in a new party with a new name, so long as the basic principles of democratic socialism were agreed upon.[18]

THE UNITED SOCIALIST ORGANIZATION OF INDIA

After several delays, primarily because of the poor health of Sarat Bose, the leftist conference was held in Calcutta on October 29, 1949. The conference was attended by 200 delegates and met at Netaji Bhavan, the old ancestral mansion of Subhas Chandra Bose.[19] Bose explained to the conference the circumstances that led to the meeting and recommended ". . . at this stage the formation of a United Socialist Congress with the firm hope that through common endeavour the existing Socialist, leftist and progressive parties will gradually dissolve themselves and a United Socialist Party will evolve out of the United Socialist Congress."[20]

It is clear then—and this is important—that the United Socialist Organization was conceived by Bose as a first step toward the eventual merger of all "Socialist, leftist and progressive parties."

[18] From an interview by the author with Ajit Roy Mookerjee in Calcutta in September 1954.

[19] The organizations represented at the conference included the Forward Bloc (both Subhasist and Marxist sections), the Socialist Republican Party, the Bolshevik Party, the Revolutionary Socialist Party, the Revolutionary Communist Party of India, the Socialist Unity Center, the Workers and Peasants League, the Revolutionary Workers Party, the Desh Sevak Party (East Punjab), the Bihar Kisan Sabha, the Workers and Peasants Party (Maharashtra), the United Trade Union Congress, the People's Party (Madhya Pradesh), Mazdoor Krishak Party (Bombay), the Praja Mandal (Bangalore), the INA Committee (Bengal), and the Bolshevik Mazdoor Party of India.

[20] Selected Speeches and Writings of Sarat Chandra Bose, 1947-1950 (Calcutta: Thacker's Press and Directories, Ltd., 1954), p. 110.

Ultimately, there was to be a single United Socialist Party to replace Congress and bring about a socialist transformation of the country.

It is also important to note that the desire for left wing unity and ultimately of left wing merger was expressed not only by Bose but by all the Marxist left leaders. In writings and in public meetings they expressed their support for the new moves. Resolutions for leftist unity were passed by nearly all the Marxist left parties.

The three-day session of the United Socialist conference was concluded following a decision to form a Provisional General Council with two representatives from each of the constituent parties and ten others to be nominated by the President from among the non-party invitees to the conference. The conference elected Sarat Bose as its President and announced a twenty-four-point program for the new United Socialist Organization of India (USOI).

In December and January, harmony marked the work of the USOI. A provisional working committee, a committee for preparing a draft constitution for the USOI, a committee on trade union unity, and one on peasant unity were all established in December. Throughout January the USOI actively sponsored several demonstrations against the government's decision to remain in the Commonwealth. At the end of the month the USOI and the leftist organizations celebrated Netaji's birthday as Anti-Commonwealth Day, sponsoring mass processions and public meetings.

On February 21, 1950, following a prolonged illness, Sarat Chandra Bose died in Calcutta. Swami Sahajananda Saraswati was subsequently elected President of the United Socialist Organization. Swami Saraswati had been the General Secretary of the All India Kisan Sabha (a national peasants' organization) and more recently a member of the Forward Bloc. He was born in 1888, became a *sanyasi* (monk) in 1907, and in 1932 formed the Kisan Sabha in Bihar along with some prominent Congressmen. He joined Subhas Bose at the Anti-Compromise Conference at Ramgarh, took part in the 1942 Quit India movement, and was a well-known advocate of left unity.[21] Swami Saraswati's tenure as USOI President was equally brief, for on June 27, 1950 he died. General Mohan Singh, of the Marxist Forward Bloc, was elected the new President.

With two leaders lost, 1950 was a year of great personal defeat for the USOI. But in spite of Bose's death, renewed effort was made during that year to effect closer unity among the left forces. The USOI General Council urged the merger of trade union organizations as well as its constituent parties. It appealed to the CPI to shed its ultra-leftism and called upon the Socialist Party of India to shed its policy of "reformism and sectarianism" so that all could join together in a socialist front.[22]

THE DECLINE OF UNITY

In spite of the fact that the leftist dream of a united socialist organization *had* come about, there was still a feeling among the leftists that no true unity had been achieved. One reason is that left wing unity had always implied more than organizational unity. It had come to mean a unity and harmony of spirit on the part of leftists. Although there was no organizational unity at the time, that spirit seemed to exist for periods between 1938 and 1940, when Netaji Subhas Bose advocated an immediate militant struggle against the British and the left was united behind him. Similarly, the attempt at left wing unity reached its high point in the South Calcutta by-election when the left was united in a common cause around a common leader. By comparison, the formation of a leftist organization was anti-climactic.

In the absence of a unifying leadership and a common cause, a feeling of disillusionment grew, in spite of continuous reaffirmations of support and praise for the USOI. In fact it was difficult to discover what was lacking in leftist unity. In mid-1950 there were no reports of specific conflicts within the USOI. The transference of leadership from Sarat Bose to Swami Saraswati seemed smooth. Efforts to forge unity in the trade union movement were progressing, and in any event the Marxist left trade unionists were already largely united in the United Trades Union Con-

[21] *Nation*, June 28, 1950.   [22] *Nation*, April 3, 1950.

gress (UTUC). The program of the USOI had been ratified by
the constituent parties, and no difficulties had developed over
accepting the USOI Constitution. In mid-1950 the USOI had
opened centers for the enrollment of volunteers for the coming
Calcutta Corporation elections. And finally, in October 1950, the
Parliamentary Subcommittee of the USOI agreed upon a Draft
Election Manifesto.

But in spite of this apparent progress, the feeling of left wing
unity was absent. By the end of 1950 the disintegration of the
USOI was under way, and by the time of the election campaign
in 1951 the USOI was split and all but finished. The first major
conflict arose in October 1950 over relations between the Marxist
Forward Bloc and Seth Dalmia, a well-known Indian capitalist.

General Mohan Singh, Chairman of the All India Forward
Bloc and, at the time, the President of the USOI, spoke jointly
with Seth Dalmia, the President of the All Indian Refugees Fed-
eration, at a meeting sponsored on behalf of Punjabi refugees.
Saumyen Tagore of the Revolutionary Communist Party, and
others in the USOI, strongly objected to one of its constituent
parties' cooperating with Dalmia. The General Council of the
USOI condemned the alliance but agreed to allow the Forward
Bloc autonomy in this matter. The RCPI subsequently withdrew
from the USOI, and for the same reasons so did Professor K. T.
Shah, an MP and delegate of the UTUC to the USOI, and
Purnananda Das Gupta, who originally resigned from the So-
cialist Party to take part in the USOI.[23] Disintegration of the
USOI had begun.

Purnananda Das Gupta later said that his differences with the
USOI dated back to the death of Sarat Bose and the election
of Swami Sahajanand as Chairman. Das Gupta felt that, as Chairman, Swami Sahajanand was ineffective. Sahajanand and he
had hoped for the establishment of an independent USOI, separate from its constituent parties. But with the death of Swami
Sahajanand, control of the USOI fell completely into the hands
of the Forward Bloc, with General Mohan Singh as its President.

---

[23] *Why RCPI, Professor K. T. Shah and Purnananda Das Gupta Resigned
from USOI* (Calcutta: Ganavani Publishing Company, 1951), pp. 10-11.

Das Gupta had hoped that Saumyen Tagore would succeed Sahajanand, but after the election of Mohan Singh he no longer felt
that any good could come of the USOI. It was then that the
question of Dalmia's connection with the Forward Bloc arose
and precipitated Das Gupta's decision to resign.[24]

The final collapse of the United Socialist Organization of
India occurred over negotiations for the general elections and
involved the USOI's relations with the Communists. When discussions of left wing unity were under way in 1949 and 1950,
the Communist Party was deeply involved in a program of terrorist activities. The CPI was not at that time interested in joining any front or left wing organization in which their own organization would be submerged with others. While they would
agree to united fronts on specific issues, the CPI would not join
any long term arrangement such as the USOI.[25] But in 1951 the
Communists had shifted from "left adventurism" to united front
tactics and were eager to enter into arrangements for the coming
general elections. The CPI negotiated with the USOI and came
to an electoral arrangement in which they agreed not to contest
the same seats.

As a result, disagreement within the USOI developed with
regard to their attitude toward the CPI. The Subhasist Forward
Bloc opposed the alliance and subsequently resigned from the
USOI. The Revolutionary Socialist Party, after disagreeing with
other constituent USOI parties, broke from the alliance over the
question of distribution of seats. And the RCPI, as already noted,
had broken with the USOI earlier. Thus the USOI-CPI electoral
alliance was largely an alliance between the Marxist Forward
Bloc, the largest remaining element in the USOI, and the Communist Party.

Several of the defecting leftist parties, along with the Socialists,

[24] From an interview by the author with Purnananda Das Gupta in Calcutta in October 1954.

[25] From an interview by the author with Jyoti Basu of the Bengal CPI in
Calcutta in June 1954; Jyoti Basu further explained that the Communists
had joined fronts in Travancore-Cochin and Hyderabad, but these were confined to the elections or the legislature and did not function outside the
legislature.

formed their own electoral front called the People's United Socialist Front (PUSF), with a joint election manifesto and an agreement concerning distribution of seats. The Socialist Party, the RCPI, and the Subhasist Forward Bloc were the three constituent members of the PUSF.[26]

Ultimately, the alliance between the Communists and the USOI was a great success. The Communists persuaded the USOI to allow them to contest those seats for which Congress Ministers were standing, and these turned out to be highly vulnerable seats for Congress. At the same time the Communists gained the prestige of being associated with a left front, especially with both the Marxist Forward Bloc and the Socialist Republican Party, both of which were associated with the names of Subhas and Sarat Bose, and the USOI benefited from the advantages of the superior Communist Party organization. When the results were announced, the CPI had won nineteen seats in the Legislative Assembly and the USOI another fifteen. In contrast, the People's United Socialist Front won only two.

After the elections the USOI was continued, but in name only. General Mohan Singh remained Chairman, but it ceased to hold meetings or carry on activities. For all intents and purposes, with the completion of the 1952 general elections, the USOI died a quiet death.

THE LEFT WING AND TRADE UNION UNITY

Closely associated with the problem of leftist unity has been the question of trade union unity. For many years the Indian trade union movement had been unified, more or less, in a national trade union organization called the All India Trade Union Congress (AITUC). The AITUC had been formed in Bombay in 1920 and had been closely tied to the Indian National Congress. In 1929 a split in the AITUC occurred which resulted in the formation of the right wing National Trade Union Federation and the Communist-led Red Trade Union Congress. The Communists returned to the AITUC in a few years, and in 1940 the National Trade Union Federation returned. A year later

[26] *Manifesto of the People's United Socialist Front* (Calcutta: July 1951).

another split occurred when M. N. Roy[27] formed the Indian Federation of Labour, but this remained a negligible force.

Throughout the war, the bulk of the trade unionists were more or less united in the All India Trade Union Congress. The AITUC was an amalgam of trade unions, each of which was dominated by a different political group. Thus, Congress, Communist, Socialist, and Marxist left political workers were active in the AITUC. In order to prevent a split within the movement, the AITUC Constitution required that political resolutions needed a three-fourths majority, but in practice effort was made in the General Council to achieve unanimity before the passage of such resolutions.

During the war years a shift occurred inside the AITUC. Since the Communists had opposed the Quit India movement and had endorsed the war effort, they alone of the major political groups were allowed to continue openly. As a result, while Congress, Socialist, and Marxist left political and trade union workers were either in jail or underground, the Communists had a free hand. It thus came about that during the war the Communists gained effective control of the three largest mass organizations on the peasant, trade union, and student fronts: the All India Trade Union Congress, the All India Student Federation, and the All India Kisan Sabha.

When the political and trade union leaders were released from jail at the end of 1945, they discovered that the Communists had gained control of the AITUC. The Congress trade union interests withdrew from the AITUC and in 1947 formed the Indian National Trade Union Congress (INTUC). With the withdrawal of Congress, conflict between the Communists and Socialists (who had remained in the AITUC) became so intense that in 1948 the Socialists withdrew and formed the Hind Mazdoor Sabha (HMS).

In the early part of 1948, as a result of a change in the leadership of the Communist Party, that party turned to an "adven-

---

[27] M. N. Roy was a leading leftist with a following of his own. He was one of the early leaders of the CPI but had broken with the Communists in the late '20's.

turist" terrorist line. The non-Communists remaining in the AITUC complained that the organization was being used for the political objectives of the CPI. Although the CPI did not have a three-fourths majority in Bengal, it did control the union offices. It called political strikes without the approval of the General Council and used the AITUC office as a meeting place. Finally, at the height of the terrorist activities, the Bengal government banned the CPI and closed the offices of the AITUC.

In December 1948 Jayaprakash Narayan, along with Jatin Chakravarty of the RSP and Saumyen Tagore of the RCPI, convened in Calcutta a meeting of trade unionists for the purpose of starting a new union organization. At this conference a dispute arose between the Socialists and the left Marxists. The leftists wanted to include a rule requiring the approval of three fourths of the organization for the passage of political resolutions, but the Socialists wanted a majority rule. The Socialists also wanted to include the phrase "democratic socialism" as the aim of the new trade union organization, but the leftists objected. The leftists felt that the Socialists were keen on starting a trade union organization of their own, so on the second day of the conference Tagore (RCPI), Bishwanath Dubey (Bolshevik Party), Jatin Chakravarty (RSP), and Mrinal Kanti Bose (RSP) disassociated themselves. The Socialists then proceeded to form the Hind Mazdoor Sabha.

In April 1949 the leftists, who had by then withdrawn from the AITUC and had refused to join the HMS, called their own trade union conference and formed the United Trades Union Congress (UTUC). Professor K. T. Shah, an MP, was elected President and Mrinal Kanti Bose was elected Secretary.

Four trade union organizations thus had emerged by 1949: the Indian National Trade Union Congress (INTUC), dominated by Congress, the largest of the four national trade union organizations; the Communist-dominated All India Trade Union Congress (AITUC), which included, apart from Communist-controlled unions, those controlled by the Marxist Forward Bloc; the Hind Mazdoor Subha (HMS), under the control of the Socialist Party and also containing the unions dominated by the

Subhasist Forward Bloc; and finally, the smallest of the four, the leftist-controlled United Trades Union Congress (UTUC), which included the Revolutionary Socialist Party, the Bolshevik Party, the Revolutionary Communist Party of India, the Socialist Republic Party, and the Socialist Unity Center.

Between 1948 and 1950 no major attempt was made to achieve trade union unity. Finally, on April 1, 1950, a joint statement was issued by Ruikar, President of the HMS, Satyapriya Banerjee, the Vice President of the AITUC (and a leader of the Marxist Forward Bloc), and Mrinal Kanti Bose, General Secretary of the UTUC, urging the merger of these three trade unions and suggesting that a conference be held of authorized representatives of the three organizations. This move was endorsed by the General Council of the USOI.[28] By this time the HMS had agreed to the three-fourths majority rule set up as a condition for merger by the UTUC. Bose and Ruikar proposed the formation of a joint committee through which the three organizations could work together until their merger. Although Ruikar was President of the HMS, the HMS rejected the proposal on the ground that while it was willing to work with the UTUC, it was unwilling to work with the Communist-dominated AITUC.

Merger talks then began between the UTUC and the AITUC, but the General Council of the UTUC was reluctant to see a merger of its organization with the AITUC without the participation of the HMS. Further efforts toward merger were made, and in June 1953 a meeting of the UTUC and AITUC was held. "In pursuance of these talks a meeting of the General Council of the UTUC was held on the 17th of August 1953. At this meeting certain difficulties were placed by representatives from other states, particularly Bombay and Kerala. They complained that the local AITUC leaders had obstructed united work by their hostility to the UTUC."[29] The UTUC General Council then passed a resolution urging that "an earnest effort be made to have a joint committee consisting of representatives of three

---

[28] *Nation*, April 3, 1950.
[29] Mrinal Kanti Bose, *Efforts for Trade Union Unity* (Calcutta: United Trades Union Congress, 1954), p. 3.

central organizations of labour, viz., AITUC, HMS, and UTUC, in order to organize joint action on all important issues all over the country and to coordinate the activities of all the three organisations on a common front in general."[30] The UTUC proceeded to set up its own "United Action Committee" to sponsor such joint action. On the 18th of August a joint meeting of the General Councils of the UTUC and the AITUC was held at which the UTUC General Secretary placed his organization's resolution before the joint meeting. He called for a three months' trial for the joint committee, but the Communists rejected the move and called instead for an immediate merger of the two organizations. This was followed by a considerable amount of recrimination between the AITUC and the UTUC when the AITUC charged that the Revolutionary Socialist Party had sabotaged the unity attempt. Meanwhile the HMS refused to participate in the unity talks, having earlier refused to join in the joint May Day celebrations sponsored by the AITUC and UTUC in Calcutta. The efforts of 1953 to achieve trade union unity had failed.

The reason for these failures is obvious, and it is closely bound to the attitudes of the parties which dominate the respective trade union organizations. The UTUC feared domination of its unions by either the Communists or the Socialists. By the end of 1949, when the HMS had agreed to the three-fourths rule, merger of the two groups seemed possible. But in 1950 the CPI had shifted to a united front policy, and the Communists were then prepared to reunite the trade union movement. The UTUC was afraid of merging with the AITUC for fear of Communist domination.[31] This fear was shared even by the pro-Stalinist groups inside the UTUC—the Socialist Unity Center and the Bolshevik Party. The UTUC was thus prepared to merge with both the HMS and the AITUC but was reluctant to merge with either alone. It thereupon rejected the Communist move for an immediate merger and proposed instead a joint

30 *Ibid.*, p. 3.
31 From an interview by the author with Jatin Chakravarty in Calcutta in June 1954.

committee which would allow it, in the course of a three months' trial period, to judge whether it was then possible to work with the Communists without being dominated by them. On the other hand the Hind Mazdoor Sabha was under no circumstances prepared to work with the AITUC. It was willing to work with the UTUC in united front programs, and even willing to merge the two organizations, but was unwilling to do either if this meant dealing with the Communists. The Communists, however, said they were prepared to work with either or both the UTUC and the HMS in joint fronts and in a united organization.

The AITUC was thus prepared to merge with either or both organizations. The UTUC was prepared to merge with both, but not with any one alone. The HMS was prepared to merge only with the UTUC.

The position was further complicated by the fact that negotiations were under way between the HMS and the Congress-sponsored INTUC toward the merger of some of their unions. The UTUC attempted to negotiate with some HMS dissidents who resented the HMS-INTUC talks. The UTUC hoped that it and the HMS dissidents together could merge in the AITUC without being dominated by the Communists. The HMS leaders thereupon attacked the UTUC and said that the UTUC would merge with the AITUC sooner or later. To disprove this propaganda, the UTUC leaders became even more hesitant to merge with the AITUC.[32] The UTUC leaders became afraid that without the entire HMS and without a non-Communist majority, the CPI might eventually dominate them. The 1950 talks thus collapsed but were revived in 1953. Meanwhile the Bombay and Madras UTUC organizations, bitter against the AITUC for its attacks upon them, advocated merging first with the HMS, and then with the AITUC. It was to satisfy these groups that Mrinal Kanti Bose proposed to the Communists that a joint committee be formed of their two organizations to demonstrate to the Bombay and Madras groups that they could work together; but for reasons of their own the Communists rejected this offer.

[32] *Ibid.*

Merger of the various trade union organizations is thus closely tied to the attitudes of the various political parties. The HMS unwillingness to deal with the AITUC parallels the Socialist unwillingness to deal with the Communists. Likewise, the UTUC's fear of domination by the Communists and the Socialists reflects the general fear which the left wing parties have of these two larger political groups. The various groups, however, felt that while unity on the political level was obviously not possible, some sort of unity on the trade union front might be feasible. They felt that each of the parties could continue to dominate its own trade unions, but that the national federation of unions would stay out of party politics as had, more or less, the pre-war All India Trade Union Congress. The leftists thus hoped that through some formula—three-fourths rule or another device —such non-political trade union unity could be effected.

For the leftists, trade union unity has been a greater need than it has been for either the Socialists or the Communists. While the Socialist and Communist parties and their trade unions have considerable strength and prestige on their own, the leftist parties recognize their own weakness and therefore hope to increase their strength by operating more closely in fronts, joint programs, etc., with the two larger parties. But while they seek to work more closely with them because they are so small by themselves, at the same time they fear domination by these larger bodies. They therefore hope that in a three-way arrangement their strength would be enhanced by Communist-Socialist rivalry.

Indian trade unions have never had any independent existence apart from political parties. The leading trade union workers, with few exceptions, come from the political parties and do their trade union work as part of their political work. Relations between the trade unions are dependent upon relations between the political parties. Without some degree of mutual trust between the political parties and an agreement to "depoliticalize" the trade union area, trade union unity seems unlikely.

THE FAILURE OF THE USOI

We have described in the preceding pages the initial enthusiasm of the various leftist groups for the United Socialist Organization of India and the disillusionment that accompanied the breakup of this major post-independence attempt at leftist unity. What were the reasons for this collapse?

First, it is essential to understand that none of the leftist parties wanted a merger in which their individual identities would be lost. This was made clear by both Sarat Chandra Bose and the leftist parties in their rejection of the Socialist Party proposal that they and the leftists unite in a single party. Bose looked forward to the time when such a party might emerge, but he realized that at the time the left parties were unwilling to take such a step.

Second, it was not a lack of agreement on basic issues which divided the parties, for no such differences were an obstacle to the creation of the USOI. Rather, the leftist groups, rank and file and leaders alike, looked upon the preservation of their own party as being of greater psychological need to them than the political advantages of having a single leftist party.

Third, in place of a single party, the left groups wanted a united front type of organization in which each group retained its identity and in effect worked in the front when it suited what they conceived to be their own interest. None of the constituent parties, for example, wanted to see the USOI have an organization of its own with its own individual members since that might compete with their party in attracting new members. Furthermore, on the question of determining candidates for assembly seats, the USOI was to be nothing more than a meeting place where each party would negotiate an electoral arrangement with others.

Fourth, so long as the commitment of each of the parties to the USOI was so limited, what united them was not an allegiance to the organization but common issues and a dominating personality. From 1947 to 1950 there were many issues on which all the leftist groups could unite with some enthusiasm: annulment of partition, rejection of membership in the Commonwealth, and attacks against the new constitution. But by mid-1950, especially after the decline of the movement of population between East and West Bengal, these issues had decreased in importance. As for a unifying dominating personality, none of the leftist parties produced anyone to replace Sarat Bose.

Fifth, with the absence of a unifying leader or one or two major issues which could unite them, the leftist leaders and rank and file lost the feeling of unity and began instead to feel the inroads which other groups were making upon their own position inside the USOI. The final breakdown, in fact, occurred not over any differences on policy but over the relations of strength between the groups. There was some feeling that the Marxist Forward Bloc had gained control of the USOI and was using it for its own purpose. In general each party felt that other groups were using the front for their own party advantage. Although the RCPI and several individuals ostensibly broke with the USOI over the policy of the Forward Bloc in taking part in a meeting with a well-known capitalist, the fact is that once they felt that control of the USOI had fallen largely into the hands of the Marxist Forward Bloc, they lost interest in the front.[33] Finally, the USOI actually fell apart over discussions on the distribution of seats in the general elections. The electoral agreement that was ultimately agreed to by the USOI and the Communist Party was, as we have seen, primarily an agreement between the CPI and the Marxist Forward Bloc, since by then the other major constituents of the USOI had withdrawn their active support. But by 1950, before the front formally disintegrated, the feeling of left wing unity ceased to exist and no sense of identification with the USOI had developed which might have overshadowed the fears each group had of the others.

The USOI was doomed to failure by the very limitation which the constituent groups placed upon it. So long as the front was built not on any organizational structure which would have allowed for the development of allegiances going beyond the constituent bodies, but rather on some common issues and a

[33] From an interview by the author with Purnananda Das Gupta in Calcutta in October 1954.

common leader, the front was likely to fall apart after the death of its leader and the decline of the unifying issues. What must be understood therefore is why the leftists were unwilling to see the development of a single party in which their own groups would be submerged. To answer this question, we must first understand something of the social background of Bengal leftism.

THE SOCIAL BACKGROUND OF BENGAL LEFTISM

Two factors were primarily responsible for the rise of sectarian leftist parties in Bengal. The first was the breakdown of the traditional social organization as a result of the Western impact; the second was the economic and cultural dislocation resulting from the partition of Bengal in 1906, the loss of Calcutta as the capital of India in 1911, the growth of competition from Bombay, Madras, and other business centers, partition in 1947, the trade war between East and West Bengal, the refugee problem, and, finally, the general rise of middle class educated unemployment in and around Calcutta.

The breakdown of the traditional social organization in Bengal has been greater than nearly anywhere else since Bengal was the earliest province and Calcutta among the first cities to feel the impact of the West. Among the Bengal middle class the rigors of both caste and the joint family in large part have broken down. In their place have grown a large number of small social groups scattered throughout Calcutta and other large towns and cities of Bengal. There are associations of writers, artists, students, and teachers, and groups of just friends who come from the same ancestral village or the same school or the same neighborhood. Social intercourse among these groups is very limited and there is little active recruitment. Within the group, warm, affectionate, and genuinely intimate relationships develop; but with those outside, such intimate relationships are not usual.

The leftist political parties are not a unique feature in Bengal social life but rather an extension of these small, "closed" social groups. As with the non-political groups, social contact outside the party is nearly nil. It is not only that members of one political party have little social contact with those in other parties (which is also true, to a lesser extent, in both the United States and Great Britain) but that members of these organizations frequently do not have any intimate friends outside their group, even non-political ones.

Social disintegration, by itself, probably would not have resulted in the rise of leftist groups, although the small social groups which have developed in Bengal would probably still be there. What has turned many of these groups toward politics in general, and leftism in particular, is the economic disintegration. That this is a major factor is indicated by the fact that Bombay, which has been influenced nearly as much by the West but which has not been subjected to the same economic crises, does not have a middle class with such intense political consciousness.

The appeal of leftism has been greatest to the middle class and intellectual groups, both of which have been socially and economically dislocated. The leftist organizations make little or no effort to appeal to those already involved in other political organizations but instead build their own student, cultural, and trade union fronts, and thereby pull non-political individuals into political activity. Their appeals have been especially successful with artists and writers who at one time had the patronage of the old zamindar landlord families. (In some cases the artists and writers themselves came from such families.) On the trade union front, the Communist Party has had little success with the laboring classes, who are largely non-Bengali and who have joined the Congress-sponsored Indian National Trade Union Congress, but have been successful with Bengali middle-class white collar workers. Finally, on the student front, nearly all the leftist parties have groups at Calcutta University. Most of the present leadership of the leftist groups joined their party in their student days. Considering the purposeless feelings prevalent among students throughout the country, but most intense at Calcutta University, there is little wonder that the leftists have their greatest recruitment there.

Why has the Bengal middle class turned toward the left rather than toward Congress or even toward the Hindu communal parties? Although Bengal first led the Congress nationalist movement, it later became separated from the rest of the movement and from the rest of India, not so much because of the extent of the Western impact and the Bengal literary and cultural renaissance which followed, but because Bengal culture was not conducive to Gandhian notions of non-violence. The main stream of the nationalist movement by-passed Bengal, or at least manifested itself in a different way. To understand the growth of Marxism in Bengal one must first understand that terrorism and the spirit of revolution and revolt against traditional values existed in Bengal long before the advent of Marxism. Lack of sympathy for Gandhi's non-violence was converted into anti-Congress feeling by the events which followed partition, not only by the refugee problem and the economic dislocation or even the language controversy over Hindi, but especially by the feeling which Bengalis had that the central government was giving preference to other states. With Congress as the ruling party, the feeling of resentment and discontent is now naturally directed toward it.

But why was the discontent not channeled into the Hindu political parties? Like the leftist parties, the communal groups rejected Gandhi's non-violence and lauded terrorist and revolutionary activities. But the communal appeal contained two other elements: the anti-Muslim feeling and anti-Westernization. When the anti-Muslim element dominated the thinking of the Hindu groups and when Hindu-Muslim riots occurred in Bengal, many middle-class Bengalis gave the communal parties their support. But when the anti-Muslim question died out after partition and especially after the 1950 movements of population between East and West Bengal, the Hindu groups lost their influence. Throughout the country the Hindu parties shifted their emphasis from an anti-Muslim appeal to an anti-Westernization appeal. To the Westernized Bengali middle class this was no inducement. It is interesting to note that the Calcutta middle-class district which elected Sarat Bose, later elected Syama Prasad Mookerjee, the Jan Sangh leader, and upon his death elected a Communist to the House of the People.[34]

[34] Paradoxically, anti-United States and anti-Western feeling comes from

What is the purpose of these leftist parties? They have two functions: to fill the psychological needs of their members in terms of providing a source of identification and a new set of values, and to channelize social discontent. But these groups have not been "rationalized" in the sense that they "calculate" ways and means of being politically effective. Their *raison d'être* is primarily that they fill psychological needs. It is only when there is a common issue on which all can unite that there is much social contact between members of different leftist parties. It is interesting that the leadership of each of these groups does not encourage much social contact and in fact discourages it wherever possible. This is understandable since the prestige of the leader depends upon the allegiance which he receives from his group, so that the preservation of the group is essential to his position. The absence of social relations between members of different parties has been more of a barrier to unity than differences over issues. When talks began for the creation of a United Socialist Organization, it was generally agreed that merger was not possible at the time although desirable in the long run. But all these groups insisted upon maintaining their own thesis, their own program, their own recruitment, and their own independent existence. This becomes understandable when we recognize that these groups are separated not so much by differences over specific issues or even in general outlook, but rather by their group allegiances. Only when the issue is sufficiently strong to pinpoint their social discontent, or when a leader emerges who can provide a common identification, do prospects of unity improve. In the absence of such unifying factors, the psychological barriers to unity—the lack of social intercourse with other groups, the strong allegiances to one's leaders, organization, and program, the fear of domination by other groups—soon came to dominate the situation, and the attempt at left wing unity failed.

---

the more Westernized groups while the non-Westernized Hindu-minded groups are more sympathetic to Western policy and more critical of Russia and China. On the other hand the Hindu groups are very critical of the Westernized Indian community, whose leadership of the country they intensely dislike.

8. The Background of Hindu Communalism

THE MEANING OF COMMUNALISM

In this and in the two chapters that follow we shall deal with three Hindu communal political parties: Jan Sangh, the newest and the largest; the Hindu Mahasabha, the oldest; and Ram Rajya Parishad, the most orthodox. And we shall deal with a non-political organization, the best organized of the group, called the Rashtriya Swayamsevak Sangh or the RSS.

The term "communalism" is generally used in India to refer to any party or organization which works for the interests of a caste or religious community as opposed to the general welfare. The word has been most frequently used to describe organizations operating on behalf of the Muslim or the Hindu community. In the eyes of most Indians, the Muslim League, the Hindu Mahasabha, and the RSS represent the best-organized expressions of "communal" politics. Since partition and especially since the death of Gandhi, the word "communal" has come to be heinous in connotation and the antithesis of "secular." Jan Sangh denies that it works in the interest of the Hindu community and categorically rejects the word "communal," while the Hindu Mahasabha proudly accepts the label. But in spite of various protests, the four groups mentioned above, including Jan Sangh, are generally labeled by most Indians as communal.

As a term used by Indians in common parlance, we have retained the word, but as an analytical tool we have avoided its use. Whether Jan Sangh or any of the other groups we shall discuss ought to be called communal is not a question with which we shall be concerned. If we use the word "communal" it is only because it is useful as a means of referring to this group of parties. The reader should not assume that the writer is passing judgment.

THE EARLY HISTORY OF HINDU COMMUNALISM IN INDIA

The early history of Hindu communalism cannot be separated from the history of Hindu reaction to the Western impact. The impact of Western culture and especially of Christianity was most strongly felt in India in the early part of the nineteenth century. Ram Mohan Roy (1772-1833), born of a leading Bengal Brahman family, was deeply impressed by Christian thought. He rejected the Hindu belief in transmigration, became a confirmed deist, and in 1828 formed the famous Brahmo Samaj.[1] The Brahmo Samaj was essentially a Hindu reform movement, but one which was strongly influenced by Christian thought.

Toward the end of the nineteenth century, however, Hindu leaders directed their activities not only toward a reform of Hinduism but toward its defense.[2] A counter-reformation had begun. The movement was at first led by the Arya Samaj, founded in 1875 by Dayanand Sarasvati. Dayanand stressed the theme "Back to the Vedas," including the belief in transmigration and karma. The defense of Hinduism grew with the work of Rama-krishna, Swami Vivekananda, and the Theosophical Society, founded by a number of occidentals.

During the early part of the twentieth century, the Hindu reform movement, on the one hand, was a revolt against Hindu orthodoxy, and, on the other, represented a revolt against Western ideals.[3] Religious revivalism was soon directed against the British. In the Punjab, Lala Lajpat Rai, a leading Arya Samajist and later a leader of the Hindu Mahasabha, actively participated in the national struggle. In Bengal, Aurobindo Ghosh, Bepin Chandra Pal, and Bhupendra Nath Dutt, a brother of Swami Vivekananda, were among the leaders of the terrorist movement.

[1] J. N. Farquhar, *Modern Religious Movements in India* (New York: The Macmillan Co., 1915), p. 38.

[2] *Ibid.*, p. 101.

[3] Valentine Chirol, *Indian Unrest* (London: Macmillan and Co., 1910), p. 27. Chirol has one of the most complete accounts of the early revolutionary and revivalist movements in India, although it is written from a British viewpoint and has been criticized by Indians. Another useful account can be found in the *Sedition Committee 1918 Report* of the Government of India Home Department (Calcutta: Superintendent of Government Printing, 1918).

In Maharashtra, Bal Gangadhar Tilak, who sponsored anti-cow-killing campaigns and revived the memories and glory of Sivaji, the great Maratha fighter, was one of the earliest revolutionary Congress leaders.

The reform of Hinduism likewise played a major role in the formation of the Hindu Mahasabha. The first Hindu Sabha was formed in the Punjab in 1907 to be "ardent and watchful in safeguarding the interest of the entire Hindu community,"[4] and took upon itself the task of organizing an All India Hindu Mahasabha. The first session of the new all-India organization met in 1915. In the 1920's, the Mahasabha increasingly directed its activities against the Muslim League and the Muslim community. Reconversion of Hindus and the question of removal of untouchability were soon taken up by the Mahasabha. In 1925 its program was enunciated as follows by Lala Lajpat Rai, who was then President: "1. To organise Hindu Sabhas throughout . . . the country. 2. To provide relief to such Hindus . . . who need help on account of communal riots. . . . 3. Reconversion of Hindus who have been forcibly converted to Islam. 4. To organise gymnasiums for the use of Hindu young men and women. 5. To organise Sevasamites. 6. To popularise Hindi. . . . 7. To request the Trustees and Keepers of . . . Hindu temples to allow halls attached to the temples where people may gather to discuss matters of social and religious interest. 8. To celebrate Hindu festivals in a manner which may conduce to the promotion of brotherly feelings amongst the different sections of the Hindus. 9. To promote good feelings with Mohammedans and Christians. 10. To represent communal interests of the Hindus in all political controversies. 11. To encourage Hindu boys to take to industrial pursuits. 12. To promote better feelings between Hindu agriculturists and non-agriculturists. 13. To better the condition of Hindu women. . . ."[5]

The Communal Award of 1932, which set up special electorates

---

[4] Indra Prakash, *A Review of the History and Work of the Hindu Mahasabha and the Hindu Sanghatan Movement* (Delhi: Dharmarajya Press, 1952), p. 13.

[5] *Ibid.*, pp. 43-44.

for Muslims and other communities, was severely condemned by the Mahasabha, especially since it gave the Muslims control of both Bengal and the Punjab.

After 1932 the Mahasabha grew increasingly estranged from the Congress Party and from Mahatma Gandhi, whom they accused of Muslim "appeasement." Throughout the early history of the Mahasabha most of its leaders and members held dual membership in the Mahasabha and the Congress Party. Lala Lajpat Rai and Pandit Malaviya, two early Mahasabha leaders, had also been President of the Congress. But in the latter part of the 1930's, the Congress forbade any of its members from being in communal organizations, including the Mahasabha.

The history of the Mahasabha can, in a general way, be divided loosely into three periods signifying the main targets of its work. Underlying all three periods has been a concern for the social reform of Hinduism. Throughout the earliest history of the Mahasabha and its predecessors—that is, sometime before World War I—the emphasis was on Hindu revivalism and hostility toward the Western impact. After the war, Mahasabha activities were increasingly directed against the Muslim League. And in the latter part of the 1930's, especially after 1939 when Veer Savarkar became President of the Mahasabha, its target was increasingly the Congress Party. Since independence the Hindu Mahasabha and other like-minded organizations have been shifting increasingly from their anti-Islam emphasis to opposition to the Westernized Indian community, which they feel now dominates the central government.

It would be a mistake to view the Hindu communal movement solely as an expression of orthodoxy, unless this orthodoxy is seen in contrast to the more Westernized leadership of the country. The Mahasabha, when it first began, was an expression of reformist elements within the Hindu fold. There were many orthodox Hindus who were dissatisfied with the relatively progressive attitudes of the Mahasabha on questions of social reform.[6] The more orthodox joined the Sanatan Dharma Sabha,

---

[6] C. Yajneswara Chintami, *Indian Politics since the Mutiny* (Allahabad: Kitabistan, 1947), p. 159.

which had been created in 1895 as a defense of orthodox Hinduism against the criticisms of the Arya Samaj.[7] And after the
Second World War some orthodox Hindus created a party of
their own called Ram Rajya Parishad.

THE MEANING OF WESTERNIZATION

No understanding of Hindu communalism would be complete
without an understanding of the meaning of "Westernization,"
which to many Indians has come to mean the antithesis of Hinduism. As Indians use the word "Westernization," it has a wide
range of meaning and that meaning varies from one individual
or group to another.

It is used by Indians in one sense to refer to certain daily acts:
that is, whether one eats Western rather than Indian food, wears
Western dress (this includes whether one wears the shirt inside
the pants, as in the West, or outside, as a kurta is worn, over a
lungi or pajama), eats with utensils rather than with the hand,
generally speaks English rather than a vernacular language, and
so on.

In a second sense "Westernization" is used to refer to certain
social acts. Prime among these is one's attitude toward pre-ar-
ranged marriages as opposed to love marriages. More important
than the attitude is the act. It is argued that the system of pre-
arranged marriages is a basic prop for the social and especially
the caste system, and that the most crucial break with the Indian
tradition is the willingness of a young man to reject a pre-ar-
ranged marriage by his parents and either choose his own bride
or, as frequently occurs, remain single.

Another social act involves the acceptance of Western notions
of social equality and a willingness to act in accordance with
those notions. Primarily, this involves a rejection of the caste
system. And for a fewer number of Indians, a further criterion
is one's general attitude toward servants and so-called "inferior"
occupations.

Some Indians prefer to define "Westernization" more in terms
of beliefs than in terms of acts. These people view the rejection

[7] Farquhar, op.cit., p. 316.

of a "religious" outlook and the acceptance of a "scientific" or "rational" outlook as the ultimate criterion of one's Westernization. On the specific level this involves one's attitude toward Ayurvedic versus Western medicine, acceptance of certain traditions, the extent to which a person is religious in the sense of observance of rituals, and in general whether one views life with a religious outlook.

Among politically active Hindu-minded or communal groups, Westernization is further viewed as the antithesis of a Hindu outlook. There is the belief that those who are in the government are "Westernized," by which is meant something in addition to the meanings above, that is, that the government performs no overt acts suggesting an *identification with Hinduism*: Western terms are used by government officials; the Constitution is based on Western concepts and institutions; government officials refrain from frequent references to Sanskrit and matters of religion; the educational system emphasizes Western knowledge; and so on.

THE POLITICAL STRENGTH OF HINDU COMMUNAL PARTIES

During the 1952 general elections there were three major political parties which were publicly labeled as Hindu communal parties: the Hindu Mahasabha, Ram Rajya Parishad, and Bharatiya Jan Sangh. The Mahasabha, as we have seen, is the oldest of the three organizations. Bharatiya Jan Sangh is the newest and the largest of the three. It was formed in 1951 shortly before the general elections by Syama Prasad Mookerjee, a former Acting President of the Hindu Mahasabha, and by members of the Rashtriya Swayamsevak Sangh, a Hindu organization largely composed of young people. The RSS had been informally connected with the Mahasabha for some time. Later we shall examine in some detail the differences which arose between the RSS and the Mahasabha, and the subsequent differences between the Mahasabha and Jan Sangh.[8] The third major Hindu communal

[8] See Chapter 10.

party, the most orthodox of the three, is Ram Rajya Parishad, which was started by a Swami Karapatri in 1948.

Since independence a major shift has taken place in the strength of the communal forces. Bengal, the Punjab, and Maharashtra are no longer the communal centers they once were. By 1952, Hindu-Muslim tensions, which had provided the basis for most of the recruitment into the Hindu communal parties, had subsided. Communal strength has since shifted into areas where the Western impact has been the weakest. Anti-Westernization rather than anti-Islam feeling is increasingly providing the new basis for Hindu communalism.

Of the approximately 1,300 seats which these three parties contested for the state Assemblies in the 1952 elections, they won only 85, of which 64 were in former princely states. They did best in Madhya Bharat and Rajasthan and picked up a number of seats in PEPSU, Ajmer, Bhopal, Vindhya Pradesh, and Madhya Pradesh. In the Punjab and in Maharashtra no seats were won. Only in Bengal, of all their old strongholds, did the communal parties win a substantial number of seats. Surprisingly enough, they did not do well among the refugees from Pakistan. Rather, communal strength is greatest among the religious-minded, non-Westernized, largely non-English-speaking lower middle class in the towns of the former princely states. These urban groups may provide a new basis for Hindu communalism in the years to come.

It is too early to say whether Hindu communalism is on the increase. Although the Hindu communal parties received 6,400,-925 votes for Parliament or 6% of the popular vote in the 1952 elections, there has been some decrease in by-elections. On the other hand, while no exact figures are available, newspaper reports suggest that they have done fairly well in a number of municipal elections, especially in Delhi State and Uttar Pradesh.

A further breakdown in relations between India and Pakistan might increase the strength of the communal parties. So may government measures to change the Hindu social structure. There may be limits as to how far the present government can go in passing laws which incense the more orthodox among the

Hindu community. Economic frustrations on the part of lower-middle-class groups such as shopkeepers, secondary school teachers, and clerks, may intensify their feelings against a Westernized leadership. The failure to provide economic satisfactions for these groups may increase their attraction to charismatic leaders dressed in the garb of either leftism or religious revivalism. It is interesting to note, for example, that the middle-class district of Calcutta which elected the leftist Sarat Bose to Parliament later elected Syama Prasad Mookerjee, the Jan Sangh leader, and still later elected a Communist. Under what circumstances the Marxist appeal surpasses the communal appeal and vice versa is difficult to say, since no comparative study of local constituencies has been made which would provide a basis for comparison. One tentative hypothesis is that the Hindu communal appeal is greatest in the non-Westernized towns (such as Gwalior in the state of Madhya Bharat) while the Marxist appeal is greatest in the more Westernized communities (such as Calcutta).

THE IDEOLOGY OF HINDU COMMUNALISM

The ultimate political objective of Hindu communal parties has always been shrouded with some ambiguity. The ideal of *Hindu Rashtra* (literally, "Hindu Nation"), or a variation of this term, has been central to the Hindu communal parties, but its exact meaning is somewhat unclear.[9] Although Savarkar has explicitly said that non-Hindus will share equally with Hindus all fundamental rights and obligations,[10] the vehemence with which the Mahasabha and other Hindu communal parties have attacked Muslim government officials has made the sincerity of the communal parties questionable. Precisely what the difference is between the present Indian government and a government un-

[9] Ram Rajya Parishad declares its political ideal to be a society in which *Ram Rajya* exists, that is the rule of Ram, a mythical golden age of Indian history, but this notion has never been clearly defined either. Jan Sangh prefers the term *Bharatiya Rashtra* to *Hindu Rashtra*, but, as we shall show in a later chapter, the difference is largely semantic.

[10] Swatantrya Veer Savarkar, *Hindu Sanghatan: Its Ideology and Immediate Programme* (Bombay: N. V. Damle, Hindu Maha Sabha Presidential Office, 1940), pp. 161-162.

der *Hindu Rashtra* has never been explicitly defined. In the minds of many of the supporters of the communal parties, *Hindu Rashtra* means a Hindu-ruled state with non-Hindus holding lesser positions, if any at all.

A second ultimate ideal of the Hindu communal parties is *Akhand Bharat*, that is, the reunion of India and Pakistan. The Hindu communal parties do not accept the present division of the subcontinent as permanent. While no method has been presented for bringing about a reunion, as an ultimate ideal and as an expression of resentment against the state of Pakistan it is ever present. It holds a central place in the political manifestos of both the Mahasabha and Jan Sangh.

The point of view of the Hindu communal parties can probably more easily be described and understood by reference to their moods and general outlook than to their explicit ideology.

There is, first of all, the anti-Westernization mood. It is a mood felt not only by members of the communal parties but by sections of Congress as well. It is essentially, as we have noted earlier, a feeling that the present leadership in New Delhi has a Westernized outlook. The anti-West feeling is thus more strongly directed against Indians who are Westernized than the West itself. The Hindu-minded not only resent legislation that changes the Hindu social structure but would like to see the country's leadership talk in more traditional terms.

Second, there is a mood of militarism and violence so aptly expressed in Savarkar's slogan, "Hinduise all politics and militarise Hindudom!"[11] The Rashtriya Swayamsevak Sangh, for example, is organized along military lines, and physical exercise and drills form a major part of its activities. Savarkar frequently urged the militarization of Hindus and before World War II personally urged Hindus to join the British army. The manifesto of the Hindu Mahasabha urges the adoption of universal military training by the government. This predisposition to violence is likewise a part of the Hindu tradition as is the tradition

[11] Satya Prakash (ed.), "The National Constitution of Hindusthan," *Hindu Rashtravad as Outlined by Swatantryaveer V. D. Savarkar* (Rohtak: Rohtas Printing Press, 1945), p. 201.

of non-violence which Gandhi followed. The Hindu communal organizations reject Gandhi's non-violent approach to India's problems and urge a more militant policy toward Pakistan even if war is the consequence.

Third, a lack of interest in the political process is another mood which characterizes the Hindu communalists. The early Hindu Mahasabha, as we have shown, had as its goal the reformation of Hinduism from within as did the Arya Samaj, the Sanatan Dharma, and other Hindu organizations. The Rashtriya Swayamsevak Sangh, since the time of its creation in 1925, has made the rejection of political activity a central notion of its ideology. Not until the formation of Jan Sangh in 1951 did large numbers of RSS members enter politics. The Mahasabha has had a longer record of political activity than other Hindu communal groups, but in spite of this there has been relatively little concern on the part of the Mahasabha's leadership for the specific task of building a political organization that could assume power. Very little of Savarkar's extensive writings, including his Presidential addresses from 1937 to 1942, have been concerned with party organizational matters.[12] Mahasabha leaders have preferred instead to write ideological tracts, issue public pronouncements, and take part in mass demonstrations and agitations. One is left with the feeling, however, that something other than formal political power has been the objective of the Mahasabha.

A further aspect of the attitude of the Hindu communal parties toward the political process has been their almost total lack of concern for economic questions and the problem of economic development. Until recently the Hindu communal parties have been almost exclusively concerned with communal questions. Savarkar's writings on constitutional questions, for example, have been largely confined to matters of minority rights. Only recently has the weekly organ of Jan Sangh, the *Organiser*, been commenting on specific economic matters.

While there is no conscious rejection of the democratic frame-

12 See Swatantryaveer V. D. Savarkar, *Hindu Rashtra Darshan, A Collection of the Presidential Speeches delivered from the Hindu Mahasabha Platform* (Bombay: L. G. Khare, 1949).

work by the communal parties, there has not thus far been any conscious understanding or defense of the democratic system. The fact is that communal questions, rather than political or economic issues, have dominated the thinking of both the leaders and the rank and file of the Hindu communal parties.

HINDU COMMUNAL ELECTION MANIFESTOS

Of the three major Hindu communal parties, Ram Rajya Parishad stands alone in the uniqueness of its program. Unlike the other two parties, Ram Rajya Parishad is orthodox in its Hinduism. Its orthodoxy is highlighted by its election promise to give untouchables "high posts" in the management of the sanitation departments and leather and hides trades—traditional occupations for outcaste Hindus. The party manifesto promised a return to the "blessed days of Lord Rama's reign," when every citizen "was contented, happy, gifted with learning, and religious-minded. . . . All were truthful. None was close-fisted; none was rude; none lacked prudence; and above all, none was atheist. All followed the path of religion."[13]

Relatively little space in the forty-page manifesto of Ram Rajya Parishad is devoted to specific policy issues, although confiscation of land without compensation is opposed, the barter system is preferred over the use of legal tender, a ban on cow slaughter is advocated, and the traditional Ayurvedic system of medicine is supported. Much of the manifesto is concerned with a description of the days of Lord Rama. "The days of slavery were not our days. We were under foreign domination. We should write off those days from our Calendar. So far as our fresh activities are concerned, we should bridge over the gulf of the foreign domination and thus link our glorious past with the budding present."[14]

The ideals of Ram Rajya Parishad are so orthodox and so politically unconventional that the English-language press in India and the Westernized intelligentsia pay little attention to

[13] *The Election Manifesto of the All-India Ramarajya-Parishad* (Delhi: Nigamabodha Ghat, 1951), p. 3.
[14] *Ibid.*, p. 10.

the program and activities of this party—in spite of the fact that over 2 million voters (including 14.2% of the voters in Madhya Bharat and 9.4% in Rajasthan) gave it their support in the 1952 general elections.

In contrast with the general ideological emphasis of the Ram Rajya Parishad manifesto, the election statements of both the Hindu Mahasabha and Bharatiya Jan Sangh are relatively specific. Jan Sangh campaigned for a nullification of partition and the reunion of India and Pakistan. It claimed to stand for four fundamentals: "one country, one culture, one nation and Dharma Raj, rule of law."[15] The party manifesto declared that "secularism, as currently interpreted in this country . . . is only a euphemism for the policy of Muslim appeasement." The party stands for the "revival of Bharatiya culture and revitalisation of true Bharatiya nationalism on its basis, with such adjustments as may be necessary to make our country truly modern, progressive and strong."[16] Precisely what "Bharatiya culture and nationalism" refers to we shall try to make clear later when we contrast the outlook and program of Jan Sangh and the Hindu Mahasabha.

Jan Sangh, in its election manifesto, declared itself in favor of measures to increase food production,[17] the abolishment of *jagirdari* and *zamindari* (landholding systems) with compensation, the distribution of land to the tillers, the prohibition of cow slaughter,[18] public ownership of defense industries but not of other large industries (for "state-capitalism may . . . lead to totalitarianism"), the encouragement of small-scale and cottage industries,[19] better labor-management relations based on profit sharing, the discouragement of strikes and lockouts and the settlement of disputes by industrial tribunals whose decisions would be binding,[20] the regulation of foreign trade "in the interest of self-sufficiency and swadeshi," and, in foreign policy, the pursuit of a policy of "reciprocity" toward Pakistan, a "re-

---

[15] *Organiser*, November 5, 1951, p. 5.
[16] *Manifesto of Bharatiya Jan Sangh* (Delhi: Bharatiya Jan Sangh, 1951), p. 3.
[17] *Ibid.*, p. 4.   [18] *Ibid.*, p. 5.
[19] *Ibid.*, p. 6.   [20] *Ibid.*, p. 7.

examination" of the question whether India should remain in the Commonwealth, the complete integration of Kashmir into India, nation-wide military training, and a strengthening of India's army and defense industries.[21]

Jan Sangh also declared itself in opposition to the Hindu Code Bill (a proposed government bill dealing with reforms in marriage, divorce, inheritance rights, guardianship, and adoption), and in favor of Hindi as the national language and the promotion of Sanskrit as "being the repository of Bharatiya culture."[22] The manifesto criticized Congress for trying to make "Bharat a carbon-copy of the west" and for having "ignored and neglected the best in Bharatiya life and ideals."[23]

During the election campaign Jan Sangh leaders made a considerable effort to distinguish their party from the Hindu Mahasabha. The Mahasabha, like Jan Sangh, had pledged itself to "reestablish Akhand Hindustan by all constitutional means."[24] It also favored a policy of reciprocity toward Pakistan, severance from the Commonwealth, military training, and the strengthening of the country's defenses.[25] Nationalization of key industries, encouragement of cottage industries, compensation in case of confiscation of land, decontrol, a ban on cow slaughter, and opposition to the Hindu Code Bill likewise found a place in the Mahasabha manifesto.

What then were the differences between Jan Sangh and the Hindu Mahasabha? To answer this, one must understand the history of the groups and personalities who made up Jan Sangh, how their differences with the Hindu Mahasabha arose, and what led them to create a new political party.

---

[21] *Ibid.*, pp. 8-9.   [22] *Ibid.*, p. 11.   [23] *Ibid.*, p. 1.
[24] *Election Manifesto of the Akhil Bharat Hindu Mahasabha* (New Delhi: Akhil Bharat Hindu Mahasabha, 1951), p. 7.
[25] *Ibid.*, p. 10.

9. The Formation of Jan Sangh[1]

Two elements contributed toward the formation of Jan Sangh in 1951: an organization called the Rashtriya Swayamsevak Sangh (RSS) and a personality named Syama Prasad Mookerjee. Both the RSS and Mookerjee had withdrawn from the Hindu Mahasabha; both broke independently, at different times and under different circumstances. Together they created Jan Sangh, which in the course of a few months was to become the fourth largest party in India.

THE ROLE OF THE RASHTRIYA SWAYAMSEVAK SANGH

The Rashtriya Swayamsevak Sangh or RSS was started in Nagpur by Keshav Hedgewar, an Andhra Brahman who had settled in Maharashtra. Hedgewar believed that the major nationalist forces in India had failed to make the Hindus aware of their essential unity and that the presence of an organized Hindu group in Nagpur would provide confidence and protection to the Hindus at a time when there were periodic Hindu-Muslim riots.[2] When the RSS was founded in 1925, it was closely associated with the Hindu Mahasabha. Hedgewar himself had been an active member of the Mahasabha before then and continued to retain his membership until 1929.

The ties between the two organizations were close. First, there was an overlapping of membership. Not only Hedgewar but other RSS leaders and members belonged to the Mahasabha and vice versa. Second, there were fairly close associations between the leaders of the two organizations. Hedgewar, for example, was for many years friendly with Veer D. Savarkar, the best-known leader of the Mahasabha. Third, the two organizations frequently took part in joint activities. The RSS often served

---

[1] The complete name is Bharatiya Jan Sangh (Indian People's Party), but it is more popularly known simply as Jan Sangh.

[2] J. A. Curran, Jr., *Militant Hinduism in Indian Politics: A Study of the RSS* (New York: Institute of Pacific Relations, 1951), pp. 11-12. Curran's study gives the most complete description available of the history, policy, leadership, etc., of the RSS.

as a volunteer corps at conventions and rallies sponsored by the Mahasabha. The two likewise worked together agitating on such issues as the Hindu Code Bill. Fourth, the organizations were similar ideologically. They both advocated *Hindu Rashtra* (Hindu nation), and, before 1932 at least, they both emphasized social reforms for the Hindu community.

What separated the two organizations, however, later became crucial to their relationship. First, there were no organizational ties between the two. As closely as they might work together, each organization had its own leaders, its own activities, and its own allegiances. This lack of formal organizational ties was later to become a decisive factor in the growing distance between them. A second dividing element was their different approach to the matter of organization. While the Mahasabha was organized loosely as an association, the RSS had rigid requirements for its members.

The RSS developed as a non-political national organization, primarily of youth, which aimed at revitalizing the Hindu community. By 1948 the actual membership of the RSS was somewhere between 400,000 and 500,000 and it claimed 5,000,000 supporters.[3]

But the strength of the RSS resided not so much in its membership or in its supporters, as large a number as that may be, but primarily in its organization. Each *Swayamsevak* or member takes part in local Sangh units known as *Shakhas*, which he attends daily. Each day, in the morning or evening, the *Swayamsevaks* participate for one hour in physical exercise drills, calisthenics, and games. There is a daily salute to the ochre-colored Sangh flag and a brief Sanskrit prayer. A host of activities—special Sangh holidays, weekly discussions, training camps—and a clear-cut ideology combine to give the *Swayamsevaks* an intense devotion to their organization.

The RSS expects strict discipline from its members. Its organization is authoritarian in form and practice. Centralization of authority is the most characteristic feature of the RSS structure.[4] Decisions are made by the top leadership and passed down,

[3] *Ibid.*, p. 43.   [4] *Ibid.*, p. 55.

and leaders lower in the hierarchy are appointed by the leaders above, although this is frequently done in consultation with the rank and file.

Since the founding of the organization in 1925, the RSS has maintained its essential characteristics. But two things have changed: first, the attitude of the RSS leaders and rank and file toward the Hindu Mahasabha; and second, their attitude toward politics and political activity. Behind these two changes lie the elements which led the RSS into active politics in support of Jan Sangh.

The RSS and the Hindu Mahasabha

Paradoxically, the break between the RSS and the Hindu Mahasabha occurred over the attitude of the RSS toward political activity. For many years both organizations had been essentially non-political cultural bodies: the RSS emphasized self-development, while the Mahasabha emphasized social reforms for the Hindu community, removal of untouchability, the encouragement of Sanskrit and the vernacular languages, "reconversion" to Hinduism, and the betterment of the conditions of Hindu women.

In the early '30's, however, the Hindu Mahasabha became more engrossed in political activity, particularly after the British Communal Award of 1932; as a result, Congress-Mahasabha relations became increasingly strained, culminating in the passage of a resolution by Congress in the late 1930's forbidding members of Congress to join the Hindu Mahasabha and other communal bodies. The Hindu Mahasabha symbolically took part in the 1936 elections by nominating one of its members for a seat in the Central Assembly.

During the years in which the Hindu Mahasabha became increasingly engrossed in political work, the RSS became more and more involved in its own cultural affairs and less in political activities. The differences between the two organizations became even more pronounced when Veer Savarkar became the President of the Hindu Mahasabha in 1937.

Veer Savarkar was born in 1883 to a family of Maharashtrian

Chitpavan Brahmans (the Chitpavan Brahmans being one of the four major Brahman castes in Maharashtra). While still a young man he became a leading nationalist terrorist. As a result of his activities he was arrested, tried, and in December 1910 sentenced for life to the Andaman Islands in the Bay of Bengal. Savarkar was released in May 1937 and was thereupon elected President of the Hindu Mahasabha, a post he held for the next four years. He then toured the country as an outspoken enemy of Congress.[5]

It was at this time, apparently, that Savarkar became dissatisfied with the unwillingness of the RSS to take part in the political activities of the Mahasabha. One RSS leader[6] pointed out that Savarkar privately complained that the RSS was not in politics sufficiently to strengthen his hand. Hedgewar, who was then the RSS leader, did not want to enter politics since he felt that people had to be prepared for independence by stressing national and private character building. Golwalkar, who succeeded Hedgewar in 1940, also urged RSS members to stay out of politics. The *Swayamsevaks*, he believed, had their drills, their songs, and their prayers to build themselves. They understood the defects of Congress and believed that there had to be something more than political organizations like the Congress and Mahasabha.

The Mahasabha took an active part in the 1946 elections, but while a few individual *Swayamsevaks* participated, as a whole the RSS did not lend the Mahasabha the kind of support it wished. The RSS continued to reject political activity or at least view it as an unsatisfactory substitute for building the Hindu community. At Ahmedabad on November 10, 1949 Golwalkar said: "We have forgotten that politics is only a part and parcel of the comprehensive life. Life is higher and wider than politics. The vital component of life is not politics but culture. . . . To regard politics as all-comprehensive is to abandon the soul of Bharat."[7]

[5] See Dhananjay Keer, *Savarkar and His Times* (Bombay: India Printing Works, A. V. Keer, Publisher, 1950). This is the most complete English biography of Savarkar.
[6] K. R. Malkani in an interview with the author in Delhi in March 1954. Malkani is the editor of the *Organiser*, the semi-official organ of Jan Sangh and the RSS.
[7] Shankar Dalikrishman Joshi, "Speech at Karnavati 10th November, 1949,"

On the surface, then, the fundamental difference between the RSS and the Hindu Mahasabha, prior to 1949, which presumably caused the two organizations to drift apart, was their respective attitude toward political activity. The Hindu Mahasabha viewed political activity as essential to the protection of Hindu rights against Muslim communalism and Congress appeasement, while the RSS considered such activity unessential to the need for rejuvenating Hindu society. By 1951, however, the RSS had completely reversed its position; if this were its sole difference with the Mahasabha one might have expected closer relations, but, as we shall see, the entrance of the RSS into politics further divided the two organizations.

The RSS and Politics

Two events led to a change in the RSS attitude toward politics: the partition of India and independence in 1947, and the assassination of Gandhi and the subsequent ban on the RSS in 1948. In 1949 several RSS leaders took steps to place their organization in politics.

In one sense it is not surprising that the RSS should enter politics; more surprising that it should not. For an understanding of this question one must examine the relationship between religion and politics in Indian life.

As we have noted earlier, the nationalist movement in India has been closely associated with some forms of religious revivalism or religious reformism. Both in Bengal and Maharashtra, the earliest centers of nationalist activity, religious revivalism played a major role.

It should be recognized, of course, that cultural revivalism of one sort or another played a part in the nationalist movements of nearly every country under colonial rule; it has always been a potent weapon in the hands of those who have opposed such rule.

Faced with the impact of Western rule and Western culture,

Synopsis of Speeches and Interviews of the Most Revered Sar Sanghchalak Sri Guruji (Poona: Vikas Mudranalaya, 1949), pp. 44-53. Quoted by Curran, *op.cit.*, p. 27.

the educated classes of India, who, more than the villagers, were confronted directly with the new culture, had to respond to that challenge. Some, like Ram Mohan Roy, accepted the new culture and tried to reform Hinduism to bring it more in line with Western concepts, i.e. to root out of Hinduism those notions like caste, untouchability, *suttee*, etc., which were unjust by Western standards. Others tried to counter the Western cultural impact by a revival of traditional Hinduism. The conflict between the revivalists and the reformists has since died out, and generally speaking the educated community accepts the point of view of the reformists. But the conflict between the Westernized and the Hinduized outlook continues.[8]

In India, religion could not be left out of politics, partly because religion and culture have been so intermingled that the use of culture as a weapon against the British invaders could not be kept separate from the use of religion, and partly because of the Hindu-Muslim conflict in politics, which gave Hindus an acute consciousness of their own identity. Furthermore the system of separate electorates established by the British was in no small measure a factor in bringing Hindus into politics as a *religious* group.

Even though the RSS did not enter formal politics, it was in a sense a political organization and was an active participant in Hindu-Muslim riots all during the 1920's, '30's, and '40's. The leaders of the RSS, Hedgewar and Golwalkar, were ardent nationalists; they differed from others only in the belief that the Hindu community had to be strengthened before victory over the British could be achieved. But this did not prevent the RSS from actively working against the British. In its propaganda it glorified the Indian and the Hindu tradition and praised the great anti-British national heroes. In its actions it went so far as unofficially to support the '42 movement. It was non-political only in one sense: *it did not take part in elections nor was it*

[8] It might be pointed out as an aside here that in this battle between Hindu and Western values, the Communist Party has become a powerful rallying force for those educated Indians who reject their traditional Hindu culture and religion but who, for one reason or another, find Western liberal values unable to fill their needs.

organized for electoral purposes. Unlike Congress, the Muslim League, or the Mahasabha, it was not concerned with building a mass organization whose members merely paid dues and offered token allegiance. Like the Communists, the RSS leaders were concerned with building an organization of devoted followers, well disciplined, well versed in the Hindu ideology, and a kind of "vanguard" for the Hindu community.

The RSS reversed its formal position with regard to political activity between 1947 and '51. RSS activity increased during the 1942 movement when Congress leaders were in jail and the Muslim League was actively agitating for the establishment of Pakistan. With the partition of India in August 1947, communal riots spread in North India, especially in the Punjab. The RSS leadership and rank and file were infuriated not only by the Muslim League but by the Congress leadership, which had accepted the British proposals for partition.

As a semi-military, highly disciplined organization, the RSS was able to play an active part in the Hindu-Muslim riots. It declared Independence Day, August 15, 1947, a day of mourning. It vilified Gandhi, Nehru, and Sardar Patel for the partition of India and found a welcome reception for its ideas among millions of North Indians suffering from the consequences of partition. In December 1947 the RSS claimed the support of 5,000,-000 Hindus.[9]

On January 30, 1948 Mahatma Gandhi was assassinated by a fanatical Hindu communalist, who was a member of the Hindu Mahasabha and a former member of the RSS. On February 4th the government placed the RSS under a ban, and immediately after, about 1,700 important RSS members were arrested. Not until June 12, 1949 was the ban removed.

It was during this period that a change in attitude took place among RSS leaders and the rank and file. As a result of the ban considerable frustration developed within the organization, accompanied by a serious rethinking of the policies of the RSS toward active political work. Many of the RSS members felt that had they been a large political force with representation in

[9] Curran, *op.cit.*, p. 18.

Parliament, it would not have been possible for the government to have banned them. The RSS members further felt that the ban was the Congress Party's way of attempting to suppress a powerful anti-Congress force. They pointed out that Godse, the man who assassinated Gandhi, was not even a member of the RSS, although years earlier he had been. They reasoned that Congress, along with the Muslim League (but the responsibility was laid on Congress), partitioned the country in spite of the objections not only of the RSS, but of the entire country. They felt that, in North India especially, resentment against the Congress ran high while the RSS, both because of its opposition to partition and the assistance it had given to Hindu refugees, had achieved high prestige. This influence had not been translated into legislative power and, as a result, the Congress Party used the assassination of Gandhi by a member of the Hindu Maha-sabha as an opportunity to suppress the RSS and intern its leaders. While the RSS was under the ban, the government had confiscated its funds, attempted to discredit the organization, and thus had temporarily destroyed its effectiveness. Furthermore no substantial group in the legislature rose to its defense. There-fore, in order to save their organization, which for the first time was threatened by the power of Congress, and to save the country from Congress misrule, the RSS leaders felt that they should re-verse their old position and actively enter the political arena.

Their political work, they felt, should be independent of the work of the Hindu Mahasabha, which they considered to be a hopelessly discredited and ineffective organization. The Hindu Mahasabha had many leaders, generally older figures, but little organization and an inactive rank and file; by not including Muslims in their work, they had failed to adjust to the situation brought about by independence. The Mahasabha even more than the RSS, they felt, was closely associated with Gandhi's assassina-tion; Godse was a Mahasabha member, and Savarkar, the leader of the Mahasabha, was being tried as a conspirator. Beyond these reasons, there was a general feeling on the part of the RSS mem-bers that what they needed was a political organization of their own and that they by themselves were an effective organization of young people with a high morale and a spirit of unity and comradeship. They did not sense any such comradeship with the Hindu Mahasabha, which they viewed as a force incapable of developing into a large political organization as the RSS felt it could.

This urge for political activity was not universally felt in the RSS. The greatest enthusiasm came from supporters in North India; the least, from Maharashtra. In the area around Delhi and the Punjab, and wherever there were refugees from Pakistan (and these included RSS members themselves who had fled from Pakistan into India), the RSS had considerable strength. It was in these areas that the RSS was particularly bitter against both partition and the government ban. Its mass strength was in complete contrast to its inability to prevent the government from suppressing its organization. Many of the RSS members came to believe that, had they been in politics earlier, partition might not have occurred. They believed that social and cultural work was not enough to bring unity to the country, for it was the political people—the Congress especially—who had partitioned the country and destroyed its political unity. *This contrast between their mass strength and their political weakness, forcibly presented to them by the government ban, activated the RSS members in North India to enter politics.*

Thus the initiative for the establishment of Jan Sangh came from North India. Upon their release from jail in 1949, RSS leaders in the North inaugurated discussions of the possibility of forming a new party. It is generally agreed that much of the initiative came from Vasantra Rao Oak, a leading RSS member. Oak, who had been released from jail in 1949, discussed the possibilities of starting a new party with Deores, another important RSS leader, and Mauli Chand Sharma, who was not in the RSS but was known to be a close sympathizer. They were joined by other RSS leaders, Professor Mahavir and Din Dayal Upadhyaya.

As early as 1949 Vasantra Rao Oak had discussed the formation of a new party with Dr. Syama Prasad Mookerjee, at that time a member of Nehru's Cabinet. In 1949 and especially in

1950, Mookerjee differed with Nehru and the government over the question of relations with Pakistan. With the exodus of Hindus from East to West Bengal, Mookerjee urged a firm policy toward Pakistan, including the use of economic pressures and, if necessary, the application of force.

Since 1949, Oak had come to know Mookerjee particularly well and had urged him to leave the Cabinet and join the opposition. In 1950 Oak assured Mookerjee that, if he left the government, the RSS would support him and start a new party.[10]

In April 1950 Mookerjee resigned from the Cabinet in protest over the Delhi Agreement between India and Pakistan. Upon his resignation a group of sympathetic citizens of Delhi sponsored a celebration to congratulate Mookerjee on his resignation from the government. In the year that followed contacts were established in the various provinces and arrangements made for creating a new party. The main plank of the new group was *Akhand Bharat*, i.e. a reunion of India and Pakistan.

It should be remembered that, in 1950, relations between India and Pakistan were particularly strained, partly over the Kashmir dispute and partly over the crisis that had occurred in Bengal with the mass exodus of Hindus to India and Muslims to Pakistan. In 1950 and 1951 the Congress Party was experiencing its own internal crises with the resignation of Kripalani and the formation of the Kisan Mazdoor Praja Party, and the conflict between Tandon and Nehru resulting in the defeat of the Hindu-minded group inside Congress.

Those who were eager to start a new party had frequent discussions with Golwalkar, the leader of the RSS. Golwalkar said he had no inclination to work in any party and that he was neither enthused about nor against the new proposals.[11] The RSS group further appealed to non-RSS people who were eager to operate in some organized opposition to Congress. One of the early leaders to be attracted to the attempt at forming a new party was Mauli Chand Sharma. Sharma is a well-known Hindu active in the Hindu Sanatan Dharma Sabha, an orthodox Hindu

[10] Told to the author by Vasantra Rao Oak in an interview in Delhi in March 1954.
[11] *Ibid.*

organization. His father had been an active leader of the Hindu Mahasabha and at one time its President. Sharma had at one time been in Congress, and was later in the service of the princely states until 1945 when he became General Secretary of the All Indian Hindi Sammelan, an organization formed to propagate Hindi as the national language. Sharma hoped that as a leader of the Sanatan Dharma movement, he would bring into the new party some of the older people not in the RSS. He felt that he was widely respected by the orthodox Hindu groups, especially because of his father, who was an active religious organizer and whose orthodoxy was well-known.[12]

THE ROLE OF SYAMA PRASAD MOOKERJEE

It was the contribution of Syama Prasad Mookerjee, however, which provided the greatest impetus to the formation of the new party.

Mookerjee was born on July 6, 1901, the son of Ashutosh Mookerjee, a well-known Bengali educator. He studied at both Calcutta and Cambridge and was admitted to the English bar in 1927. In 1934 he became the youngest chancellor of Calcutta University. His political record showed an ability to shift from one organization to another and, when necessary, to be a free lance independent. In the late '20's he was a Congress member of the Bengal Legislative Council. In 1937 he was elected to the Council as an independent. He soon fell under the influence of Savarkar and in 1939 joined the Hindu Mahasabha. A year later he was elected working President, and then President, of the Mahasabha, posts he held for four years. In 1941 he joined the Bengal government as Finance Minister, but the following year resigned. In the 1946 elections Mookerjee was elected to the Constituent Assembly of India and a year later joined the first Nehru Cabinet as Minister of Industry and Supplies, a post he held until April 1950 when he resigned over differences with Nehru on Indo-Pakistan relations.[13]

[12] From an interview by the author with Mauli Chand Sharma in Delhi in March 1954.

[13] Biographical information from Balraj Madhok, *Dr. Syama Prasad Mookerjee, a Biography* (New Delhi: Deepak Prakashan, 1954), pp. 1-44.

Almost immediately after independence, Mookerjee began to have differences with the Hindu Mahasabha. These differences became particularly intense after Gandhi's assassination in January 1948.

Mookerjee proposed that the Mahasabha leave political work and confine itself to social and cultural activities. The Mahasabha had obviously failed in the 1946 elections to prove itself a political force and Mookerjee believed that it would be best if it more narrowly confined its activities while others, perhaps a new group, could enter the political sphere. If the Mahasabha was unprepared to accept this, Mookerjee alternatively proposed that the Mahasabha reorient its "communal" emphasis and admit members of all communities, Muslims included.

Mookerjee's proposal that the Mahasabha leave politics was rejected until February 1948, after Gandhi was assassinated by a member of the Mahasabha, and when the Government of India arrested Savarkar and other Mahasabha members on charges of being involved in the death of Gandhi. A wave of anti-communal, and specifically anti-Mahasabha, feeling swept the country. Almost immediately after Gandhi's death, the Mahasabha Working Committee met in Delhi and agreed to suspend all political activity and concentrate on the relief and rehabilitation of refugees, and social and religious problems. This decision was to be operative until the All India Committee of the Mahasabha could meet. At the end of the year the Working Committee again met and agreed to propose to the All India Committee that the Mahasabha resume its political activities. Mookerjee strongly opposed this decision and urged instead that a new party be formed and that the Mahasabha merge with it or suspend its political activities and work only in the cultural field. When the Working Committee rejected Mookerjee's proposals, he resigned from the Committee and from his position as Vice President.

Savarkar was subsequently acquitted in the Gandhi murder trial, and in May 1949 the Mahasabha officially returned to political activity. The Working Committee accepted Mookerjee's resignation, and the Mahasabha reaffirmed its belief in *Hindu*

Rashtra and its policy of admitting only Hindus into the party.[14]

Although Mookerjee left the Mahasabha, dispute over his point of view continued within the organization. The leadership of the Mahasabha was virtually unanimous in its policy of continuing political activities, but some disagreement arose over the question of admitting non-Hindus. Mookerjee had proposed that non-Hindus be allowed to join the Mahasabha, but the leaders of the Mahasabha were looking for a formula whereby non-Hindus could be admitted into the electoral work of the party as non-members. After some dispute a special session of the Mahasabha was called in Jaipur in April 1951, shortly before the general elections. A resolution was proposed by N. C. Chatterjee, the President, and seconded by V. G. Deshpande, the General Secretary, authorizing the Working Committee to "enlist the sufferage and support of non-Hindu citizens and to set up candidates wherever possible from amongst them."[15]

But by this time Mookerjee had left the Mahasabha completely, and no effort was made to woo him back. In any event the proposal of Mookerjee to open the party to all was defeated.

Mookerjee's resignation from the Mahasabha left him without a party. For a short time he continued in Nehru's Cabinet. During the last months of his stay in the Cabinet and in the months following his resignation Mookerjee was in a "quest for a political platform," to quote from a biography written by one of his followers.[16] Although a close friend of Mookerjee urged him to join the Congress Party, to strengthen the position of Sardar Patel and ultimately become a leader of the anti-Nehru conservative forces of Congress, Mookerjee felt that this was not possible. Instead Mookerjee was very much impressed with the work of the Rashtriya Swayamsewak Sangh. As previously mentioned, even while he was in the Cabinet he was led to understand by RSS leaders that they would be prepared to support him in the formation of a new party which would stand for

[14] See V. G. Deshpande, *Why Hindu Rashtra?* (New Delhi: Hindu Mahasabha, 1949).
[15] *Full Text of the Resolutions Passed at the Special Session of the Akhil Bharat Hindu Mahasabha* (Jaipur: 1951), p. 1.
[16] Madhok, *op.cit.*, p. 45.

"Bharatiya culture" but which would be open to members of all communities.

THE FORMATION OF BHARATIYA JAN SANGH

In early 1951 it was reported in the press[17] that a high RSS source "in intimate touch with inner developments" had confirmed that there was an increasing demand within the RSS that it should change its policy and assume a political role in addition to its cultural one. This source said that a significant section within the RSS was of the opinion that in view of the "disintegration" that had occurred in certain political parties the chances of strong, independent candidates had become brighter for the coming elections. The report went on to say that RSS candidates might run as independents, with RSS support, but that the RSS as such might not adopt any political program, since the high command of the RSS felt that it was not the time for placing an ambitious program before the country. But—and this signified what was to come, the source said—the RSS would not withhold support to members who may form an independent party to contest elections.

As we have already noted, there was considerable disagreement within the RSS over what role it should take in active politics. A section in Maharashtra, in particular, was reluctant to assume political work, and Golwalkar himself was not prepared to endorse any political party. A compromise took place within the RSS. The large section of the RSS which favored political activity decided to work with Syama Prasad Mookerjee toward the creation of Jan Sangh, but agreed that on the official level the RSS would remain out of politics. This was in accordance with the RSS Constitution, which provided that the RSS should abjure politics and devote itself to cultural activities only, but that its members were free to join any political party except those believing in violence.[18]

After lengthy negotiations a conference was held in Calcutta to inaugurate the Bharatiya Jan Sangh in Bengal, with Mooker-

[17] *Hindu*, January 8, 1951.
[18] RSS Constitution, Articles 4, 6, and 9, cited by Curran, *op.cit.*, p. 22.

jee as its President.[19] A few weeks later, in the city of Jullundur in the Punjab, 250 citizens from the Punjab, PEPSU, and Himachal Pradesh met to form Bharatiya Jan Sangh in those states. Both conferences were applauded by the *Organiser*, the unofficial organ of the RSS.[20]

From the very earliest the new party sought to dispel the notion that it was a "communal" party. This was done in a number of ways. First, the party leaders emphasized that, unlike the Hindu Mahasabha and Ram Rajya Parishad, Jan Sangh was open to all. And second, the new party was for *Bharatiya Rashtra*, not *Hindu Rashtra* as advocated by the Hindu Mahasabha.

In Maharashtra there was less sympathy for the establishment of a new party. There the RSS was closely involved in the social conflict between the Brahman and non-Brahman communities. The RSS membership, more so than in other parts of India, tended to be confined to the Brahman castes, especially to the Chitpavan Brahmans (one of the four major Brahman castes in Maharashtra). While partition was opposed in Maharashtra, the bitterness of feeling could not equal that in North India. There were no Hindu-Muslim problems in Maharashtra comparable in seriousness to those in the North; partition had not directly affected the economic life of Maharashtra as it had that of the Punjab and Bengal; there was no refugee problem, and therefore none of the personal consequences of partition to be felt.

While the RSS grew in the North, it did not have a comparable increase in strength in Maharashtra. With the assassination of Gandhi by a Maharashtrian Brahman, an outbreak of violent anti-Brahmanism occurred in Maharashtra. Lootings of shops and attacks on homes and individual Brahmans were almost daily occurrences for a period of several weeks. It was apparent that the RSS was more narrowly confined to a single community in Maharashtra and did not have the same appeal there that it had in the North. There was also the feeling on the part of some of the RSS members in Maharashtra that the Mahasabha's organi-

[19] *Organiser*, May 7, 1951.   [20] *Organiser*, June 11, 1951.

zation and activity in that region should not be duplicated. Some RSS members felt that the Mahasabha in Maharashtra was more of a living organization there than elsewhere since Savarkar, the Mahasabha leader who was revered even by the RSS, was in the Maharashtra Mahasabha. So long as he was there some of the RSS members hesitated to form a rival political party.

Differences of opinion developed in the Maharashtra RSS. These differences, to the knowledge of the writer, never became public, nor has it been possible to ascertain with any certainty who favored and who opposed entering politics. It should be understood by the reader that such discussions within the RSS are private. As in the Communist Party, decisions are made after some discussion, but the cleavages which develop during discussions are hidden from the public. There are a number of indications, however, that cleavages did exist, enough so as to delay the formation of Jan Sangh in Maharashtra. The RSS in Maharashtra, unlike its counterparts in the North, did not enter politics during the 1952 elections, and the Maharashtra provincial branch of Jan Sangh was not formed until Syama Prasad Mookerjee personally came to Poona about a year and a half after Jan Sangh had been established.

With the general elections beginning in the latter part of December 1951 and extending through the early part of 1952, there was considerable haste to start the new party. Between May and October intense efforts were made to start Jan Sangh organizations in several provinces and during the latter part of October it was officially established on the national level at a convention in New Delhi. Three hundred delegates selected Syama Prasad Mookerjee as President and agreed upon an election manifesto which amplified the points in Mookerjee's Presidential address.[21]

In his address Mookerjee declared that while Jan Sangh would function as "the principal party in opposition" it would not "hesitate to take upon itself the reins of administration should it succeed in winning the confidence of the majority of the

[21] Details of the convention can be found in the *Organiser*, October 29, 1951, and the *Hindustan Times*, October 22, 1951.

electorate."[22] He further said that while the program of the party would be settled in detail by the representatives at the convention, the party had been functioning on the provincial sphere for several months and the main points of its program were already known. The party is open "to all citizens of Bharat irrespective of caste, creed or community."[23] Congress, Mookerjee said, was pursuing "a suicidal policy of appeasement of Muslims," and, he continued, "Our Party firmly believes that the future of Bharat lies in the proper appreciation and application of Bharatiya Sanskriti and Maryada. . . . This must be suitably reflected in our system of national education."[24] On the economic level the party "has laid great stress on the solution of the basic problems of food and cloth." He called for an integrated scheme of development of "large, medium and small scale industries," and declared that "sanctity of private property will be observed and private enterprise will be given a fair and adequate play, subject to national welfare."[25]

In foreign policy Mookerjee called for withdrawal from the Commonwealth, and declared that "partition of Bharat was a tragic folly. We believe in the goal of a reunited Bharat . . . through peaceful means. . . . So long as Pakistan continues we will urge a policy of strict reciprocity."[26] He said that Jan Sangh favored the withdrawal of the Kashmir case from the United Nations and that there should be no plebiscite. At some length Mookerjee attacked the policy of "Muslim appeasement" pursued by the Prime Minister.[27]

Mookerjee, as Jan Sangh President, nominated a provisional Working Committee, with Professor Mahavir and Mauli Chand Sharma as General Secretaries, and included representatives from U.P., Madhya Bharat, the Punjab, Madhya Pradesh, Ajmer, Rajasthan, Vindhya Pradesh, Bihar, Mysore, Delhi, and West Bengal. With few exceptions, the bulk of the leadership and the convention delegates appeared to come from northern and cen-

---

[22] *Why Bharatiya Jana Sangh—The Presidential Address of Dr. Syama Prasad Mookerjee at the Opening Convention of Akhil Bharatiya Jana Sangh* (Delhi: Bharat Mudranalaya, 1951), p. 2.
[23] *Ibid.*, p. 3.   [24] *Ibid.*, p. 4.   [25] *Ibid.*, p. 5.
[26] *Ibid.*, pp. 6-7.   [27] *Ibid.*, pp. 7-9.

tral India. No organization had gotten under way in South India, and, for reasons we have already described, Jan Sangh was not organized in Maharashtra until the following year.

Jan Sangh, from the very first, achieved considerable prominence in the public eye, partly because of the popularity of Mookerjee, and partly because the new organization had the benefit of the vigor, discipline, and organizational efficiency of the RSS. Within not more than six months, party organizations were established in most of the northern and central Indian states.

Touring the country in the latter part of 1951, Mookerjee denied in his public statements the charge that Jan Sangh was "communal" and in turn accused Congress of "communalism" through its policy of "Muslim appeasement." He laid emphasis on Jan Sangh's open membership and pointed to that as the distinguishing factor which separated Jan Sangh from the Mahasabha. Mookerjee further denied that the RSS and Jan Sangh were one, arguing that while some RSS members joined Jan Sangh, many members of Jan Sangh were not in the RSS.[28] This was reinforced officially by Golwalkar when he declared that the RSS would not back the Hindu Mahasabha or any other party, but that the Swayamsevaks were free to vote as they pleased.[29]

It should be clearly understood here that at no time was there any formal constitutional or legal arrangement between Jan Sangh and the RSS. In that sense the leaders of both organizations could honestly deny that the two organizations were one. However, RSS members played a key role in organizing the new party and without their participation it is not unlikely that Jan Sangh could have achieved such prominence. It is also true that, among the top leadership of the party, RSS leaders were in major positions. But it is important to note that at all times the RSS insisted that those who were office bearers in one organization could not be office bearers in the other.[30]

---

[28] Organiser, October 29, 1951.   [29] Ibid., October 29, 1951.

[30] It is conceivable that this division between the RSS and Jan Sangh could become a source of conflict between the two organizations at some future date. It should be recalled that while the RSS never controlled the Mahasabha, many Swayamsevaks were members of both organizations in the 1920's and

GENERAL ELECTION RESULTS

For a new party Jan Sangh did remarkably well in the general elections. While the Hindu Mahasabha and Ram Rajya Parishad were older organizations, Jan Sangh received as many votes as the other two parties put together. By obtaining 3,246,288 votes or 3% of the national vote for the House of the People, Jan Sangh received recognition from the Election Commission as a national party.

Several obvious but interesting features of the Jan Sangh voting strength are worth noticing. Most important of all is that Jan Sangh is almost exclusively confined to northern and central India with no strength in the South. In Madras, Hyderabad, Mysore, and Travancore-Cochin, Jan Sangh either did not contest any state Assembly seats or lost those contested. Only in Uttar Pradesh, Bengal, Madhya Bharat, PEPSU, Rajasthan, Ajmer, Delhi, and Vindhya Pradesh did Jan Sangh win any Assembly seats. It is also interesting to note that Jan Sangh is not confined area-wise to the same extent that the Mahasabha and Ram Rajya Parishad are. Its appeal and influence seems to be wider. Eleven of the Mahasabha's twenty Assembly seats are in Madhya Bharat while twenty-four of Ram Rajya Parishad's thirty-two seats are in Rajasthan, in contrast to the wider distribution of Jan Sangh seats. Only nine of its thirty-two seats are in Bengal, where it won its largest number (see Tables 4 and 5 below).

The elections thus demonstrated to the communal parties that Jan Sangh had the widest appeal of them all. And while it is true that, as a national force, Jan Sangh's strength was minor compared with that of either Congress, the Socialists, or the Communists, it was strong, like the Communists, in certain regions. Jan Sangh also did quite well in comparison with the Hindu Mahasabha and Ram Rajya Parishad, and it was with a feeling of some satisfaction that Jan Sangh members saw that they had surpassed these other parties, especially the Mahasabha. And finally, while most of the leaders of other parties were defeated in the elections, Syama Prasad Mookerjee had been elected

---

1930's. So long as two separate organizations exist, they are a source of potential conflict.

TABLE 4

General Election Results for Hindu
Communal Parties in the
Legislative Assemblies

	Jan Sangh	Hindu Mahasabha	Ram Rajya[a] Parishad	Hindu[b] Total	Assembly Total Seats
U.P.	2	1		3	429
W. Bengal	9	4		13	238
M. Bharat	4	11	2	17	99
PEPSU	2			2	60
Rajasthan	8	2	24	34	160
Ajmer	3			3	30
Bhopal		1		1	30
Delhi	3	1		4	48
V. Pradesh	2		2	4	60
Madhya Pradesh			3	3	232
Bihar			1	1	330
Totals	33	20	32	85	1,716

[a] *Indian Press Digests* (Berkeley: Bureau of International Relations of the Department of Political Science, University of California, Vol. 1, No. 4, September 1952), Table III.

[b] The Hindu parties won no seats in Madras, Hyderabad, Mysore, Travancore-Cochin, Coorg, Assam, Bombay, Orissa, the Punjab, Saurashtra, and Himachal Pradesh.

Source: Ministry of Information and Broadcasting, Government of India, *India, A Reference Annual 1953* (Delhi: Publication Division, Government of India, 1953), p. 98.

TABLE 5

General Election Results for
Hindu Communal Parties

	HOUSE OF THE PEOPLE		STATE ASSEMBLIES	
	Popular Vote	Seats	Popular Vote	Seats
Jan Sangh	3,246,288	3	2,866,566	33
R. R. Parishad	2,151,603	3	1,260,049	32
H. Mahasabha	1,003,034	4	848,415	20
Totals	6,376,000	10	5,036,000	85

Source: Election Commission, *Report on the First General Elections in India 1951-52*, Vol. II (Statistical) (Delhi: Manager of Publications, 1955).

and became a leading figure in Parliament. Mookerjee was widely viewed as a major spokesman for the opposition and, in the minds of some, a possible alternative leader to the Prime Minister.

THE ORIGIN OF JAN SANGH—A SUMMARY

Essentially, Jan Sangh grew out of an estrangement between the RSS and the Hindu Mahasabha, and a subsequent urge of the RSS leadership and rank and file (or at least a large part of it) to enter active political life. This estrangement between the two organizations was not so much the product of differences over issues (although such a difference did exist) as it was centered around a set of organizational allegiances which developed on the part of the RSS. Having developed in its own way, with traditions, leaders, and activities of its own, the RSS resented any effort by the Hindu Mahasabha to make its organization a subsidiary of the Mahasabha. Ostensibly the drift occurred over the question of the attitude of the RSS toward political work, but that this was not the decisive factor is indicated by the fact that when the RSS decided to enter politics, it did not consider entering the Hindu Mahasabha.

There was an age difference between the Mahasabha and the RSS (which contained younger elements); there was a feeling on the part of the RSS that the Mahasabha was an ineffective organization with no future and no mass support; there was a feeling that communalism had been discredited and that the Mahasabha had failed to adjust to this situation. While ostensibly there was a difference over whether a political party should be open to all—the Jan Sangh being open even to Muslims while the Mahasabha was not—the difference was more theoretical than real. Even the Mahasabha eventually said it was willing to admit Muslims for its political work but could not admit them for cultural activities. And in practice, while the Jan Sangh admitted Muslims to actual membership in their organization, there were few joiners and few Muslims ran on Jan Sangh tickets.

In private, RSS leaders admitted that even if the Mahasabha were open to all, they themselves would be reluctant to join. Basically, there was a feeling on the part of RSS leaders and rank and file that they needed a party of their own which would be a tightly knit organization of RSS members.

It is interesting to note that while Vasantra Rao Oak and a

few other RSS leaders were eager to expand the party to take in non-RSS people, a substantial section of the RSS felt that there was little scope for non-RSS people who lacked the discipline which they shared; they believed that in the final analysis Jan Sangh depended upon the work and contribution of its RSS members.[31] It was this lack of reliance upon non-RSS members and leaders which enabled the party to survive and grow even after the death of Syama Prasad Mookerjee in 1953.

[31] See report in the *Statesman*, November 2, 1954 on the RSS–non-RSS dispute within Jan Sangh involving the attempts by RSS members to gain complete control of the party. As a result of this dispute, Mauli Chand Sharma, the non-RSS President of the party (elected after Mookerjee's death), resigned his office.

10. The Unsuccessful Merger Attempt of Jan Sangh and the Hindu Mahasabha

Why is it possible for two political parties to merge while other parties fail in the attempt? In an earlier chapter we described the successful merger of the Socialist Party and the Kisan Mazdoor Praja Party. In this chapter we shall describe the attempt made by the Hindu Mahasabha and Jan Sangh to merge, the failure of that attempt, and the reasons for the failure. At the close of this chapter we shall make some comparisons with the SP-KMPP merger and try to explain the differences between the two.

THE MERGER STORY: THE ATTEMPT

Almost immediately after the elections, as early as March 1952, Syama Prasad Mookerjee, the leader of Jan Sangh, invited several parties to attend a conference in New Delhi to consider forming an opposition Parliamentary front in the House of the People.[1] As a result of this conference the National Democratic Party was formed in Parliament in June 1952, made up of thirty-four MP's; they included members of Jan Sangh, the Hindu Mahasabha, the Commonweal Party and the Tamilnad Toilers (both from Madras State), Akali Dal (from the Punjab and PEPSU), and Ganatantra Parishad (from Orissa), and several independents.

Mookerjee, speaking at the annual conference of the West Bengal Jan Sangh, felt that the Congress election victory was the result of the "existence of far too many candidates and small parties. . . . It was therefore vital that the opposition parties should not fritter away their energies but consolidate their position by presenting a united front based on a common programme dealing with urgent and vital problems. This was especially necessary inside the legislature so that due pressure might be brought to bear upon the ruling party and efficiency and purity of administration secured."[2]

[1] *Organiser*, March 17, 1952, p. 1. [2] *Ibid.*, May 12, 1952, p. 8.

The parliamentary front got underway under the leadership of Mookerjee. In the year that followed his prestige increased as a result of his forceful speaking in Parliament and the recognition given to him by the opposition as being their best spokesman.

In the early months of 1953, circumstances developed which brought the Mahasabha, Jan Sangh, and Ram Rajya Parishad even closer together. At that time an organization called the Jammu and Kashmir Praja Parishad launched an agitation in Jammu, south of the Kashmir valley. The Praja Parishad advocated the full and unconditional accession of the state of Jammu and Kashmir to India, and their slogan, "Integrate Kashmir," was supported by Jan Sangh, the Mahasabha, and Ram Rajya Parishad. The three organizations agreed to meet to consider what steps could be taken to aid the movement in Jammu.

On February 8th talks were held between Dr. Mookerjee and Mauli Chand Sharma of Jan Sangh and N. C. Chatterjee, Dr. N. B. Khare, and V. G. Deshpande of the Hindu Mahasabha, concerning the Praja Parishad agitation in Jammu. As a result of these meetings a joint program was formulated. N. C. Chatterjee said that there was a great desire for a merger on the part of the rank and file of the Hindu Mahasabha. There was already a good measure of programmatic unity between these two parties and a greater coordination of activities should be sought, he declared.[3]

Greater unity between these organizations seemed to be evolving. In late February they took part in a four-day conference inaugurated by Swami Karapatri, leader of Ram Rajya Parishad, demanding a government ban on cow slaughter.[4] A few weeks later the three organizations jointly launched a *satyagraha* in support of the four-month-old Jammu Parishad agitation. Shortly after, Mookerjee, Chatterjee, Nand Lal Sharma (General Secretary of Ram Rajya Parishad), Guru Dutt (President of the Delhi State Jan Sangh), and eighteen others were arrested in Delhi for leading a procession in defiance of a government ban on processions, but a few days later were released from jail. In

[3] *Hindustan Times*, February 8, 1953.   [4] *Ibid.*, February 22, 1953.

the months that followed, the agitation over Kashmir and Jammu increased in intensity until some 1,200 persons from these organizations were under arrest.[5]

That sentiment existed at this time for merger of the various organizations was suggested by Ashutosh Lahiri in an article in the *Hindu Outlook*. He noted that Dr. Khare (a former President) and Mr. Deshpande (the General Secretary) of the Mahasabha along with some MP's favored merging with the other organizations, but that the rank and file were opposed. Lahiri said that the Sabha is *not just interested in capturing political power*, and he expressed the fear that in the event of a merger the Jan Sangh leadership would absorb the Hindu Mahasabha.[6]

On May 12, 1953 Mookerjee was again arrested, this time for attempting to enter the state of Jammu without a permit. Dr. Mookerjee had been served with an order that his entry into Jammu was prejudicial to the security of the state and was arrested under Section 3 of the Preventive Security Act. Mookerjee remained in a Kashmir jail through May and June but as a result of the sudden occurrence of an ailment was moved to the Srinager State Hospital. On June 23, 1953 it was announced to a surprised nation that Dr. Mookerjee had died from pleurisy.

In early July the Joint Action Committee of the Mahasabha, Jan Sangh, and Ram Jajya Parishad announced that the movement in Jammu had been called off and that their *satyagraha* was to be terminated. Almost simultaneously with the termination of the movement, N. C. Chatterjee, the Mahasabha President, called for the merger of the three organizations and declared that it was Syama Prasad Mookerjee's last wish that such a merger take place. This statement by Chatterjee was dramatically made on the "Shradi" day (the last day of ritual mourning) for Mookerjee at a large public meeting at Gandhi grounds in New Delhi. As a result of their suffering for a common cause, said Chatterjee, the workers and leaders now had realized the need to stand together under a single banner. He added that

5 *Hindu Outlook*, May 3, 1953.
6 Ashutosh Lahiri, "Immediate Problem before the Mahasabha," *Hindu Outlook*, May 3, 1953, p. 2.

although the agitation had been called off, the Joint Action Committee would not be dissolved.[7]

The movement for merger seemed to be gaining momentum. Mauli Chand Sharma, the new acting President of Jan Sangh, said in his Presidential address at the annual conference of Jan Sangh that the time had now come for a merger. The conference adopted a resolution welcoming the move for unity.[8] On the following day, at a press conference, V. G. Deshpande, an MP and General Secretary of the Mahasabha, said that he favored a merger or some sort of alliance between the Mahasabha, Jan Sangh, and Ram Rajya Parishad in order to forge a united front of all organizations believing in Hindu ideology.[9]

The sentiment for merger seemed universal. The Working Committee of the Mahasabha, meeting in Delhi, quickly passed a resolution calling on "all Hindu nationalist forces to combine to face the crisis of the present times and present a united front against all anti-national forces."[10]

THE MERGER STORY: THE FAILURE

But the early enthusiasm for merger, which for a time seemed irresistible, was soon dampened. At a meeting of the Working Committee of Ram Rajya Parishad, Swami Karapatri gave a guarded answer about the possibilities of merger. "If the other parties sincerely wanted a merger, they should take concrete steps toward it. The Parishad was willing for cooperation but he emphasized that they would not forsake their principles in respect of religion."[11] Pandit Mauli Chand Sharma of Jan Sangh, speaking at a public meeting in Agra, said of his party's merger with the Mahasabha: "We are, of course, interested in that *if the Mahasabha accepts our policies.*"[12] A further damper came from an editorial in the *Hindu Outlook*. Indra Prakash, the editor, wrote that Chatterjee had threatened to resign if there was not a merger of these organizations and that, as a result of this threat, the Mahasabha Working Committee had passed the

---

[7] *Hindustan Times,* July 6, 1953.   [8] *Ibid.,* August 17, 1953.
[9] *Ibid.,* August 18, 1953.   [10] *Ibid.,* August 24, 1953.
[11] *Hindustan Times,* August 27, 1953.   [12] *Ibid.,* August 27, 1953.

resolution calling for consolidation. But, Prakash declared, this move to merge with Jan Sangh and Ram Rajya Parishad was really started by the Congress to weaken the Hindu movement. He added that while Jan Sangh denied being communal, the Mahasabha proudly believes that communalism is "bliss."[13]

A week later, at a press conference in Jaipur, Mauli Chand Sharma, referring to the possibilities of merger, said that both Jan Sangh and Ram Rajya Parishad favored the idea, but that the Hindu Mahasabha executive wanted a joint front without obliteration of the separate identities of the three organizations. He said that the policy of the Hindu Mahasabha was endorsable, but that the constitution of that organization, by restricting membership only to Hindus, savored essentially of communalism. He urged the Mahasabha to throw open its membership to all citizens alike. He added, in a note which suggested that prospects for merger were dim, that efforts for the merger had not been abandoned.[14]

In December, talks between Jan Sangh and the Hindu Mahasabha completely fell apart. Early in the month a three-day session of the Working Committee of the Mahasabha was held in Delhi, presided over by N. C. Chatterjee, the party's President. In a lengthy statement the Mahasabha Working Committee announced that it was terminating the merger talks and charged Mauli Chand Sharma with having misrepresented the Mahasabha and its ideology during his Bombay press conference by saying that "the Hindu Mahasabha is a communal body and welcomes princes, zamindars and vested interests in its midst."[15]

Mauli Chand Sharma immediately issued a statement denying that he had misrepresented the Hindu Mahasabha and its ideology. He explained that at his press conference he had said that Jan Sangh was a national organization open to all Indians while the Hindu Mahasabha was restricted to one community. "The Jan Sangh does not accept the concept of majority and minority communities based on religion and stands for one nation and

[13] Indra Prakash, "Liquidation under the Garb of a United Front," *Hindu Outlook*, August 30, 1953, p. 3.

[14] *Hindustan Times*, September 14, 1953.   [15] *Ibid.*, December 8, 1953.

one culture. As such, merger could only take place with bodies which accepted this stand," he said.[16] Sharma stated that, while Jan Sangh welcomed the merger move, at the last meeting of the Hindu Mahasabha Working Committee "it had become evident that Mr. Chatterjee could not carry his committee with him as the latter rejected his move for merger."[17] Jan Sangh, he said, favored merger and felt that mere coordination, as advocated by the Mahasabha, was no substitute.

During the remainder of December, considerable recrimination passed between the leaders of the two organizations. The basic theme of each organization was that the merger talks had failed because the other organizations never wanted a merger. Newspapers reported that a speaker was shouted down at a Mahasabha public meeting at Gandhi grounds in New Delhi when the speaker, the President of the U.P. Mahasabha, charged Jan Sangh with having betrayed the trust of the Mahasabha. "Pandemonium prevailed, and the proceedings of the meeting were interrupted, when the Jan Sangh withdrew from the meeting and created noise and shouted slogans such as 'Dr. Mookerjee Amar Rahe' (Long live Dr. Mookerjee)."[18] In another statement V. G. Deshpande, MP and General Secretary of the Hindu Mahasabha, sought to refute the charges by Jan Sangh leaders that the merger talks were terminated as a result of the rejection of such a move by the Mahasabha. Speaking at a press conference, Deshpande said that "the real difficulty was that some of the Jan Sangh leaders did not wish any real alliance. Their meaning of merger was that all Mahasabhaites would join Jan Sangh. This formula was not acceptable to a party which has been in existence for the last thirty years." Discussions could have continued, he felt, but some leaders of Jan Sangh "indulged in vilifying or misrepresenting the Mahasabha. Statements were issued calling Hindu Mahasabha communal and a body composed of capitalists. . . . I need not answer the baseless charge of Princes, Rajas, jagidars being in Hindu Mahasabha. Much can be said about the real position of the Jan Sangh itself."[19]

[16] *Ibid.*, December 8, 1953.   [17] *Ibid.*, December 8, 1953.
[18] *Hindustan Standard*, December 7, 1953.
[19] *Hindu Outlook*, December 20, 1953, p. 2.

The Jan Sangh Working Committee meanwhile retorted by pointing out that while the August session of Jan Sangh authorized its President to negotiate a merger with the other two organizations, the Mahasabha Working Committee had called only for "closer cohesion," not a merger. The Jan Sangh Working Committee felt that the Mahasabha had utilized Mauli Chand Sharma's statement as an excuse for calling off the talks.[20]

The merger talks thus collapsed over the relationship between Jan Sangh and the Mahasabha. Ram Rajya Parishad apparently played no part in the collapse and in general played a secondary role in the merger efforts. It was generally agreed that without the merger of the other two major organizations, Ram Rajya Parishad would not merge with either group.

Given the above basic facts, the question arises as to why the attempted merger of the Hindu Mahasabha and Jan Sangh failed? What were the obstacles to a merger? To answer this question we must consider what proposals for unity were considered, what the attitudes of the leadership of both parties were, and what differences existed between the two parties and their leaders, ideological or otherwise.

UNITY PROPOSALS

Although both organizations had officially called for some kind of "cohesion," "united front," or "merger," at no time were there any formal talks between delegates of the two parties. There were, however, informal meetings of party leaders to discuss the various alternatives. In attempting to get at the attitudes held by those involved in merger and united talks, it is useful to examine the proposals considered.

In our chapters on the left wing parties we noted that discussions on closer cooperation between the various left parties centered primarily around the need for some kind of permanent united front organization, but with each constituent organization retaining its own identity. A proposal for a united front on an *ad hoc* basis, operating only when key agitational issues were available, was rejected as being too unstable, while a proposal for complete merger of the left parties was rejected as politically impossible at the moment. On the other hand, talks between the Socialist Party and the Kisan Mazdoor Praja Party, from the very first, centered around the need for organic unity and the complete merger of the two organizations into one. The very nature of merger proposals in itself points to the extent to which the participants are prepared to adjust and compromise.

Sometime in August 1953 an informal meeting was held in New Delhi at the home of N. C. Chatterjee, the Mahasabha President. Several other Mahasabha members were present along with Mauli Chand Sharma and others from Jan Sangh. Four proposals were raised at this meeting: first, that the three organizations liquidate themselves and a single united organization be created; second, that there be a single united political group but that the Mahasabha continue its work as a non-political cultural organization, just as the RSS would continue its non-political cultural work; third, that the three organizations continue, but that a presidium be formed to decide on joint candidates for elections and a joint political program; fourth, that two organizations merge into the third.[21]

VIEWS OF THE LEADERSHIP

N. C. Chatterjee, the President of the Mahasabha, made it clear that he supported the complete merger of the three organizations and the creation of a united Hindu Party. Chatterjee felt that both the Praja Socialist Party and the Communist Party had become strong as a result of mergers and united fronts, and that the Hindu groups might likewise increase their strength. Together they might be able, at some future time, to form a ministry in Madhya Bharat and improve their position in Bengal, Uttar Pradesh, and the Punjab.[22] Chatterjee was thus apparently guided by political calculations.

Other leaders of the Mahasabha were less concerned with the political consequences of a merger. L. B. Bhopatkar, a former

[21] From an interview by the author with N. C. Chatterjee in New Delhi in January 1954.
[22] *Hindu Outlook*, July 12, 1953.

Hindu Mahasabha President, said that he could not speak freely in a party which accepted Muslims. Furthermore, he felt that if they merged with Jan Sangh his views might be submerged in the new party. He felt that he would also not be free to express himself in the new party if the majority voted against him, but that this could not happen in the Mahasabha because he knew the mentality and views of its members.[23]

Savarkar, the ideological leader of the Mahasabha, told members that he opposed any merger so long as Jan Sangh insists upon admitting non-Hindus. He felt that in any event Jan Sangh had failed to attract non-Hindus, but that Jan Sangh members wanted to maintain their own organization and attempted to justify their separatist tendencies by raising the membership principle.[24]

V. G. Deshpande, General Secretary of the Mahasabha, favored a joint front which would allow each party to retain its identity as much as possible. He felt that the rank and file of his party was totally opposed to any kind of merger that would destroy the identity of their organization. Deshpande felt that the Mahasabha could thus continue its social reform work, including removal of untouchability and reconversion of non-Hindus, etc. It could then carry on its political work through the joint front and could continue as a social and cultural unit, just as Jan Sangh had its RSS and Ram Rajya Parishad had its own cultural front, called Dharma Sangh.[25]

The most outspoken opposition to merger was voiced by the *Hindu Outlook* and its editor, Indra Prakash. Prakash felt that Jan Sangh was eager for a merger so as to get N. C. Chatterjee to replace Mookerjee as a mass leader. He felt that the real intention of Jan Sangh was to get the Mahasabha to merge with it and lose its identity. Prakash declared that he was also firmly opposed to liquidating the political work of the Mahasabha and having

---

[23] From an interview by the author with L. B. Bhopatkar in Poona in April 1954.

[24] From an interview by the author with V. D. Savarkar in Bombay in April 1954.

[25] From an interview by the author with V. G. Deshpande in New Delhi in December 1953.

it continue as a cultural organization, since the purpose of the Mahasabha is to protect Hindus in the political sphere. The Mahasabha is almost exclusively involved in political work, and were it to merge with another party, argued Prakash, the Mahasabha would for all practical purposes cease to exist.[26]

Except for N. C. Chatterjee, it was apparent that the leadership of the Mahasabha would not accept any merger which would destroy the independence of its own organization. Apparently, the rank and file shared this view. If there were a merger, it would be acceptable only if Jan Sangh and Ram Rajya Parishad merged into the Mahasabha.

What were the views of Jan Sangh? Officially, Jan Sangh welcomed the move toward merger and authorized Mauli Chand Sharma to carry on negotiations on its behalf. Sharma said he favored a merger but felt that since partition there was no longer need for a *Hindu* Mahasabha as an antidote to the Muslim League. He felt what was needed was a truly nationalist party of Hindus and Muslims. The problem, he felt, is to make Muslims feel Indian and to absorb them into the national life. "One country, one nation, one culture" was the aim of Jan Sangh. It was essential, therefore, that any political party be open to all communities and on this point he opposed the Mahasabha's policy. Sharma proposed that the Mahasabha merge into Jan Sangh. The Mahasabha could continue as a cultural body, but Jan Sangh would be its political party. But even though he proposed a merger, Sharma felt that so long as there were some people in the Mahasabha who believed that Hindus as Hindus must be in politics, the movement would remain split.[27]

Din Dayal Upadhyaya, General Secretary of Jan Sangh, said that he supported merger of the two parties, but that it must be on the Jan Sangh program and the party must be open to all. Like Mauli Chand Sharma, he felt that, of the top Mahasabha leadership, only Chatterjee sincerely favored a merger.[28]

[26] From an interview by the author with Indra Prakash in New Delhi in March 1954.

[27] From an interview by the author with Mauli Chand Sharma in Delhi in March 1954.

[28] From an interview by the author with Din Dayal Upadhyaya in Delhi in April 1954.

Vasantra Rao Oak, a leading founder of Jan Sangh and a member of its Working Committee, said that he was prepared to see a merger of the two parties with a new name if necessary, but it was important that the new party retain the Jan Sangh program and be open to all. He pointed out that Jan Sangh was unwilling to join the Mahasabha because it is a party with no political future. Like other Jan Sangh leaders, he believed that the Mahasabha leaders really did not want a merger and that the merger failed because N. C. Chatterjee was unable to convince his Working Committee.[29]

K. R. Malkani, the editor of the *Organiser*, the semi-official Jan Sangh–RSS organ, said that since the Mahasabha and Ram Rajya Parishad had few political workers, these workers ought to join Jan Sangh. He noted that most of those who took part in the Jammu and Kashmir agitation came from Jan Sangh and the RSS. The Jan Sangh leaders and rank and file, he said, were virtually unanimous in opposing the creation of a new party. The rank and file in particular have "contempt" (the word, he said, may be too strong; "lack of respect" might be better) for the Mahasabha people, who have been armchair politicians. Furthermore the Mahasabha has the reputation of being a party of reaction. In any event the Mahasabha was clearly against any merger, as shown by the resolution of its Working Committee calling for increased cooperation rather than merger. He felt that this August resolution ended the possibility of a merger and that talks had actually broken down even before Mauli Chand Sharma's statement at the Bombay press conference. Malkani further admitted that the question of Muslim membership was a formal issue between the two organizations, since in any event Jan Sangh does not have many Muslims, and if the Mahasabha wanted a merger they would have come to accept some Muslims in the party.[30]

It is apparent that while the Jan Sangh leaders were prepared

[29] From an interview by the author with Vasantra Rao Oak in Delhi in March 1954.
[30] From an interview by the author with K. R. Malkani in Delhi in March 1954.

to merge with the Mahasabha, a considerable number of conditions were set up. First, by merger they meant that the other parties would merge into Jan Sangh. Second, they felt that if a new party were established, with a new name (which they were reluctant to have in any event), that such a party should be based on the political program of Jan Sangh and that, above all, the party should be opened to all communities.

The Mahasabha and Jan Sangh had each set up conditions for merger which were not acceptable to the other. Neither organization would accept any merger that infringed upon the independence and integrity of its own organization. Both thought in terms of one party's merging into another. Mahasabha leaders would not accept any proposal which involved relinquishing control over the political policy and activities of their party, while Jan Sangh leaders would accept a merger only if the Mahasabhaites joined their party or a new party were formed which accepted the basic political program of Jan Sangh.

PROGRAMMATIC DIFFERENCES

What was the reason for the reluctance to merge on the part of the leaders and rank and file of both parties?

It should first be pointed out that whatever the policy differences were between the two parties, they were never seriously discussed among the leaders. There were no formal meetings between the leaders of the two parties, and at the informal meeting at N. C. Chatterjee's home there was no discussion of a program for a united party. Unlike the merger talks between the KMPP and the Socialist Party, where discussion and ultimately an agreement on the basic program of the merged party occurred very early, the talks between Mahasabha and Jan Sangh leaders primarily centered around the various organizational alternatives. No joint program was drawn up for a new party and none was discussed. But there were, however, a number of issues which ostensibly separated the two organizations and were frequently referred to in public and in the party presses.

First, there was the surface difference over the question of *Hindu Rashtra* (literally, "Hindu Nation") versus *Bharatiya*

Rashtra (literally, "Indian Nation"), the former being the goal of the Mahasabha, the latter that of Jan Sangh.

Both Jan Sanghists and Mahasabhaites have privately admitted that between *Hindu Rashtra* and *Bharatiya Rashtra* there is no essential difference in meaning. Privately, Jan Sanghists and RSS members admit that the word "Bharatiya" was preferred to "Hindu" because of the communal overtones of "Hindu." In terms of long-range objectives, both the Mahasabha and Jan Sangh feel that there must be Hindu rule, although there is no precise and universally agreed upon definition of this concept.

The second supposed difference between the two organizations centered around the question of admitting non-Hindus into their parties. Jan Sangh said that the Mahasabha was a "communal" organization since it was open only to one community, while Jan Sangh accepted all.

A third supposed point of difference between the two organizations, occasionally referred to by party workers, concerned economic programs. Jan Sanghists accused the Mahasabha of being sympathetic to zamindars and of not having a progressive economic program. But a careful examination of the manifestoes of both parties and the speeches of their leaders shows that in terms of what each party advocates there are no essential differences.[31] On the question of land reform, both parties expressed their sentiment on behalf of land to the tillers, and both parties urged fair compensation for the confiscation of land. "The Hindu Mahasabha stands for ultimate ownership of the land by the State on behalf of the people." Mahasabhites, however, "recognize the sanctity of private property and guarantee its possession and inheritance to its owners. . . . In case it becomes absolutely essential to take over the proprietary rights, the Hindu Mahasabha assures them reasonable compensation."[32] Jan Sangh was prepared to go further by openly advocating the abolishment of jagirdari and zamindari rights but with compensation,[33] but

[31] See above, Chapter 8, for description of election manifestoes of both Jan Sangh and the Hindu Mahasabha.

[32] *Election Manifesto of the Akhil Bharat Hindu Mahasabha, op.cit.,* pp. 11-12.

[33] *Manifesto of Bharatiya Jan Sangh, op.cit.,* p. 6.

Mookerjee in a number of speeches made clear his sympathy for the system of private property.[34]

These three issues, then, seemed to be the programmatic differences between the two parties: *Bharatiya Rashtra* versus *Hindu Rashtra*, the question of admitting non-Hindus into their parties, and the economic programs of the two parties. A careful examination of these differences, however, reveals that they themselves could not have been the major obstacles to a merger. Apart from the fact that no difference in meaning existed between *Bharatiya Rashtra* and *Hindu Rashtra, what is important is that both parties recognized this*. Differences over admitting non-Hindus, upon examination, likewise prove not to be differences. The RSS, as a cultural organization, does not admit non-Hindus, nor does the Mahasabha in its cultural work allow the participation of non-Hindus. But just as Jan Sangh, as a political group, takes in non-Hindus, the Mahasabha in its political work was prepared to accept non-Hindus. The only point of difference involved was that the Mahasabha, while willing to work with non-Hindus in elections and in the parliamentary front, would not admit them into its organization as members. Had the Mahasabha leaders genuinely desired a merger, no compromise in principle would have been involved in allowing the merged party to be open to all while the Mahasabha continued its cultural work as a Hindu organization. In addition it is important to note that Jan Sangh leaders privately admitted that even if the Mahasabha had been open to all, they, as RSS members, still would not have considered joining the Mahasabha rather than creating a new party.

On questions of economic policy, as we have already noted, differences were slight. Again, looking at it not from the point of view of an outsider but from the viewpoint of the Mahasabhaites and Jan Sanghists themselves, the differences were minor and generally irrelevant largely because *the issues which occupied the attention and interest of the members of both organizations were essentially not economic. Akhand Bharat* (re-

---

[34] Syama Prasad Mookerjee, *Why Bharatiya Jan Sangh?* (Delhi: Bharat Mudranalaya, 1951), p. 5.

union of India and Pakistan) was the key slogan of both parties. Their emphasis on cultural questions—Sanskritized Hindi as the national language, a ban on cow slaughter, their opposition to the Hindu Code Bill, and their charge of favoritism toward Muslims by the government—these were the key issues for both parties, not land reform and other economic questions. Furthermore whatever differences in policy may have existed, it was possible for Syama Prasad Mookerjee to resolve them in the creation of the National Democratic Party in Parliament, which contained both these organizations along with several others. Obviously, given their agreement on a parliamentary program it would not have been too difficult to agree on specific issues for the manifesto of a party. In any event the important thing to note is that in the informal discussions between Jan Sangh and the Mahasabha, no discussion took place on these specific issues and no effort was made to draw up a joint manifesto for a merged party.

OBSTACLES TO MERGER

If these issues were not involved, what then were the obstacles to a merger? Essentially and rather obviously, neither party, with the exception perhaps of a few of their leaders, ever wanted a merger in which both parties would merge into one and something new would emerge. They were willing to accept a merger only if one party were merged into another; the leaders of each party wanted to retain the identity of their own party. From August, when both organizations passed resolutions, until December, when the talks terminated, few members or leaders of either party had any real expectation that a merger would come about, for each party felt that the other did not want a merger.

The Mahasabhaites continually emphasized the lengthy tradition and history of their organization and the great figures who had been associated with them. The RSS Jan Sangh were seen as "upstarts," whose ideology, if they had one, was derived from that of Savarkar, the leader of the Mahasabha. The Mahasabhaites regretted that the RSS had not become a mass-volunteer organization of the Mahasabha, and were particularly bitter that the RSS had "sabotaged" the Mahasabha by creating a new party. This bitterness toward the RSS and Jan Sangh, and the strong allegiances of the Mahasabhaites for their organization which prevented any consideration of any proposal that would have liquidated their party, overshadowed any argument as to the beneficial effects of a merger upon the mass strength of their movement.

While the Mahasabhaites emphasized the lengthy traditions and history of their organization as an argument for maintaining the continued existence of the party, Jan Sangh emphasized the unity and discipline of its organization. Jan Sanghists, especially those in the RSS, pointed out that as a result of their drills, games, and other activities, the ideology which they had all come to accept, and the discipline inculcated into them, they had a feeling of unity and comradeship which they did not share with others. Even the non-RSS members of the Jan Sangh recognized the strength contributed to their organization by the RSS members. All of them felt, therefore, that this organizational strength and discipline should not be injured by any merger with the Mahasabha. This feeling received further emphasis from their assessment of the Mahasabha. They felt that it was an organization of leaders, with no rank and file and little organization.

Many Jan Sangh rank and filers further felt that, since the Mahasabha members were generally older than those in Jan Sangh, they would seek to dominate a new organization. As one Jan Sangh member put it: "The Mahasabha has no youth and no working group. They are easy chair politicians with no following. There is a wide gap between the youth of today and these easy chair politicians. These Mahasabha people want to dominate the youth."[35] Jan Sangh leaders and the rank and file further felt that the Mahasabha had been an ineffective organization and that by being labeled "communal" it had lost its political effectiveness. In part, then, the rivalry between Jan Sangh

[35] From an interview by the author with Vasant Geet in Poona in April 1954. Mr. Geet is the editor of *Bharat*, a Jan Sangh–RSS Marathi paper published in Poona.

and the Mahasabha assumed the character of a dispute between older and younger people.

As one RSS member put it, a certain amount of "contempt" or at least "lack of respect" existed between the members of the two organizations; each for its own reasons looked down upon the other. Much of this "lack of respect" was on an impersonal level, since few members of either organization had any social contact with the other. This lack of communication extended from the rank and file up through the leadership. When asked what he felt was the main obstacle to unity, L. B. Bhopatkar, a former Mahasabha President, replied that it was the fact that the people of one organization did not freely talk with those of the other.[36]

Given all these obstacles and the unwillingness of the leadership and of the rank and file of either organization to merge, one wonders not so much why the merger attempt failed as why it was attempted at all.

ADVOCATES OF MERGER

The merger attempt primarily grew out of the efforts made by Syama Prasad Mookerjee to unite the communal forces first in a parliamentary front, then in a Joint Action Committee to deal with the Jammu and Kashmir situation. During this latter agitation, rank and file workers of both organizations found that they were constantly asked by sympathizers to explain the differences between the two organizations. At mass meetings of either party or at joint mass meetings during the agitation, frequent cries were heard for uniting the "communal" parties. Mookerjee gave encouragement to these cries. With the death of Mookerjee, N. C. Chatterjee took up the cause, and primarily through his efforts the Working Committees of both Jan Sangh and the Mahasabha agreed that talks should be held. Chatterjee persuaded his own Working Committee to appoint a subcommittee to carry on negotiations, and then personally had talks with Golwalkar, Savarkar, and Mauli Chand Sharma. Mookerjee, and

---

[36] From an interview by the author with L. B. Bhopatkar, *op.cit.*

then Chatterjee, seem to have been the prime movers behind the merger proposal.

Both Mookerjee and Chatterjee had been brought into the Mahasabha in 1939 by Savarkar, then the nationally known President of the Mahasabha. In the years that followed, Mookerjee and Chatterjee likewise became nationally known. Mookerjee's reputation grew as a Minister in the Bengal government during the war, as President of the Mahasabha after Savarkar, and finally as a Minister in Nehru's government. As a leader and spokesman for a sizeable opposition in Parliament after the first general elections, his reputation transcended his position as Jan Sangh President. His election as an MP from Bengal for the seat previously held by Sarat Chandra Bose, the leftist leader of Bengal, indicated that Mookerjee's reputation did not depend upon either the RSS or Jan Sangh or any other organization. While the RSS component of Jan Sangh had a long tradition and strong allegiances, Mookerjee had no such firm attachment to Jan Sangh. His earlier break with the Mahasabha, and before that his break with Congress, demonstrated that his ties with political organizations could be weak and that he felt his political strength went beyond any single political party. As a leader of the opposition in Parliament, Mookerjee achieved a nationwide reputation and he became the only opposition leader (with the exception of Jayaprakash Narayan of the Socialist Party, who has been drifting from political work to Gandhian constructive work and Bhoodan) who threatened to rival the Prime Minister. He felt that a strong united opposition party of Jan Sangh, the Hindu Mahasabha, and Ram Raja Parishad (Mookerjee also took steps to attract the Ganatantra Parishad Party in Orissa and the Sikh Akali Dal Party in the Punjab and PEPSU) might develop into a powerful opposition force which, with himself at the helm, might eventually replace the Congress Party.

After the death of Mookerjee, N. C. Chatterjee became by far the best-known man among the Hindu communal groups, although he did not approach the stature of Mookerjee. He was well respected as a capable Supreme Court barrister, and achieved some fame as an effective speaker and as the President of the

Mahasabha. With the death of Mookerjee the possibility existed of Chatterjee becoming the spokesman for the opposition. Many of the Jan Sangh leaders, feeling the need for a new leader to replace Mookerjee, informally told Chatterjee that if a merger took place, he would naturally become the leader of a united party. Many Jan Sanghists were prepared to accept Chatterjee as the President of their own party even if no merger were effected, but Chatterjee rejected this informal offer.

In trying to bring about a merger, Chatterjee operated against the wishes of the Mahasabha Working Committee, but rather than lose him as President, it reluctantly agreed to set up a subcommittee to carry on negotiations. When Sharma's statement attacking the Mahasabha as a "communal organization" appeared in the press, members of the Mahasabha Working Committee who opposed the merger talks used the statement as an opportunity to advise the subcommittee not to proceed further.

Mookerjee and Chatterjee were men whose ambitions transcended their allegiances to any one organization and who sought to strengthen their movement partly as a means of strengthening their own position. Their popularity did not depend solely upon their organizations; they were men who had wide and varied associations. Mookerjee was at different times a member of Congress, an independent, a member of the Mahasabha and finally of Jan Sangh. Chatterjee first entered the Mahasabha in 1939, but even while there he built up, as a result of his law work, a reputation and a following apart from the Mahasabha. Thus Mookerjee and Chatterjee were men who had learned to look beyond their own political group for mass support, and were therefore able not only to advocate the merger of their own party with that of others, but to build support for themselves outside their own party.

The merger attempt of the Mahasabha and Jan Sangh, then, was primarily the result of the efforts of Syama Prasad Mookerjee and N. C. Chatterjee, both of whom thought in terms of building a national pro-Hindu party.

Both men were encouraged by their success at creating a Parlia-

mentary front and then a Joint Action Committee. After Mookerjee died, Chatterjee was prepared to see the creation of a national party with himself as the head, even though such a merger
meant the liquidation of the Mahasabha as a political party.
But he was unable to overcome the basic reluctance on the part
of the rank and file and leadership of his own party, and of
Jan Sangh.

THE PRAJA-SOCIALIST MERGER AND
THE HINDU PARTIES

What are the differences between the KMPP–Socialist Party
merger and the Hindu Mahasabha–Jan Sangh attempt? What
were the elements which permitted a merger in one case, but
prevented it in another?

First, there was a basic difference in the relationship that had
existed between the organizations in each case. The KMPP,
which had been formed as a result of a break with the Congress,
was not involved in merger talks with the Congress but with a
third party. On the other hand, Jan Sangh was involved in
merger talks with an organization with which it had had, through
one means or another, close associations; Jan Sangh, as we have
described in an earlier chapter, actually grew out of the Mahasabha, partly as a result of the early relationship between the
RSS and the Mahasabha and partly because its own President
had at one time been the President of the Mahasabha. When
Jan Sangh was formed, therefore, it was under greater compul-
sion to explain its differences with the Mahasabha than the
KMPP was in relation to the Socialists. (The KMPPers were
more concerned to explain their differences with Congress than
to explain those with the Socialists.)

A second point is that after the general elections almost the
entire leadership of both the KMPP and the Socialist Party advocated a merger. The incentive for a merger thus involved more
than the personal ambitions of one or two people.

A third element leading to the successful merger of the KMPP
and the Socialists is that the leaders of each party believed that

the leaders of the other party were genuinely in favor of a merger. Once this mutual confidence had been established, it became easier to compromise. In the Jan Sangh–Mahasabha talks, neither side believed in the sincerity of the other, so that neither side was prepared to make any compromises for the sake of a merger, particularly compromises which would have affected the policy of the party were a merger not to succeed.

But this still leaves unanswered the question as to why both Socialist and KMPP leaders sincerely desired a merger while the leaders of the Jan Sangh and Mahasabha did not. What is apparent in the pre-merger statements of both KMPP and Socialist leaders is their consciousness of the political needs favoring a merger and the political results that would follow, a consciousness which, except with a few persons, was a minor consideration in the minds of Jan Sangh and Mahasabha leaders. The political needs—in the case of the KMPP and Socialists they were the growing strength of the Communists, the feeling that between the Congress and the Communists the democratic socialist left was being squeezed out, the recognition that a merger of the two parties would make them together the largest opposition group—all overshadowed the question of organizational and group allegiances, which played such a dominant part in the Mahasabha–Jan Sangh relationship.

The KMPPers had little identification with their own organization. Their party not only was new, but was primarily made up of a number of separate groups in different areas—Kelappan and his followers in Malabar, Prafulla Ghosh's group in Bengal, Prakasam's in Andhra, and the personal followers of Kripalani. In both Bengal and Andhra, where the KMPP was strongest, it easily overshadowed the smaller Socialist Party so that there was no question of the KMPP's being submerged in a merged party there. Furthermore, having just brought their groups out of one organization, the allegiance of the KMPP leaders to the new organization was far from fixed. On the other hand, the Mahasabha was an older organization and even Jan Sangh had already built up strong allegiances; not that the members had a strong identification to Jan Sangh as such, but that the RSS members had a strong attachment toward their own group, which they feared might be submerged in any new party.

While it is understandable why the KMPPers did not have a strong loyalty to their own organization, it is more difficult to understand the willingness of the older Socialist Party to merge with the KMPP. After all, the Socialist Party, having extended back to 1934, and having grown in the '42 movement, had traditions, a history, a leadership, and an ideology of its own. One would expect that the same feeling against liquidating their party which was felt by the Jan Sangh and the Hindu Mahasabha would have been shared by the Socialists.

The fact is, as we noted in our chapter on the KMPP–Socialist merger, that the rank and file of the Socialist Party were generally against a merger. If it had not been for the persistence of the Socialist Party leadership, it is likely that a merger would not have come about. The question of "Why a merger?" therefore revolves around the attitude of the Socialist Party leadership.

It is interesting to note, first, that the leadership was generally united in its desire for a merger with the KMPP. Not only were Jayaprakash Narayan, Acharya Narendra Deva, and especially Asoka Mehta active in bringing about the merger, but other members of the National Executive of the Socialist Party gave their support.

This eagerness to see further unity among democratic forces was not merely a product of the results of the general elections, although the incentives increased as a result of the election returns. The Socialist leadership, even before the elections, sought to bring other leftist groups as well as the Congress dissidents into their party, and they further attempted to establish closer relations with the Scheduled Caste Federation (a national party of untouchables led by Dr. Ambedkar) and the Jharkhand Party (a tribal party in Bihar). These attempts at alliances and merger were part of a larger "expansionist" attitude, on the part of the Socialist Party leadership and some of the rank and file, that seems to have begun with the decision of the Socialist Party at its Patna Convention in 1949 to drop its Marxist-Leninist democratic centralism and build instead a mass organization, a decision which resulted from some basic changes in the ideology of the Socialist Party.

In the period following the break of the Socialists from Congress in 1948, the Socialist Party moved away from its Marxist moorings and more and more fell under the influence of democratic socialism and, more dramatically, of Gandhi's ideas. This rethinking of the Socialist Party ideology may in part be the result of a series of sharp failures experienced by the Party, which seem to have resulted from the failure of the Marxist ideology to coincide with the facts of the political situation. The coming of independence, without the violent upheaval expected by the Socialists, suggested that something was wrong with the Party's ideological line. Furthermore, in the last year or so of Gandhi's life, he grew considerably closer to the Socialists, not only because of the mutual opposition to partition, or Gandhi's renewed emphasis on the need for economic reforms, but also because of his personal interest in the Socialists. Gandhi went so far as to attempt to persuade the Congress leadership to accept a Socialist as President. Gandhi's personal influence on many of the Socialists should not be minimized.

Partly as a result of Gandhi's influence and partly as a result of the growing awareness in the Socialist Party of the limitations of Marxism, a rethinking occurred. Some Party leaders—Achyut Patwardhan, Kamaladevi Chattopadhyaya, and even later Jayaprakash Narayan—became increasingly active in non-party constructive work.

Asoka Mehta and Rammanohar Lohia, as Party theoreticians, laid the foundations for a new ideological orientation. Mehta, who became the architect of the policy of mergers and absorption of other groups which accepted the basic ideas of nationalism, secularism, democracy, and social change, emphasized democratic socialism as the basic Party ideology. While he agreed that there had to be militant struggles, demonstrations, and even *satyagraha* (civil disobedience) against the Congress governments, he felt that essentially power had to be won through the democratic electoral machinery.[37] Mehta turned his attention, and the attention of many others in the Party, toward the elections coming in 1952. He recognized that a willingness to struggle for power within the electoral system and the parliamentary framework necessarily meant a less dogmatic approach to other ideologies and other parties and a willingness to join with similarly oriented groups.

Large numbers of Party members did not then, and do not even now, fully appreciate all the implications of this new orientation; many in fact do not accept the basic propositions. But the new approach had a drastic effect on the attitude of the Socialist Party, especially the Party leadership, toward other political groups.

Our final point, then, is that one of the basic differences between the Jan Sangh–Hindu Mahasabha merger attempt and the attempt made by the Socialists and the KMPP was that the Socialists—and this is equally true for the KMPP, but was not fully appreciated by them until after the general elections—accepted the parliamentary electoral system and were prepared to learn to operate within its rules. Syama Prasad Mookerjee and N. C. Chatterjee, both men with considerable parliamentary experience, may have understood the rules to some extent, but their followers were more oriented toward communal and cultural issues.

[37] In his Presidential address to the national conference of the Socialist Party in 1950, Mehta said that "The elections will teach the political parties that there is no short-circuiting the people. The impatient 'revolutionary' who pins his faith in minority action and dreams of barricades will realise when he sees the release of mass energy through elections that the march of history has outgrown his romantic beliefs. Socialism in India can come only through the conscious co-operation of the people. Democracy is the inescapable *ethos* of socialism." *Presidential Address of Asoka Mehta to the Seventh National Conference of the Socialist Party* (Madras, 1950), p. 16.

PART III

11. The Development of a Multi-Party System

In this chapter we will try to answer the question, Why has a multi-party system developed in India? In the previous chapters we have focused on the role of party leaders and the rank and file in the process of party formation, and have tried to lay the foundation for an answer to this question in a series of case studies dealing with splits, mergers, and attempted mergers of political parties in India.

Although the splits described in these cases occurred within the major opposition parties, they are only a few among the many schisms which have occurred. Nearly every Indian party has been subjected to factional disputes or splits, and even within the Congress Party there have been factional disputes in virtually every state. The disputes within Congress have most frequently been between the Chief Ministers and their supporters in the state governments, on the one hand, and, on the other, the Presidents of the Pradesh (State) Congress Committees and their followers, who control the Party organization.

Among the left parties, factional disputes are so much a matter of course that only when a major split occurs do newspapers bother to report the event. In 1954, for example, there was another split in the Marxist Forward Bloc. The Revolutionary Communist Party of India had undergone three splits at the last count, and within its large Andhra State organization the Communist Party has also been torn by factional disputes. In 1955 the Praja Socialist Party was split by the withdrawal of Rammonohar Lohia and his supporters, who formed a new Socialist Party.

The Hindu communal groups have been no less subject to schisms. In the latter part of 1954 there were reports of growing differences between the RSS members of Jan Sangh and the non-

RSS members. The Hindu Mahasabha has also been ridden with factionalism, especially in Delhi and in Bengal.

In addition to these, a large number of parties which were in existence before the general elections are still on the political scene. Many more parties actually participated in the general elections than won seats, but even the number which won seats is impressively high. In the House of the People alone some twenty-three parties are represented,[1] and about fifty parties, including most of those with seats in Parliament, won seats in the state legislative assemblies. A few of these parties have merged with others, but most of them retain their independent status. Others may yet merge and still others may be eliminated by the electorate in subsequent elections, but a large number of parties participated in the 1957 elections.

Why have so many parties developed? There are many obvious difficulties in assessing motivation, but sometimes the behavior of large numbers of people suggests patterns of motivation without deep probing into the mind of any one person. The political scientist must often make such judgments where the psychologist would probably be far more cautious.

The case studies do not suggest that any one variable is involved in party fragmentation, or that any group of variables is definitively crucial. It would appear, however, that the electoral system is less relevant than, first, the characteristics of party members and leaders—the personnel of politics—and second, their orientations toward politics, that is, the attitudes and framework which guide behavior.

THE ELECTORAL SYSTEM AND PARTY FORMATION

Many Western writers have argued that there is a direct correlation between a country's party system and its electoral system. "The simple-majority single-ballot system," wrote Maurice

[1] Congress, Socialists, KMPP, Bharatiya Jan Sangh, Communists, Ram Rajya Parishad, Scheduled Caste Federation, Hindu Mahasabha, Jharkhand, Lok Sewak Sangh, Janata, Peasants and Workers, Commonweal, Tamil Nad Toilers, Muslim League, Marxist Forward Bloc, Ganatantra Parishad, Shiromani Akali Dal, Revolutionary Socialists, Krishikar Lok, Kerala Socialist, Travancore Tamil Nad Congress, and People's Democratic Front.

Duverger, "favours the two party system. Of all the hypotheses that have been defined in this book [Duverger's], this approaches the most nearly perhaps to a true sociological law. An almost complete correlation is observable between the simple-majority single-ballot system and two party system; dualist countries use the simple-majority vote and simple-majority vote countries are dualist."[2] Duverger concludes that both "the simple-majority system with second ballot and proportional representation favour multi-partyism."[3]

According to this hypothesis, therefore, the great multiplicity of political parties in India should be in part attributable either to a system of proportional representation or to a run-off system in which there is a second ballot. In fact, this is not the case.

India's electoral system is outlined in its Constitution and in two major acts of Parliament, the Representation of the People Act, 1950, and the Representation of the People Act, 1951. The electoral system created by the Constitution and enlarged by these acts of Parliament, provides for a system of universal adult suffrage. Direct elections are provided for both the House of the People in New Delhi and for state legislative assemblies. Of the 489 seats in the House of the People, 98 are set aside for scheduled castes (untouchables) and scheduled tribes; likewise of the 3,283 seats in the various legislative assemblies, 477 are reserved for scheduled castes and 192 for scheduled tribes. These provisions for backward castes and tribes are temporary and are to be dropped ten years after the effective date of the Constitution, that is, in 1960. But for all seats, including those that are reserved, victory is obtained by a plurality. There is no proportional representation, and no run-off ballot. It was decided that as a general rule every constituency of the House of the People and the state legislative assemblies would elect only one member and that two-member constituencies would be set up only where seats were to be reserved for the scheduled castes or the scheduled tribes.[4] For the House of the People (with its 489

[2] Maurice Duverger, *Political Parties—Their Organization and Activity in the Modern State* (London: Methuen and Co., Ltd., 1954), p. 239.
[3] *Ibid.*, p. 239.
[4] Election Commission, *Report on the First General Elections in India,*

seats) there are 314 single-member constituencies, 89 double, and 1 triple. For the legislative assemblies there are 2,124 single-member constituencies, 578 double, and 1 triple.

Only members of scheduled castes or tribes may be candidates for reserved seats, and only members of those communities may vote. In double- and triple-member constituencies members of these communities cast two or three votes, but the votes for the scheduled caste or scheduled tribe seat are kept separate from those for the general seat; there is no transfer of votes as in a system of proportional representation. Even in multi-member constituencies, therefore, the effect on the parties is virtually the same as in single-member constituencies. To use the words of Duverger, India has a "simple-majority single-ballot system." The one notable exception is that the reserved seats facilitate the growth of separate parties for the scheduled castes and scheduled tribes. For example, the Scheduled Caste Federation, a national party of untouchables, derives its strength from the reserved seats. Likewise, the Jharkhand Party, a tribal party in Orissa, gets added strength from the reserved seats. But the bulk of the opposition parties have not been affected in any apparent way by the reserved seats. They compete for them in much the same way that they compete for general seats, and none of them have any special strength in the reserved constituencies.

The Indian electoral system, with its simple majority and single ballot, has the usual consequence of giving the plurality party a disproportionate number of seats in the legislature and reducing the seats of the smaller parties. For the House of the People, Congress with only 45.0% of the popular vote received 74.4% of the seats, while the Socialists with 10.6% of the popular vote received only 2.5% of the seats. For the state legislative assemblies Congress won 68.4% of the seats with only 42.2% of the popular vote, while the Socialists won only 3.8% of the seats with 9.7% of the popular vote. The electoral system, therefore, ought to discourage minor parties, as it has in the United States

---

Vol. I (Delhi: Manager of Publications, Government of India Press, 1955), p. 46.

and Great Britain. That it has not raises the question, Why? If we examine party development in India *only* in relation to the electoral system, there are several possible explanations.

First, it may be that the opposition would have been even more splintered without a single-ballot, simple-majority system. Proportional representation might have encouraged other dissidents within Congress to break away. The present electoral system may therefore contribute to the ability of the Congress leaders to hold divergent elements within the Party.

Second, before the general elections the opposition parties may not have realized what the effect of the simple-majority, single-ballot system would be. In this first election with universal suffrage, many parties mistakenly over-estimated their strength. Realization of how the electoral system affects smaller parties is probably a major reason for the attempt by many of these parties to affect mergers after the general elections. But it obviously does not explain why, with the exception of the Socialist Party and the KMPP, none of the major attempts at merger were successful. The Hindu communal parties still remain divided as do the bulk of the Marxist left parties. And in 1955, in spite of the fact that the newly formed Praja Socialist Party was increasing its seats in by-elections, a split occurred within the Party.

Finally, it is possible that in spite of an electoral system which discourages small parties, the opposition parties may not have felt the pressure to consolidate because Congress is so far ahead. It can be argued that as long as power is beyond reach there is little point in opposition groups' compromising their programs and ideologies for mergers that would have few political consequences. But is power beyond the reach of the opposition? With the exception of its success in the tiny states of Delhi and Coorg and the state of Saurashtra, Congress failed to win a majority of the popular vote for any of the state legislative assemblies. A merger of the three Hindu communal parties—the Hindu Mahasabha, Jan Sangh, and Ram Rajya Parishad—would give them a total of 28.8% of the popular vote in the state of Madhya Bharat, compared with 47.3% for Congress. They would still be far behind but in a better position to win seats and further popular support. In Bengal a combination of the Communist Party and the Marxist left parties would have 19.1% of the vote compared with 38.9% for Congress and 11.9% for the Socialists and KMPP combined. While there are few states where a combination of the "left" or the "right" would bring the opposition within a hair's breadth of defeating Congress, in many states such combinations would serve to present a clear-cut opposition to the voters and thereby encourage dissidents to vote for a major opposition party rather than split their votes among a large number of small splinter opposition parties. Again it should be noted that the combined opposition vote (obviously it is rather unlikely that the entire opposition could be united, but these figures do indicate the size of the discontent with Congress) exceeded that of Congress in the elections for the House of the People and for virtually every state legislature.[5]

A closely related argument is that, never having been in power and always having been in opposition, first against the British and now against the Congress Party, the opposition parties have no clear experience as to how power can be won. As a result, opposition parties tend not to aggregate interests in order to build a broad-based movement, but tend instead to be ideologically dogmatic and frequently unwilling to take steps which would bring them closer to political power. The further a party is from political responsibility, the greater the concern for ideology. While there is considerable truth to this proposition, the fact is that some of the opposition groups have had experience holding power. The Praja Socialist Party formed a minority government in the state of Travancore-Cochin in 1954 which lasted for about a year—over the opposition, it should be noted, of a large part of its own rank and file. Likewise, in PEPSU, the

---

[5] If the total number of opposition votes for candidates to the House of the People is divided by the number of seats won, then in effect each opposition MP "represents" 466,229 voters compared with 130,950 for Congress. Likewise, in the state legislative assemblies, each opposition member "represents" 57,858 voters compared with 19,502 for each Congress member. This great disparity results from the splintering of the opposition, which allowed Congress to win most of its seats by a plurality.

Sikh Akali Dal and other opposition parties formed a short-lived coalition government which fell apart as the constituent units in the coalition failed to work together.

Although it is possible that another type of electoral system in India might have resulted in an even more splintered party system, and the opposition parties may have been, on the one hand, over-optimistic, or, on the other, discouraged by the over-whelming strength of Congress, existing evidence does not suggest that the electoral system in India played any major role in the present multiplicity of parties.

THE PERSONNEL OF PARTIES

In the case studies we have seen that the greatest enthusiasm for splits has come from the rank and file and the greatest reluctance to merge has also come from the rank and file. When the Socialists broke from Congress in 1948, the rank and file were more eager to do so than the Socialist leadership; likewise, the Socialist rank and file were not eager for a merger with the KMPP. The membership of the RSS was more willing to form a new party than many of its leaders and, like the rank and file of the Hindu Mahasabha, was more reluctant than the leaders to see a merger of the Hindu parties. Again, the membership of the Marxist left parties was not eager to see a merger of the leftist parties. Who are the party rank and file? What is their relationship to the party leaders? Who are the personnel of parties and what is their orientation toward politics? In the following pages we shall explore first the personnel of parties—the recruitment of party members, the nature of party factions, and the role which factions play in satisfying their members' needs—then the links which tie factions together within a party and how a break in these links may occur which precipitates splits within a party, and finally the role of party leaders in splits and mergers.

Party Membership

No precise membership figures are available for most of India's political parties. Official claims are often made but there is no way to check their validity. At best a rough estimate can be obtained by noting the published figures for a few of the parties. A dispatch from the *New York Times* correspondent in India, A. M. Rosenthal, said that the Communist Party had about 50,-000 to 80,000 members and the Praja Socialists about 200,000 compared with 6,000,000 for Congress.[6]

In 1951, before the general elections, the leader of Ram Rajya Parishad claimed a "following" of 100,000.[7]

No official estimates of party membership are available for either Jan Sangh or the Hindu Mahasabha, but estimates have been made for the Rashtrya Swayamsevak Sangh. J. A. Curran, in his study of the RSS, estimated that in 1951 membership was probably a little more than 600,000.[8]

Among the Marxist left parties, again there are no accurate figures. The general secretary of the Bolshevik Party of India claims about 3,000 members for his party while the Revolutionary Communist Party of India claims a membership of from 4,000 to 5,000. These are, however, among the smallest of the Marxist left parties. The Marxist Forward Bloc in Bengal, the Revolutionary Socialist Party, also in Bengal, and the Peasants and Workers Party in Maharashtra are all larger.

Party Recruitment

Little information is available in India on either party recruitment or party organization. What follows, therefore, are unverifiable impressions based on the few available studies, occasional writings in the party press on problems of recruitment and organization, interviews, and personal impressions of the author from meetings with party members and attendance at party conventions. Thus the hypotheses suggested here are particularly tentative.

Recruitment of party members, especially by opposition parties, appears to occur largely in the cities and is conducted, for the most part, among office employees, shopkeepers, members of

[6] *New York Times*, January 2, 1956. The official number claimed by the general secretary of the PSP is 189,339 (*Hindu*, December 28, 1955).

[7] *Hindustan Times*, June 24, 1951.

[8] J. A. Curran, *Militant Hinduism in Indian Politics—A Study of the RSS* (New York: Institute of Pacific Relations, 1951), p. 43.

professions, and others in the middle classes. The Hindu communal parties, the Communists, the Socialists, and the Marxist parties all seem to recruit from similar social groups. Jan Sangh, for example, draws its membership from the RSS, which in turn attracts students and other young people in towns and cities in northern and central India.

The General Secretary of the RSS estimated that approximately 60% of the RSS members are between eighteen and twenty-five years old.[9] In the past most of these youth, especially in Maharashtra, were from Brahman castes, but more recently membership has been cutting across caste lines. Both the Hindu Mahasabha and Jan Sangh also recruit among small shopkeepers, and to a lesser extent clerks and teachers. These organizations once had their greatest appeal in areas with large Muslim concentrations, but more recently there has been a spurt of activity in central India and in the former princely states.

The Marxist left parties and the Communists have also been most active in urban areas but in different localities. It is true that some of these groups, especially the Communists, have expanded to rural areas, but the recruitment of rank and file members is still largely from urban centers. In Calcutta, a leftist stronghold, party members come from student groups for the most part. Many of these students are landlords' sons who have migrated to the city for their education. (This is also a common pattern in Andhra and other parts of South India.) Others are the children of clerks, low government officials, and professionals. It is not unusual for a government official who is a member of the Congress Party to have a Communist son. This is true for at least one Minister in the central government and for a large number of state officials. The Marxist left parties and the Communist Party are also full of intellectuals, some unemployed and others who are teachers, artists, and writers. A large number, too, are clerks for the government and private businesses. But in general, nearly all party members, whatever their present occupation or lack of it, joined during their student days.

The Socialists also recruit heavily among student and intel-

9 *Ibid.*, p. 50.

lectual groups, but do so in different areas than either the Marxists or the communal Hindus cover. The strength of the Socialists tends to coincide with the areas in which Gandhi was most popular. A large number of Party activists come from the universities at Allahabad, Lucknow, and Banaras, all in Uttar Pradesh. The Socialists have also recruited heavily in the city of Bombay. The Socialists, like the Marxist left and the Congress Party, do a great deal of work on the trade union front, but like other parties, they have had little success in recruiting members from unions. Rather, unions are an area of activity for the Party members themselves. This is equally true on the peasant front.

Some estimates are available on the composition of the Praja Socialist Party. One survey of the PSP has been conducted by the Party's Bombay City organization, and there is another on delegates to the Party's convention at Betul in 1953. Of 469 "active" members surveyed in Bombay City, 136 were industrial workers while virtually all the remainder were in the "middle classes." Office employees totaled 109, businessmen 47, lawyers, doctors, teachers, technicians, and journalists totaled 68, 13 were cooperative workers, 8 were students, and 21 miscellaneous, including 17 women. Another 66 members were recorded as full-time Party workers.[10]

Asoka Mehta, General Secretary of the Praja Socialist Party, circulated a questionnaire to the 609 delegates attending the national Party convention at Betul in 1953.[11] From the 111 delegates who answered the questionnaire, Mehta provided the following information:

Age		Education	
Between 20 and 30 years	32	School education	20
Between 30 and 40 years	54	Matriculation	19
Between 40 and 50 years	13	Undergraduate	14
Between 50 and 60 years	11	Graduate	26
Over 60	1	Double graduate	32

[10] M. R. Dandavate, *Report: Political and Organizational* (Bombay: Praja Socialist Party, December 1953).

[11] Asoka Mehta, "Composition of the Party Elite," *Janata*, Vol. VIII, No. 23 (July 5, 1953), pp. 7-8.

Over 80% of those surveyed had studied up to matriculation (high school) and beyond.

The Party members were asked how much time they devoted to Party work. Three-fourths (74) said they were full-time workers. Eleven worked over 28 hours a week, 24 from 14 to 28 hours, and 2 under 14 hours. Three-fourths of those surveyed were full-timers. Of 30 part-timers describing their occupations, 11 were in law, 7 in agriculture, 3 in journalism, 2 each in business, medicine, teaching, and government, and 1 in social work.

The Party members were also asked how long they had been in political work. Ten had been since 1920, 12 since 1930, 13 since 1932, 50 since 1942, and 27 since 1947 or after.

Thus Mehta's study shows that the bulk of the Party leaders are under forty years of age and joined either during or since the '42 movement. These figures tend to confirm the impression that Party recruitment is particularly heavy among students and others of student age.

Although the study did not ascertain whether Party members came from rural or urban areas, a partial answer can be deduced from the type of activities Party members engage in. Only thirty-nine said they did any peasant work. Mehta complained that "the entire sector of kisan (peasant) work has [a] disproportionately small number of leading cadres engaged in it."[12] He further pointed out that "overwhelmingly the leadership is middle class or of those elements from the peasantry and working class who through education etc., have become middle classish."[13]

The same seems to be true for the membership and leadership of the other opposition parties. Even the Communist Party has admitted that so far it has been unsuccessful in recruiting outside of the middle classes. Ajoy Ghosh, the general secretary of the CPI, tactfully wrote: ". . . we cannot afford to ignore the fact, as emphasized in the Central Committee's review of the elections, that despite the big headway we have made in the recent period, our position among the working class, among the

12 *Ibid.*, p. 8.
13 *Ibid.*, p. 8.

agricultural workers and poor peasants . . . is still extremely weak. . . ."[14]

If the various opposition parties recruit from more or less the same social class, one may ask why some people join one party rather than another. To some extent, this may be related to the fact that these parties recruit from different geographical areas and have had their maximum recruitment at different times. Socialist expansion was greatest during the '42 movement and was concentrated largely in U.P., Bihar, and Delhi State in the North, and Bombay and Maharashtra in the Southwest. The Communists grew during the popular front movement of the late '30's—especially in South India, where they gained control of the Congress Socialist Party in Malabar, Madras, and Andhra. They expanded further in South India after 1947 when the Party entered a terrorist phase. Hindu communal groups, especially the RSS, grew in North and Central India during the height of the Muslim-Hindu riots and expanded enormously after partition.

Recruitment of party workers, therefore, has been largely from urban centers and from classes in which the breakdown of the traditional order has been the greatest. One can surmise on the basis of what is generally known about those who break from traditional patterns that a loss of status, roles, and values has been involved or that there is a desire for more status than the traditional order has provided.

No statistical evidence is available to describe the background of party members, such as their caste, their role in the joint family, and the like, but some patterns can be illustrated from the writer's personal knowledge. Many young Socialist, Communist, or RSS members have broken entirely with their joint families. Often they have left the family in the village to attend college in the big city, and frequently they joined a party over the objections of their father and other members of the family. Other party workers remain in the joint family physically, but their differences with the family are so great that they do not

[14] Ajoy Ghosh, *Some of Our Main Weaknesses* (Bombay: People's Publishing House Limited, 1952), p. 16.

participate in it, except perhaps to eat and sleep at home. A young Indian often finds that he has little about which to communicate with his parents. Neither the mother nor the father can guide the young person in his problems. The problems of deciding an occupation, or planning a university program, for example, are outside the experience of most elder members of a joint family. The elders are often religious, while the young person considers himself "modern." The joint family, the village organization, the caste system, no longer fit into his way of looking at the world. He has been caught in the process of Westernization. The process may seem abstract, but it operates on the most personal and human level.

Having moved from the village to the city, or having been brought up in the city or town but broken physically or spiritually with his family and caste, the young person feels that he has lost his role in the family, his status in his home community, and the values with which he judged the world. In the traditional social structure his values were provided by members of the joint family. His role was fixed: as an elder son or as a younger son, he knew his place. His occupation was to be the same as his father's. His own role as a father and ultimately as an elder in the joint family was clearly understood and seen by him through a lifetime of experience in the joint family. His status in the community as a member of his caste was fixed. Status mobility was rare and involved not his own mobility but that of his caste. His caste may have moved up or down the status ladder, but he rarely moved beyond caste limits.

As a result, a person who has wholly or in part left this traditional system is in search of new values and a sense of belonging. It is a feeling like that of immigrants who came to the United States. But in the United States there is a basic consensus of values which could be adopted by the immigrant, whereas in India there are many value systems to choose from. Furthermore, in the United States, status in the society can be won by success in business, since the prestige of business is high and wide opportunities exist. Without such opportunities, Indian young people look to other areas of activity. In India the frustrations of a rapidly changing social system are compounded by the lack of economic opportunities for young people and by widespread educated unemployment.

At the end of October 1955, 700,000 unemployed were registered at the various government-run employment exchanges throughout the country, and, of these, 227,000 were termed educated. "Most of the country's exchanges report an excess of untrained teachers, clerks, freshers from schools and colleges, unskilled office workers, motor drivers and carpenters."[15] A staff reporter for *The Statesman*, reporting on the unemployment situation in Delhi, wrote:

". . . the greatest majority of those without jobs do not even register themselves at the exchange. They come fresh from schools and colleges, from far and near, to a capital where, they imagine, there are jobs waiting for them. . . . The result is that they spend their time solving crossword puzzles in the capital's cafes or at matinee shows at Delhi's cinemas. . . .

"Many of these young men, after feverish efforts to secure 'white collar' jobs, reconcile themselves to the idea of being permanently unemployed. They are helped in this attitude by their families or relations in Delhi to whom they can turn for help in times of distress."[16]

Much of the recruiting by political parties is among this community of educated unemployed. A young person may join a political party both as an outlet for the expression of his discontent with the society and to find a psychological substitute for the roles and status and values provided by the traditional system. It is significant that young people in India—and it is the young people who constitute the bulk of the party workers—have traditionally joined opposition groups, whatever they may be. In pre-independence days, when the Congress Party was in opposition, young people flocked to it; now that independence has come and Congress is the governing party, young people express their discontent by joining the opposition parties. One indication of a growing weakness in the Congress Party is its failure thus far to attract young people into its ranks.

[15] *The Statesman*, December 21, 1955.   [16] *Ibid.*, December 21, 1955.

It is not our intention to argue that all who join Indian political parties have broken with their caste or joint family or
have left their village. Mention should also be made of the large
number of party workers who have entered politics because their
caste or community has been threatened by others. For example,
the author knows a young RSS leader who came from a Muslim
majority area in the Sind and became conscious of his Hinduism
as a result of the threats to his group from the majority community. Another illustration is of a Brahman student in Maharashtra whose caste has been so threatened by the rising non-
Brahman communities that he joined the RSS as a means of
gaining security. In still other instances low-caste non-Brahmans
and untouchables have formed or joined political parties to
raise the status of their groups. But even among these groups a
large number of the younger party recruits, although they have
intensely identified themselves with their religious, caste, or
tribal community, have themselves broken with the traditional
joint family system.

Party Factions

Those who join a political party in India invariably become
members of a faction. A faction can be defined as a group with
an articulated set of goals, operating within a larger organization
but not created by or with the approval of the parent body. The
faction may range in size from several dozen members to several
hundred. It is generally characterized by a uniformity of goals
and basic values and usually has sufficient permanence to allow
members to develop a sense of identification with the faction.
There is little movement into and out of the faction. Except in
its formative stages, it does not generally recruit members openly.

A person who joins a political party in India apparently feels
the need to be a member of a tightly knit face-to-face group.
This need, incidentally, is not confined to political joiners.
Nearly every high school and college in India contains a large
number of student "cliques." These groups are usually closed to
outsiders; the members provide their own social life and have
their own leaders. Frequently a group of students who are mem-

bers of one of the politically dominated student organizations will later become a faction within a political party. This was the origin of many factions within the Congress Socialist Party, for example.

Cliques within schools and colleges are not unknown in Western countries, but after students enter the job market the cliques usually break up and other friendship, business, and family groups take their place. In India, however, as in many other Asian countries, where the break between the new and old generations is so severe, these cliques continue outside the universities and become factions inside political parties or other types of associations.[17]

An essential characteristic of an Indian faction is not only the strength of its members' allegiance to it, but the amount of time devoted to its activities. Indian parties have an enormously large number of full-time and nearly full-time party workers. In fact, the social life of a party member is built within the party, and consequently within his faction. There are few multiple group memberships. A party member, whether socialist, communist, or communalist, rarely belongs to outside groups unless they are some kind of "front" organization. This is in fact a problem for the Communists and others who find it difficult to recruit new members as long as the Party rank and file is unwilling to engage in much social intercourse with those outside. There may be social intercourse and communication among factions within the same party, but not with those outside the party.

The faction assumes many of the functions of the traditional joint family, caste system, and village organization. Like groups in the traditional order, the faction is virtually "closed" to outsiders. One Indian politician recently said that Indian parties are like castes, since they often regard each other as untouchables. In other ways, too, the factions are like the traditional organizations. The party member will talk to the faction head

[17] It is interesting to note that a recent investigation described factional groups operating even within Indian villages. Many of these, however, appear to be organized along kinship lines. See Oscar Lewis, *Group Dynamics in a North Indian Village—A Study of Factions* (Delhi: Programme Evaluation, Planning Commission, 1954).

about personal problems in much the same way that he might, in the old days, have gone to his father or older brother. It is not uncommon, for example, for a party member to see his faction leader to discuss whether he ought to take a specific job. Even when personal problems are not discussed, strong bonds of affection develop between the party member and his leader.

By being within a political party, the party member also assumes a new role. He attends party meetings, sells the party journal and other literature, delivers agitational speeches, and organizes demonstrations. In some instances he may even be paid by the party. (All the larger political parties have a great many paid party workers, sometimes numbering in the hundreds.) But whether he is a full-time, part-time, or occasional party worker, a role is assigned to him. In many of the political parties, as in the Indian joint family, the role is part of an authoritarian hierarchy. He may play a very small part in active decision-making. Work is assigned to him and he may be disciplined if he fails in his responsibilities. Such discipline is more or less characteristic of the Communist Party, Jan Sangh, the Marxist left parties, and, until only a few years ago, the Socialist Party.

The political party also provides its members with status, or a position in the community. People in a community will generally know who in their area is a member of which party. So-and-so is known as a Congressman or a Socialist, or as an old-time revolutionary, or a member of the Mahasabha. If he is a Congressman or a Socialist, he is likely to wear the distinctive party hat or the party dress. Almost no party workers hide the fact that they are members.

How does a party achieve status in the community? It may be derived from the sacrifices made by the leaders or the party members. A militant *satyagraha* (civil disobedience demonstration) resulting in mass arrests of party members may do more for the prestige and status of the party than a large number of votes. Both the Communists and Socialists have done their best in elections in areas where they have launched agitations, non-violent or otherwise. Status may also be achieved by virtue of the charismatic qualities of the party's leader.[18] The respect given to men like Jayaprakash Narayan, Syama Prasad Mookerjee, and Veer Savarkar, for example, provides enormous prestige and status to their parties. A faction within a party may have high status in its local community because the factional leader is someone of local importance. Party leaders, whether local or national, are generally highly educated, or from a highly respected family, or a combination of both. The leader may have achieved some prominence through a sacrifice—renunciation of his wealth, fasting, physical deprivation as a result of being imprisoned, etc. More recently, especially within the Congress Party, status may be associated with holding a position in the government, although status is not necessarily lost through resignation. A leader may in fact gain for having renounced office; but if he is defeated in a contest for power, his status may be lowered.

Since the party member gets status largely by virtue of his leader's status, threats to the leader will be strongly resisted. Should the faction or party leader lose position within the party or the government, his supporters will be eager to split and create a new party so as to reassert the position of their leader. When the Socialist leadership, for example, failed to gain positions within Congress commensurate with the prestige which CSP members thought was due them, pressure for a split grew among the rank and file. Likewise, when Congress leaders in Andhra and Bengal lost their party and government positions before the general elections, their followers wanted them to leave Congress to create a new party. Again, when Saumyen Tagore was not elected Chairman of the United Socialist Organization of India, many of his followers wanted to withdraw from the USOI.

[18] Weber called charisma "the absolutely personal devotion and personal confidence in revelation, heroism, or other qualities of individual leadership." From Max Weber, *Essays in Sociology*, edited by H. H. Gerth and C. W. Mills (New York: Oxford University Press, 1953), p. 79.

Factional Links

As we have noted, all Indian parties have a large number of factions. What keeps the factions working together within the same party?

1. There is, first of all, the unique role of the party leader as a unifier. What makes the party leader a unifying force is his "detachment" from the various factions. If you ask a Socialist what it is which he most respects about Jayaprakash Narayan or Acharya Narendra Deva, he will tell you that these men are thoroughly impartial and without personal ambition. Congressmen will say the same for Jawaharlal Nehru, and the same was said for Gandhi. These men are not only detached from the factions, but they often seem to be detached from the formal structure of the party organization itself. Nearly every political party in India has as its leader a man who does not wield formal power in the organization and who has little to do with the day-to-day workings of the party. Gandhi proudly said that he was not even a four-anna-dues-paying member of Congress, and, except for a brief period of his life, he held no formal office in the Party. Today, the most respected man in the Praja Socialist Party is Jayaprakash Narayan, yet he recently announced that he is leaving active political work and is no longer a member of the National Executive of the Party. Nevertheless his influence in and leadership of the Party are likely to continue in an informal way. The leader and founder of the Ram Rajya Parishad is Swami Karapatri, who, in the tradition of a *sanyasi* (monk), does not even hold membership in the Party. The most important figure in the Hindu Mahasabha, the "giver" of its ideology of *Hindu Rashtra*, is Veer Savarkar, who lives in virtual retirement in Bombay. He holds no formal position in the Party, but he played an active, although not decisive, role in the recent negotiations to merge the Mahasabha with Jan Sangh. The Jan Sangh leader is formally Pandit Premnath Dogra, but the man most respected by Jan Sangh members and leaders is Golwalkar, the RSS leader who holds no position in Jan Sangh.

Dhebar is the President of the Congress Party, but Nehru is its leader.

The leader has three key functions. He is, first, the compromiser of factional disputes. Second, he is a source of prestige to the members of the party. And, third, he is an absolute source for the articulation of values held by the group, and he may, as Gandhi did, articulate a new set of values.

How important the leader is as a unifying link and symbol for the party factions is indicated by what has happened upon the death of various leaders. While the loss of the leader was not the only factor involved, in at least three of the case studies described here it was a major element in subsequent splits. The Socialist-Congress break was preceded by the death of Mahatma Gandhi. The break between the Hindu Mahasabha and the RSS followed the death of Hedgewar, the RSS leader. And the break-up of the USOI came after the death of its leader, Sarat Bose.

2. A second unifying factor is the level of toleration which one faction has for the other. This toleration was at its greatest within the Congress Party during the pre-independence era, when a wide variety of groups—Socialists, Communists, Marxists, and even Hindu communalists—worked together inside Congress. The Congress Party Constitution did not at that time prohibit organized groups from functioning within the Party; in fact the leadership made a considerable effort to keep the various groups satisfied. Not until after the war was a systematic effort made at eliminating some of these groups. But although organized parties are no longer allowed within Congress, the Party even now tolerates a wide variety of factions. As we have already noted, this is a major source of the strength of the Congress Party today.

The Congress Party is able to keep these factions together for a large number of reasons. First, it is the governing party. A faction which breaks from Congress knows that it loses power, while factions in opposition parties often feel that they lose little by starting anew. Second, those who plan to win power through the electoral system, unless they feel they have fundamental ideological differences with Congress, tend to join it rather than the opposition parties. Those who reject the democratic electoral system are more likely to join one of the opposition parties. A third factor is that, as a result of having been a collection of diverse factions for so many decades, the Congress Party has built up a fairly effective machinery for dealing with factional disputes. There is a Congress Parliamentary Board which deals with disputes in the various state legislatures and those that arise between the Party organization and the government. Three General Secretaries of the Congress Party serve as trouble shooters, visiting the various states and settling disputes as they arise. The factions have come to accept the General Secretaries as unbiased figures who can arrange an honest election within the Party and can settle a dispute impartially. These Secretaries treat most of these factional disputes for what they usually are: not disputes between interest groups over pieces of legislation, but conflicts between factions who want more status and prestige by holding more important positions in the government or the Party.

Since the Socialist Party broke from Congress and converted itself from a Leninist-type revolutionary organization to a party of democratic socialism with membership open to all, it too has begun to assume some of the characteristics of the Congress Party. Like Congress, the Socialists are becoming a party with a wide variety of factional groups with a broad-based ideology— a mixture of Fabian socialism, Gandhism, and Marxism. As a result of this growth, the Party has been subjected to an increase in factional disputes. Its tolerance is great, but so is the number of factions. The Party has yet to develop an effective machinery for dealing with internal disputes.

The level of toleration for factional differences in the leftist parties is very low. The leftist parties are organized along Leninist lines with rigid limitations on members and rigid rules of discipline. As a result, the leftist parties in Bengal are almost one-faction parties with a single leader.

Larger parties in India tend to be more tolerant of divergent factions than the smaller parties. Obviously, any party which tries to have a mass base must of necessity be fairly tolerant of its factions and have machinery for dealing with internal disputes. The more rigidly a party enforces discipline, i.e. is not tolerant of its factions, the more likely it is that splits will occur. There are two exceptions to this: the Communists and the RSS. While the margins for differences of opinion are very narrow in both these organizations, they prevent splits by making so many demands on their membership that powerful party allegiances are built which transcend factional loyalties. The RSS has been even more effective in this than the Communists. While the top leadership remains fairly constant, local leadership is rotated fairly frequently, thus preventing the rise of personal followings on the local level. Their national leader, Guruji, visits local RSS meetings as frequently as is humanly possible and several times a year local RSS units can expect visits from some of the national leaders. National and regional training camps for RSS members are frequently used; these strengthen the ties between local leaders throughout the country. RSS members attend daily drill exercises and, as we have described earlier, share a host of symbols, slogans, holidays, and the like. Two factors, then, combine to mitigate factional differences within the RSS. One is that local factions have little opportunity to get started since leadership is rotated fairly frequently. And, second, RSS members develop nearly fanatical devotion to their national leaders and their organization. A split would, for most RSS members, be unthinkable.

But in other organizations factions have developed which share and often overshadow party allegiances. A threat to the existence of a faction is almost always sufficient to cause its members to break their allegiance with the parent organization. When the Congress Party, for example, demanded the breakup of the Congress Socialist Party and later of the Congress Democratic Front, the factions in these groups no longer felt they could operate within Congress. Members of such factions do not think in terms of working as a loosely organized interest group inside a party, influencing the party as individuals. Many Congress Socialists, for example, were prepared to remain inside Congress in spite of their differences, if they were tolerated as a party within Congress. But when Congress became unwilling to tolerate an organized party within its framework, the Socialists decided to leave. The psychological need for maintaining the faction was apparently so great that it overshadowed whatever aim the faction members may have had to attempt to convert the parent organization to their point of view.

In sum, where the level of tolerance is high a split is not likely in a party, but when tolerance is low, when there are threats to the existence of the faction, a split is likely. In Indian opposition parties the level of tolerance is generally low. This is essential to understanding why a multi-party rather than a two-party system has developed. A two-party system necessarily means that both parties contain the enormous number of divergent groups which make up the society. In a two-party system each party has a high level of tolerance for disagreements within its ranks. In the United States, where disagreements within parties are so great, the tolerance must also be great. In more homogeneous Great Britain the two major parties are able to discipline dissidents who stray too far from the basic party policy, but there is still considerable tolerance for differences.

It is significant that most Indian parties have as their organizational model either the British parties or the Leninist-type parties of the Soviet Union and continental Europe. Both of these models require varying degrees of discipline. Thus far, rigid rules of discipline have not proved workable for mass national parties in India. Any large party seeking power must define what it considers to be "indiscipline." But how rigid can the party line be without destroying the unity of the party? This is a fundamental problem for Indian political parties. It raises the question as to whether the American pattern of party organization is more suitable to large parties in India than the British or Leninist type.

3. A third unifying factor is that an Indian opposition party is generally united by a consensus on the basic party thesis which cuts across factions. As long as such unity continues, the factions are likely to remain within the party. But a split is usually unavoidable once disagreement over the party thesis arises. What

appear to outsiders as minor ideological differences on theses assume enormous proportions within the party. Furthermore we have seen that factional disputes, almost irrespective of their cause, tend to center around ideological issues, and this lends an appearance of rationality to the disputes. Threats to the leader or to the existence of the faction are frequently reinforced by ideological differences, sometimes genuine, sometimes not; but what is important is that the ideological differences do appear genuine to those involved.

It has been a source of strength to the Congress Party that factional disputes during the past few years have not always coincided with ideological differences. The concomitance of factional disputes and ideological differences involved in the Socialist break from Congress in 1948 made that break particularly bitter. But it is significant that the KMPPers, who broke from Congress in 1951 over non-ideological questions, are among those in the Praja Socialist Party who are least adverse to closer cooperation with Congress. Nor is it a coincidence that while several KMPPers defected back to Congress, no major Socialist leader has.

In summary, then, the urban middle-class Indian who joins a political party is in search of a sense of belonging to a group, a role within the group, a status in the society, and a set of values by which he can judge the world. The party recruit joins not just a party, but one of the many factions which most of the political parties contain. These party factions are held together by a common party leader, a tolerance within the party for the existence of various factions, and a general agreement on the basic ideology of the party. If any of these three links is broken, a split in the party is likely to occur. A threat may come from loss of status in the party by the factional leader, thus endangering the status of the members of the faction, from the parent organization which wants the faction to disband, or in the form of a challenge to the faction's values.

Party Leaders

How do the needs and the behavior of a party leader affect the splits and mergers that occur? When does a leader want a split and when not? When does he favor a merger and when does he oppose one? Are there any differences between the faction leaders and the party leaders in their attitudes toward splits and merger? Who are the initiators? Who exert the greatest pressures for splits and mergers—the leaders or the rank and file? The six case studies presented lend themselves to a number of tentative generalizations about the behavior of party leaders.

Politicians everywhere seek recognition for either themselves, their point of view, their party, or a combination of these. Indian politicians, like their counterparts elsewhere, seek recognition for themselves, but Indian politicians can be broadly divided into two categories: those who tend to feel that their point of view is tied irrevocably and solely to one party and those who do not. The first group will almost never advocate a merger; the second often will. Whether an Indian politician is prepared to look outside of his party for support for his point of view appears to be the result of whether or not his influence extends beyond his party. Invariably, those who look outside are more likely to be party leaders than factional leaders. In the three case studies dealing with mergers, four figures consistently advocated greater unity: Jayaprakash Narayan, Syama Prasad Mookerjee, N. C. Chatterjee, and Sarat Bose. Each of these men had a reputation which extended beyond the confines of his party. The latter three had, in fact, transferred their allegiance from one party to another, and Jayaprakash is in the process of developing new identifications with the Gandhian constructive workers. In each case the identifications, or, as the social psychologists say, "group memberships," were "multiple." In addition all these men have reputations for being undogmatic in their ideologies. Jayaprakash's ideology is a mixture of Gandhism and socialism without a dogmatic adherence to either. Neither Syama Prasad Mookerjee nor N. C. Chatterjee has ever been a fanatic communalist or a bitter attacker of Muslims. And Sarat Bose was a socialist, but one who did not adhere to any special brand of socialism.

If Mookerjee, Chatterjee, and Bose failed to bring about a merger, it was not only because their party rank and file were opposed, but also because there was opposition from the second-ranking leaders, including the factional leaders. The men who opposed merger had reputations more narrowly confined to their own factions or their own parties. The leaders of the Marxist left parties, such as Tridib Chaudhuri in the RSP and Saumyen Tagore in the RCPI, and the leaders of the communal parties, Din Dayal Upadhyaya in Jan Sangh, V. G. Deshpande, Indra Prakash, Dr. Khare, and others in the Mahasabha, are less well known outside their parties; the recognition and allegiances they receive are almost exclusively from within their own parties. One is left with the impression that they consciously or unconsciously feared that a merger would lessen their own importance within the party. While a merger might in the long run improve their political position in the larger society, they were more concerned with maintaining their position within the party. In contrast, men like Mookerjee, Chatterjee, and Bose did not spend their political lives in one party, but, in fact, came in as outsiders. There associations with the "outer world" were greater, their allegiances to the "inner world" weaker.

If the hypothesis is correct that the advocates of merger and cooperation with other groups are those who have achieved recognition outside their own party, then the behavior of two groups of leaders needs to be explained: Why did the second-ranking figures of the Socialist Party favor a merger and why did the top leadership of the KMPP at first oppose a merger? The answer to the latter is simple. Kripalani, Prakasam, and Prafulla Ghosh are in fact men whose reputations extend beyond their group and who are not rigid adherents to any dogma. Like Mookerjee, Chatterjee, Bose, and Jayaprakash, they are almost "natural" advocates of closer relations and unity with other groups. If they were not advocates of merger before the 1952 elections, it was only because in the flurry of the break with Congress they had badly miscalculated both their own strength and that of Congress. After 1952 they were not only willing to merge with the Socialists, but are among those in the present Praja Socialist Party who favor closer relations with Congress and other parties.

As for the Socialist Party leaders like Asoka Mehta and Acharya Narendra Deva, it is true that they were as eager for a merger as Jayaprakash was. But apart from these men, the members of the National Executive of the Socialist Party supported merger. Perhaps the explanation lies in the fact that after its split from Congress in 1948, the Socialist leadership moved the Party away from its "exclusiveness." The Party drifted away from Marxism and closer to both Gandhism and democratic socialism. Its Leninist type of closed organization was revamped and membership opened to all. The Socialist leadership—or at least sections of it—came to accept the parliamentary system and its implications for tactics and strategy. This is not to say that the entire Socialist Party changed its outlook. To the contrary, there are still large sections of the Party, including the bulk of the rank and file and many of the factional leaders, who have not yet accepted the parliamentary system as the sole means of winning power, who are still dogmatic in their ideology and in many cases unsympathetic to the move from Marxism to Gandhism, and who, consequently, were critical of the merger.

There are indications—and this leads us to our second hypothesis about the kinds of leaders who are likely to favor mergers—that once individuals accept the parliamentary system they tend to lose their feelings of "exclusiveness." There are several other examples apart from the Socialists. When the Subhasist Forward Bloc consciously rejected Marxism and moved toward democratic socialism and an acceptance of the parliamentary system, its leaders were prepared to merge with the Praja Socialist Party. This was accomplished in late 1952. Again, a section of the Marxist Forward Bloc in the Punjab, which turned against the communists and presumably moved away from their revolutionary tendencies, merged with the Congress Party in March 1955. If this hypothesis is correct, then it is quite possible that other small but democratically oriented parties may eventually merge either with Congress or with the Praja Socialist Party.

The parliamentary system, by its very nature, requires the acceptance of certain rules. Ideologies cannot be so rigid that there is an unwillingness to compromise. Parties seeking to win within the system must have a fairly broad-based membership and must be prepared to tolerate wide intra-party differences in order to capture a majority of legislative seats. Exclusiveness, whether in ideology or in attitudes toward others, has little place in a parliamentary framework.

In the preceding pages we have discussed the role of leadership in the various mergers that have occurred or were attempted. A word is due on the role of leadership in party splits. Many of the same factors which operate in mergers likewise operate in splits. A leader whose reputation extends beyond his party and who does not depend upon the party for recognition can more easily leave the party. Sarat Bose left the Forward Bloc to create his own Socialist Republican Party. Mookerjee left the Hindu Mahasabha and later formed Jan Sangh. The nationally known leaders of both the Socialist Party and the KMPP who led their parties in the break from Congress were later the same people who pressed for a merger of their two parties.

But if nationally known figures find it easy to shift allegiances from one party to another, factional leaders are even more eager to split when the unity and the status of their faction are involved. The smaller leftist parties, for example, have been full of factional leaders who have broken from a parent organization to create their own party. The factional leaders of the Socialist Party were even more eager to split from Congress before 1948 than the national leaders of the Party. The common factor in a split, both for factional and national leaders, is loss of prestige within the party. Prakasam, Prafulla Ghosh, Professor Ranga, and Suresh Banerjee all broke from Congress as a result of a serious demotion. In other instances local Congress factional leaders have demanded posts in the government, but, having failed to receive status commensurate with their demands, have either left Congress or become disgruntled factional leaders.

The leftist parties are also full of examples of factional leaders, usually young and "up and coming," who challenge the party leaders, fail to win their way to dominance or an important post, and then leave with their supporters to form their own parties.

Does the initiative for a split or merger come from national party leadership or the rank and file? The evidence suggests that whenever a split occurs the rank and file are more in favor than the leadership, and whenever a merger is involved the leadership is more in favor than the rank and file. This accords with the general pattern that *allegiances to the party are more exclusive for the rank and file than for the party leaders.* But to this general pattern must be added the qualification that differences between the rank and file and the leadership, whether on the question of merger or splits, are less likely to be as great within the Marxist left or the communal right parties as in the democratic parties. This suggests the hypothesis that *the leaders of the democratic parties who accept the parliamentary framework are inclined to be more tolerant of differences within their party and are more likely to be influenced by calculations for electoral advantage in their attitude toward a merger.*

But whether it be in the Marxist left, the communal right, or the democratic center, factional leaders in one degree or another are likely to be influenced by their need for recognition within the party since their failure to receive recognition may endanger their relationship with their followers. Consequently, if the party fails to provide adequate recognition, pressure from followers to leave the party is likely to be great.

Just why the need for recognition by political leaders is so great, is beyond the scope of this study, although we have tried to show earlier how consideration of some of the disintegrating features of Indian social life may help us to understand Indian political behavior. To what extent these insecurities also result from certain child-rearing practices, or the failure to achieve status in the society by other means, or other factors, cannot be examined here because of the present lack of data.

ORIENTATION TOWARD POLITICS

No analysis of the factors involved in the development of a multi-party system in India would be complete without a consideration of the various ideologies, attitudes, moods, feelings, and the like of those who take part in politics. Here we shall discuss the diverse effects of ideologies, the role of feelings toward governmental power and democratic institutions and values, and the difficulties not only in effecting compromises among parties but in communication itself.

The Role of Consensus

In the broadest sense, the existence of a multi-party system in India can be traced to the absence of a consensus on basic values and to the failure of the political parties to make political calculations which would improve their prospects for winning political power.

Fundamental disagreement on the kind of state India ought to have, and the functions of such a state, divide the major political groupings in India. Indian political parties do not agree on the value of either a secular or a democratic framework. The Hindu communal parties, for example, are not fully committed to the secular state. They have not made clear their views on the role of religious minorities in the state and have implied that minorities might have something less than a position of complete equality. The Communists and the Marxist left do not support the democratic framework, and the Hindu communal parties do not always fully understand the implications of that framework. There is even a lack of consensus about the legitimate forms of political activities. Opposition parties are generally willing to violate laws passed by the popularly elected state legislatures and Parliament, while many, especially those in the Congress Party, go so far as to reject the use of the Gandhian technique of civil disobedience in a democratic state.

Nor is the nationalist ideal completely shared by all political groups. Strong support of the national state has been tempered on the one hand by groups with strong provincial feelings[19] and on the other hand by political groups, like the Communists and some of the Marxist left parties, which have emotional ties to the Soviet Union and China.

Although the Indian Constitution is predicated on a belief in nationalism, secularism, democracy, and a society built on non-violence and social, political and economic equality, these values probably belong more to the ruling elite than to the society at large. They may be shared by top Congress Party leaders, the top echelon of the government, the administrative services, and the military, but they are not shared in entirety by many intellectuals and a large section of the lower middle classes, not to mention the unorganized masses.

One may ask how it was possible for the pre-independence Indian National Congress to contain factions which differed on such basic questions. In pre-independence days, nationalism, expressed in terms of opposition to foreign rule, was so intense as to overshadow all other conflicts. It was this agreement on an overriding question that made it possible for Congress to operate as a broad-based national movement made up of many groups. With the fulfillment of the goal of independence in 1947, conflicts which had hitherto been submerged by the national struggle came forward.

When we say that there is no consensus in India on certain questions, we mean not merely that differences exist, for differences on issues exist within the United States as well. But in India, as in many other Asian countries, differences are on fundamental questions concerning the nature of the society and are felt so strongly that those who differ cannot work together.

In a society where values are in the process of rapid change, a sense of insecurity about one's beliefs is unavoidable. The result is that each party clings to its values tenaciously and value differences are met with hostility. When differences emerge within

[19] The Akali Dal in the Punjab, the Kerala Socialist Party, the Tamilnad Congress, and other language groups, for example, have been so strongly in favor of reorganizing the states along linguistic lines that national consequences have not always been fully considered.

a party organized around a well-articulated ideology, feelings of hostility are likely to grow. When there is "deviation" from the party manifesto by a section of the party, the charge of "betrayal" is raised. Each phrase in the manifesto has some special importance and disagreement over any part of the manifesto may result in a party split.

But if unity on basic questions is essential to the unity of an ideologically oriented party, it does not follow that agreement on basic questions will necessarily result in a merger of two or more parties. Such an agreement may be a prerequisite to merger, but it is not the sole prerequisite. As we have seen in the case studies, especially those dealing with the Hindu communal parties and the Marxist left parties, agreement on basic questions does not necessarily result in political unity. The absence of a consensus, therefore, does not of *itself* explain the existence of such a wide variety of political parties in India, but it is certainly a crucial contributing factor. The divergent orientations to politics of the Communists, the democratic center, and the Hindu communalists represent real dividing lines.

Anti-Power Feelings

Another element which may contribute to the reluctance of opposition parties to merge is the ambivalence which many Indians feel toward political power as an objective. Perhaps this appears to be a contradiction in terms since supposedly political parties are by nature instruments for achieving power. But it is possible for a political party to exist, to have an ideology, to make demands upon the government, to organize demonstrations and strikes, and yet be essentially unwilling to assume the responsibility of running a government, and to feel at heart that there is something "dirty" and unpleasant about the whole business of politics.

How widespread such anti-political-power feelings are in India can be easily illustrated. Many members of the Rashtriya Swayamsevak Sangh believe that their objective of changing Indian society and revitalizing Hinduism will be achieved, not through political power, but through propaganda and by the example set by RSS members. This was always a guiding principle of the RSS before it entered active politics; it can hardly fail to influence the thinking of those RSS members in Jan Sangh.

There are also sections of the Praja Socialist Party who view the entire political process skeptically. Many of the party workers are Gandhians who want to devote their lives to constructive work in the villages or to *bhoodan* work (voluntary land collecting), hoping thereby to bring about a change in society without government intervention. There are followers of the late M. N. Roy, who advocated a society in which there are no political parties but where change would be brought about by activity in villages and factories. And then there are those Socialists who, without being articulate ideological anarchists, nevertheless feel a general contempt for the political process and for political power itself.

These anti-power feelings, which can be found in nearly every opposition party in India[20]—including even the Marxist left parties, many of whose members have abandoned politics to become *sanyasis* (monks) at the Aurobindo ashram in Pondicherry—are in large part the product of certain traditional Hindu values. High status in India has not traditionally been associated with political power. Ideally, status is a function of one's position in a caste hierarchy in which the *Brahman* priest rather than the *Kshatriya,* or ruler-warrior, was at the top.[21] Special status, almost irrespective of caste position, was accorded to those persons who strove for *moksha* or salvation, an ideal achieved through renunciation, sacrifice, and, above all, detachment from this world. "Renunciation," "sacrifice," and "detachment" are not the ideals by which all men can live; only a few can choose this path. For the rest, each man must live in accordance with the duty assigned to him by his caste. In the West, too, the religious life of withdrawal has been confined to relatively few; what makes this notion unusual in India is, first, the number of people who

[20] The one exception is the Communist Party, perhaps the most Westernized of all the Indian parties and one which is completely concerned with the objective of winning power.

[21] D. Mackenzie Brown, *The White Umbrella: Indian Political Thought from Manu to Gandhi* (Berkeley: University of California Press, 1953), p. 17.

leave established positions to devote themselves to the search for salvation, and, second, the fact that these ideals are still widely accepted in modern India and have considerable impact even on the lives of those who do not withdraw.

It is also interesting to note that while Hindu tradition accords high status to the *Kshatriya* ruler, it is important that others should not strive for positions of authority. Each man must accept his own *dharma* (duty) and perform his duty well. Better to perform one's own duty poorly, say the scriptures, than to perform someone else's duty well. Authority is acceptable, but to struggle for a position of authority is not.

To what extent traditional Hindu notions affect contemporary political attitudes, it is difficult to say. Westerners are often tempted to magnify the differences between the Hindu religious tradition and Christianity; perhaps what is most important to note here is that, apart from whatever doctrinal differences exist, Hinduism plays a far more conspicuous part in contemporary Indian life than Christianity does in the West. How much traditional Hindu notions actually affect *attitudes* and *behavior* rather than *speech* would require more of an analysis than we are prepared to make here.[22]

But however religious notions affected Indian attitudes toward power and the struggle for power, there is little doubt that the West had a substantial impact on Indian thinking about government. Under British rule, Indian feelings toward government were ambivalent, just as attitudes toward the West in general and toward the British were ambivalent. On the one hand, politics grew in importance as the state took on more functions. But on the other hand, as the nationalist movement grew, cooperation with the alien British rulers became anathema. Indians who accepted office were looked upon with suspicion (although, interestingly enough, those who held office under the British are now widely respected and used in important government positions). Even after 1936 when the Congress party agreed to

[22] For a further elaboration of some of these points see Myron Weiner, "Struggle against Power: Notes on Indian Political Behavior," *World Politics*, VIII, No. 3 (April 1956), pp. 392-403.

assume office in a number of provinces, virtually the entire leftist section of the Party denounced the move. And while one section of Congress talked of the uses to which an Indian national government could be put when independence came, another section, under Gandhi, continued to emphasize the need to change society through non-governmental activities. With this in mind, Gandhi created a large number of constructive work organizations in the villages. Gandhi's attitude toward power is illustrated by the story of his reply to a proposal by some of his friends that he become first Governor-General of India to highlight India's newly won freedom. Gandhi is reported to have said that were he to accept office for even one minute, he would negate all the principles for which he stood.

Today, even under a national government, there are widespread feelings against the "scramble for ministerial posts," especially among those in opposition. Many Indian intellectuals tend to feel a certain contempt for those in political office and to question their motives. These feelings are not so widespread within the Congress Party since most of those with anti-political-power feelings, including many Gandhian constructive workers, have left the Party. For Congressmen today, a government post confers considerable prestige and status. But this feeling is not shared by those outside Congress. Any mention of a "bargain" for ministerial posts is likely to be looked upon with some scorn. Part of the criticism of the Socialists' assumption of power in Travancore-Cochin in 1954 with the support of the Congress Party undoubtedly arose because many believed that some kind of "deal" was involved, and that somehow this arrangement was morally incorrect.

Among the opposition parties, status is achieved by means other than political power. Status may be won by the extent to which sacrifices are made and deprivations undergone by the party leaders or the rank and file. The "renunciation" of office may in fact bring one greater status than victory in a contest for power. Imprisonment, fasting, renunciation of wealth and/or power are sources of status for a political party.

As long as many Indians feel that the search for power is somehow degrading, it is easy to understand why they have some difficulty in learning to accept all the rules of a parliamentary system. When the objective of winning political power plays a secondary role in the behavior of political groups, it follows that pressures for mergers will not be great.

Anti-Democratic Feelings

The unwillingness or inability of many opposition parties to make political calculations which would improve their electoral prospects can also be attributed to the fact that many of them are not committed to working within the parliamentary system. Of the major parties, only the Congress and the Praja Socialists are committed to a democratic electoral structure.[23] Anti-democratic feelings, in the sense of an unwillingness to accept a system of elections as the sole means of achieving power, are expressed by two groups: the violent revolutionaries and the non-violent revolutionaries.

The violent revolutionaries include the Communists and the Marxist leftists, who believe that free elections are a bourgeois institution, and that the bourgeois ruling groups will never allow them to achieve power through elections. They go even further in their positive feeling for violence. As we have seen in our examination of the leftist parties in Bengal, there is a feeling that in the final analysis a social revolution can come to full fruition only through violent action. The Communists and the Marxists may therefore work in elections, but they may at any time attempt to win power through violent revolutionary means.

The non-violent revolutionaries include sections of the Praja Socialist Party and of the Gandhians. Although these groups say they accept and fervently believe in the democratic way, and will work in elections, they also feel that Gandhian techniques of civil disobedience, i.e. law breaking, are not contradictory to the democratic process. Many Socialists feel that as long as such acts are non-violent, they are democratic. It is not merely that some

[23] Not even all sections of the Praja Socialist Party believe that power can be won through elections. A large part of the rank and file and some leaders believe that it can be won only through non-violent civil disobedience.

Socialists and Gandhians feel that injustices can be called to the attention of society and pressures exerted on the government by civil disobedience movements; some go further in believing that an actual *change* in the government may be democratically brought about by some kind of mass civil disobedience campaign that will force the Congress out and bring the Socialists in. This feeling is somewhat analogous to syndicalist notions about the general strike.

Feelings against political power and feelings against the electoral process are often found in the same people. Such feelings are perhaps strongest among party rank and file. This helps to explain not only why they do not calculate in terms of the relation of a merger or a split to winning power through an election, but also why their discontent against the government. and against society is very often expressed in rather vague ways. Rank and filers generally have little concern for specific issues of government policy—except to condemn the government on all questions. It is rare to find a party worker who can reduce ideological differences to differences on specific issues of state policy. None of the opposition parties have research staffs studying specific government bills or proposing new legislation. Several Socialist leaders, especially Asoka Mehta, the former General Secretary of the Praja Socialist Party, have talked of starting a research division for the Party, but none has been started yet—in large part because there is little interest within the Party.

Some of the opposition leaders, especially in the Praja Socialist Party, have been concerned about this. But these leaders either have had extensive contact with British or American democratic practices, have read widely, or have had some experience in Indian legislatures. Many of these leaders have come to accept the electoral system as a means of winning power and can therefore calculate accordingly.

But among those who are not committed to a democratic system with free elections there is little pressure to merge. Members of the Marxist left parties, for example, believe, as do revolutionary Marxist parties throughout the world, that when the revolutionary situation develops, their party irrespective of its size will come to lead the revolution by virtue of having the "correct" line. Those who are "incorrect" will fall away in the revolution. One may take part in the elections and even have electoral arrangements and alliances with others, but a genuine revolutionary party does not believe that society can be changed through bourgeois institutions. Electoral arrangements are allowable, but mergers of parties, except between those who share the same "correct" line, would have little meaning in a revolutionary situation.

Among those groups which have accepted the democratic secular order and are prepared to struggle for power within the electoral process, there is a willingness to learn to operate within parliamentary rules and calculate accordingly. The absence of proportional representation and the existence of single-member constituencies where a plurality determines the seat, have put pressure on the democratic parties to merge. During the past few years the few mergers of parties that have taken place have been almost exclusively among the democratically oriented groups. The Socialists and KMPP merged in 1952. Early in 1955 an anti-Communist section of the Forward Bloc in the Punjab merged with Congress. Likewise, the Krishikar Lok Party (Peasants People's Party) of Andhra merged with the Congress Party, after that state's February 1955 elections.

That the non-democratic parties have been less able to merge and consolidate their strength has, thus far, aided the Congress Party by enabling it to win a clear majority of parliamentary seats in the 1952 elections with less than a majority of the total popular vote. To that extent the fragmentation of the opposition has served to stabilize Indian politics. But the absence of proportional representation and the presence of a system where a plurality vote wins, may eventually force some of the smaller non-democratic groups either to merge or to resort to extra-legal, extra-parliamentary devices in order to avoid extinction.

Perhaps still another reason for party splintering in India, a point that we have noted earlier, is that politics has become so central to the lives of those who take an active part in it that compromise is exceedingly difficult. In the United States and

Great Britain, politics is highly instrumental. Business groups, unions, farmer organizations, and others join together in various combinations to try to put into office those who will enact legislation on their behalf. Compromises and "deals" are constantly made. Fights are generally over specific questions of state policy, rarely over involved "ideological" issues. A large national party in either the United States or Great Britain is a collection of a number of interest groups, sometimes harmonious in their demands, but often divided and conflicting.

In India, only the Congress Party can be said to be a mixture of many interest groups in the same sense that political parties are in many Western countries. The fact that Congress is in power and that no other party has yet emerged as a clear-cut rival has tended to make Congress a natural focus for various interest groups. The provincial groups, for example, who have tried to get a reorganization of the Indian states along linguistic lines have focused their attention not on the Cabinet or Parliament but on the Congress Working Committee. These groups apparently believe that the locus of power is not in the government but in the ruling party. Apart from these provincial interest groups, trade unions, business organizations, and peasant groups all attempt to exert influence on Congress. On the other hand, the opposition parties receive little interest group support. Perhaps this is one of the reasons that the opposition parties can be so engrossed in ideology. Some of the opposition parties, it is true, are not engrossed in ideology—the Jharkhand Party (a tribal party of Orissa and Bihar), the Scheduled Caste Federation (of untouchables), Ganatantra Parishad (a princely sponsored party of Orissa), Kedut Sangh Lok Paksh (a landowners' party of Madras), etc.—but in many respects these political organizations, with their narrow set of demands, more closely resemble interest groups in the West than they do political parties. On the other hand, the national opposition parties in India tend to make total demands—Socialism, *Hindu Rashtra, Bharatiya Rashtra*, Communism, etc.--over which there is little room for compromise.

Perhaps, too, these parties make total demands because the

parties themselves are "total" organizations. Those who belong to an opposition party do not belong to many other groups. Their entire lives center around the party: values, roles, status, sometimes even livelihood, are derived from the party. They are almost self-contained "societies." As long as there are few economic and social opportunities for the educated in India, as long as unemployment continues at its present high rate, then individuals will join parties and make politics central to their lives. And as long as parties are not, to use Max Weber's and Talcott Parson's language, "functionally specific"—as long as they do not think in terms of limited demands and public policy—then compromise and closer collaboration between groups is not likely.

Not only is compromise difficult, but communication itself is restricted. Party rank and filers find that they have little in common which would allow them to communicate with rank and filers of other parties. Not only are there physical barriers to communication—parties are often in widely-separated regions where different languages are spoken, and so on—but there are social barriers as well. The traditional emphasis on closed social groups, the persistence of caste and regional identifications, the general lack of political experience all tend to prevent the bringing together of people who share opinions. As a result there is a tendency on the part of each faction and party to feel that it is grossly different from all others.

SUMMARY

We have offered several possible explanations for party splintering in India:

1. Prior to the general elections the various opposition parties had little knowledge as to how they would be affected by the single-ballot, simple-majority electoral system. In the absence of knowledge as to who had a sizeable electoral following, opposition parties refrained from mergers.

2. After the elections the opposition parties were more aware of the effect of the electoral system upon their strength, and so there was some incentive toward merging with other parties.

3. Merger of all the opposition parties was obviously out of

the question since, apart from their opposition to the victorious Congress Party, there was nothing to unite them. There was no consensus as to the kind of state India ought to have or the functions of such a state.

4. Even among those parties which seem to agree on basic issues—the Hindu communal parties or the Marxist left parties, for example—there appears to be an unwillingness or an inability to make calculations which would improve their electoral prospects.

5. One possible reason for the absence of such calculations is the existence of strong anti-power feelings or somewhat ambivalent feelings toward power. These discourage "deals" that might result in political advantage.

6. Another possible reason is that many of the opposition parties are not committed to working within the parliamentary system as a means of achieving power. Some of these parties hope to achieve power by revolutionary means and are therefore more concerned with "correctness" of policy than with making compromises that might enlarge their party and improve their electoral prospects.

7. Even where apparently like-minded parties seem interested in merging, the rank and file are generally reluctant. This seems to be related to the fact that political groups in India assume some of the functions which the traditional groups performed, especially for the large number of "displaced" intellectuals in India's urban centers. The intensity of devotion of members to their political groups, the absence of continuous and ready communication with outside groups, the importance of the group and factional leaders to their members, the development of a *Weltanschauung* in many political parties which provides a new orientation toward life, the absence of multiple group memberships, all indicate the enormous needs which political groups fulfill for so many of their members. Is there any wonder that the rank and file are so concerned with maintaining the integrity of their organization and "purity" of ideology? And so long as party manifestoes center around an ideology rather than specific issues of public policy, it is particularly difficult to make the

compromises which may be required for closer collaboration and mergers with other parties.

8. The absence of large numbers of strong and independent organized interest groups in Indian politics is a major factor inhibiting the growth of parties concerned with issues of public policy rather than broad ideological questions. Interest groups, especially when they are concerned with the specifics of public policy, tend to be a bridge between professional politicians who are often forced to unite and to make compromises in order to win their support. In the absence of such groups on a large scale, parties and especially the rank and file of parties are inclined to make decisions on the basis of internal rather than external considerations. The needs of the rank and file and their emphasis on the "purity" and integrity of their organization are not balanced by the pressures of independent trade unions, peasant organizations and the like for the building of effective parties which can win power and effect specific changes in public policy.

9. Finally, like-minded parties are subjected to a large number of physical and social barriers to communication—illiteracy, traditional caste and regional allegiances, language barriers, etc.— and a general lack of experience with democratic parliamentary institutions. Communication even between like-minded parties is at a minimum, with rank and filers of one party rarely in contact with those of other parties. The absence of such communication constitutes a further barrier to closer collaboration and mergers of political parties in India.

One final point. The reader may wonder whether these hypotheses are applicable to other countries besides India. Indonesia, Ceylon, Pakistan, Burma, and the Philippines, like India, have suddenly been thrust into the world arena with Western-type democratic systems. As in India, traditional modes of behavior and values are likely to play an important part; but the question of whether the specific hypotheses offered here are valid for other Asian countries cannot be answered until comparable studies are available.

12. Prospects for Stable Government

In Chapter 11 we examined some of the factors involved in the rise of a multiplicity of parties in India. In this final chapter we shall explore some of the basic problems which, in the broadest sense, affect India's prospects for stable government and the survival of democratic institutions. We shall examine first the major issues in Indian politics which challenge the political system; then we shall turn to the agents of stability and instability; and finally we shall explore the way parties affect the outlook for stable government, with special attention to the prospects of the Congress and Praja Socialist parties.

ISSUES

Whether or not democracy succeeds in India depends in large measure upon the ability of the government to deal with some of the country's basic problems: the problem of national unity, the problem of "cultural integration," and the problem of "fulfilling expectations," or, more narrowly, of economic development.

Perhaps most striking of all is the problem of achieving a sense of national unity and mitigating sub-national allegiances. Foremost in this is the linguistic problem. A large number of political parties and groups, especially in South India, have been agitating for the reorganization of the present India states along language lines.[1] These demands have existed for several decades. In 1920 the Congress Party reorganized its provincial organizations to coincide with linguistic divisions. Since the areas of the twelve major and many minor languages spoken in India do not coincide with existing administrative divisions, many of the Congress Provincial Committees cut across state lines. Virtually all other political groups subsequently followed the Congress reorganization.

Surprisingly enough, these provincial, or rather linguistic, sub-national loyalties intensified once independence was achieved.

[1] See Marshall Windmiller, "Linguistic Regionalism in India," *Pacific Affairs*, xxvii (December 1954), pp. 291-318.

Although the Congress Party promised to reorganize state boundaries along linguistic lines when independence was achieved, the first Congress government decided that the administrative and economic difficulties involved were too great to warrant tampering with boundaries at that time. Why these sub-national loyalties have grown even after a national state came into existence is a basic problem which has to be studied further.

It is interesting to note that some of the intense local loyalties come from caste or religious groups that feel threatened in one way or another. In the Punjab, for example, pressure for a Punjabi-speaking state comes from the Sikh community, which is rapidly being absorbed into the Hindu fold.[2] In the South, agitation for a Telugu-speaking state came from the Telugus of Madras, who feared domination by the majority Tamils.[3] The agitation there grew so great that in 1952 Nehru's government agreed to partition Madras to form a Telugu-speaking state called Andhra. The new state, the first to be formed along language lines by the new government, was created in October 1953. But demands to include the Telugu-speaking area of Hyderabad in Andhra State soon followed.

Agitation for linguistic reorganization was also voiced in the Marathi-, Tamil-, and Malayalam-speaking areas. Demand for linguistic reorganization became so strong that in 1954 the Government of India appointed a commission to inquire into the entire matter. The commission, which issued its report in October 1955, called for reorganizing India's twenty-seven states into sixteen, for the most part along linguistic lines, though other considerations were taken into account as well. Although the plan met the demands of a number of linguistic groups, there were some—including the Naga tribesmen of Assam, the Sikhs of the Punjab, and the Maharashtrians of Bombay—who expressed their dissatisfaction, and demonstrations flared in the wake of the commission's report. After considerable agitation, a modified reorganization plan was adopted which went into effect on Novem-

[2] See Khushwant Singh, *The Sikhs* (London: George Allen & Unwin, Ltd.), 1953, pp. 177-185.
[3] Windmiller, *op.cit.*, p. 302.

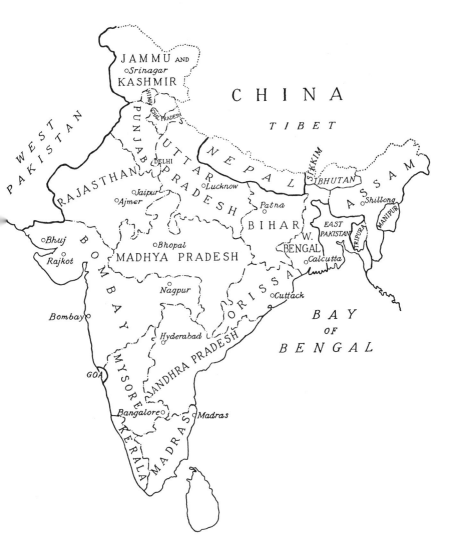

INDIA SINCE THE REORGANIZATION OF STATES
ON NOVEMBER 1, 1956
(Based on a map in *India News* and used with permission)

For a map of India before the reorganization, see page 9

ber 1, 1956. The twenty-seven states were reorganized into four-teen. Six territories are now administrated directly by New Delhi. Only the Punjab and Bombay states remain bilingual. In Bombay, sentiment for the creation of a Maharashtrian state is still strong and in the 1957 elections the Congress majority in the Bombay state legislature was reduced. The extent to which un-reconciled irredentists in Bombay and elsewhere continue their struggle is likely to have considerable effect on building a sense of national unity in India.

But the problem of developing a sense of national unity is broader than the linguistic problem. There are a large number of tribes which have still to be integrated into the new nation (including the tribes of Bihar, which have been agitating for a Jharakand tribal state). Likewise, although the Government of India has made a considerable effort to aid Anglo-Indians, Mus-lims, Sikhs, and other minority communities, government of-ficials would probably agree that communal feelings have not been completely wiped out. Nevertheless, by providing for a secular state the Indian Constitution established the basic frame-work within which the struggle against communalism, casteism, and linguistic provincialism can be carried on.

A second basic political problem is that of reconciling the Indian cultural tradition and social structure with the needs of a modern state. In the broadest sense the Western impact on Asia has brought new ideas as well as new techniques for in-creasing material wealth. In India the Western impact has had profound effects upon both social structure and attitudes. The political system and political ideas, the caste system, the practice of suttee, attitudes toward the role of women, the joint family, and other religious practices and notions have all been influenced by the West.

The Indian leadership during the past century and a half has attempted to achieve what one might call a "cultural integra-tion." Since the reform movement of Ram Mohan Roy in the early part of the nineteenth century, basic changes have been brought about in the Indian way of life. Today's Indian leaders are attempting to reconcile the Indian cultural tradition and social structure with what they feel are the needs of a modern state. Steps have been taken by the Government of India to remove untouchability, grant equal rights to women, and introduce other social reforms. The concept of equalitarianism, although far from being universally practiced in India, has been making major inroads.

Opposition to these reforms has come from some of the non-Westernized Hindu-minded groups. Their hostility has been directed primarily against various provisions of the Hindu Code Bill and recent legislation affecting marriage, divorce, and property rights. They have also agitated for a ban on cow slaughter and for adoption of a Sanskritized Hindi as the national language.

On the other side, the Government of India has been under considerable pressure from Western-minded, frequently Western-educated, intellectuals who have become impatient with the slow pace of social change. Having rejected their own cultural tradition, many intellectuals are often attracted more to the dogmatic system of Marxism than to the more flexible notions of Western liberalism and democratic socialism.

Still other Indians are inclined to have ambivalent feelings toward the West. Whether to accept or reject Western techniques and culture and precisely how much to accept or reject is a difficult and personal problem for nearly all educated Indians. It involves not only one's attitudes toward clothing, movies, music, and the like but one's fundamental attitudes toward "materialism," science, religion, the joint family, and democracy. While both the Hindu parties and the Communists have rejected the democratic liberal tradition—each because of its own viewpoint and philosophy—the convictions of most Indian intellectuals remain somewhere between the two.

For many Indians seeking to integrate Indian and Western notions, the core of the problem is how to reconcile material development with man's "spiritual" life—what George Kennan referred to in an address on June 1955 when he asked, "what environmental conditions are most favorable to man's enjoyment of the experience of life and to the dignity of his relationship with other men?"[4] There is considerable fear in India, and with some justification, that industrialization may bring with it not only slums, juvenile deliquency, and crime, but mass cultural vulgarity, the breakdown of religious values, and the loss of the intimacy of the village and the ancient joint family. At what point, many Indians ask, does a man become so concerned with his material prosperity that he ceases to be concerned with his inner life?

In an effort to maintain the ancient values, some Indians, including some disciples of Gandhi, reject the process of industrialization and look toward the creation of self-sufficient villages in which living standards are raised to the minimum needed for healthy living without impairing the village culture and its values. Others are prepared to see great material development, but advocate the growth of small-scale, decentralized, semi-mechanized industries located in the rural areas. Discussion of these proposals has often been accompanied by accusations of "revivalism" and "feudalism." Even the advocates of decentralization have frequently been fearful of presenting what must inevitably be an intangible argument for the perpetuation of cultural values; they have often chosen the easier way of arguing almost exclusively along economic lines for cottage industries, decentralization, and the like. None of the techniques of the social scientist and little of the thinking of the social philosopher have been applied to this problem of integrating material development with cultural values; but unless the problem is faced, it is likely that change will occur at its own pace with little conscious human intervention, with unpredicted and perhaps undesirable effects.

If the problem of achieving some kind of cultural integration involves adapting Western notions to traditional beliefs and practices, it also involves developing some kind of national agreement on basic values. Unless there is some basic agreement on the desirability of a democratic, secular, and national state, political divisions are likely to become even more rigid. This may

---

[4] George F. Kennan, "How Stands Our Pursuit of Happiness?" *The New Leader*, xxxviii (June 20, 1955), p. 18.

be why many have felt that the major task of the present Indian government is to achieve a national consensus. The fears of the orthodox Hindu must be dispelled; the impatience of the intellectuals must be satisfied; particularistic tendencies must be broken down. Perhaps it is in an effort to achieve these ends that Nehru's Cabinet is a mixture of those who speak to the Western-minded and those who speak to the Hindu-minded, and why many government officials and public leaders attempt to justify government legislation in traditional language as well as in modern socialist jargon. Perhaps this is also why so much attention has been paid in India to reforming the educational system and encouraging the arts.

A third political problem in India is that of keeping up with mass expectations. Virtually all the underdeveloped countries of Asia are characterized by an enormous gap between what people have and what they have learned to want. This problem is not merely the much-discussed problem of poverty. In Rajasthan, for example, one of the poorest states in India, the level of discontent is not as great as in areas where there is less poverty but greater consciousness of that poverty. The gap between the consciousness of reality and expectations is greatest in the cities where Western education and influence has intensified expectations, but it is also felt strongly in much of the countryside where Gandhi's mobilization of the peasantry during the national struggle awakened the masses to their poverty.

The Government of India aims to solve these problems of reconciling reality and expectation through the Five Year Plan, and more specifically in the villages through its Community Projects and National Extension Service. However, there is considerable impatience, especially in the cities, with the slowness of development. This is probably inevitable in a country so underdeveloped. The problem is twofold: on the one hand, the government must aim to increase productivity and satisfy demands, and, on the other, it must restrain demands. Over-ambitious promises can have very severe consequences in underdeveloped areas. Political parties must be cautious about building up hopes which they cannot reasonably expect to fulfill.

Myths inevitably play a large part in filling the gap between expectations and reality. The Soviet government has always relied very heavily on propaganda to the effect that living conditions outside the Soviet Union, especially in the capitalist countries, are far worse than conditions in the Soviet Union. Likewise, exaggerated statements have frequently been made about the pace of Soviet development. The myth of "capitalist encirclement" also has served to justify the emphasis on development of capital goods industries rather than consumer commodities; as long as such "threats" existed, it has been argued, the gap between expectations and reality of necessity had to be great. Soviet myths have aimed either to deny the existence of a gap or alternatively to find some justification for it.

But in a democracy many of the myths employed by the Soviet Union cannot be used. The promulgation of such fiction is possible only when the media of communication are under rigid government control and when outside contact is minimized, neither of which is feasible in a democratic state. This is not to say, however, that other kinds of myths may not be effectively utilized.

The myth of the "spiritual" East versus the "material" West has already played, and is likely to continue to play, a major part in minimizing expectations. Lin Yutang, in a recent speech, complained of the tendency of Asian nations to justify their "backwardness" by reference to their "spirituality." Whether "spiritual" questions play a more important part in Asian thought than in the philosophy of the West is not our concern here, but what is important to note is that the belief of many Indians in the spirituality of their life has assumed the proportions of a popular conviction and has served the useful function of providing alternative satisfactions to a higher living standard.

Similarly, there is a widespread belief in India in the "sanctity" of Indian history and enormous pride in its centuries of tradition. A host of European, especially German, scholars have contributed a great deal toward giving Indians a sense of pride in their cultural tradition. This pride plays a large part in minimizing the frustration that is otherwise likely to develop from an awareness of India's economic backwardness. Likewise, Hindu notions of asceticism and self-restraint, now being propagated by Gandhi's disciples and by many of the orthodox and communal groups, have contributed toward minimizing demands and keeping the gap between expectations and fulfillment narrow.

When a foreigner tends to deprecate Indian life, Indians are likely to make their defense by reference to their spiritual life, their ancient traditions, and their ideals of detachment and sacrifice. In all cultures myths and ideals of one sort or another play a major part in reconciling contradictions in the system or discrepancies between expectations and reality. Where the gaps are as great as they are in India, these notions help prevent widespread disillusionment and cynicism. Disillusionment and cynicism, when it is found among Indians, tends to be among those who have been abroad for long periods of time and among those who have ceased to believe in the Indian traditions and myths. Widespread breakdown of these notions could have catastrophic consequences for Indian society.

Whether democracy succeeds in India depends in large measure upon the ability of the Indian government to minimize the present divisive tendencies of linguistic and other provincial groups, develop a consensus in the country, integrate culturally both the Westernized elites and the Hindu-minded groups, and bridge the gap between economic expectations and fulfillment. Our study has been primarily concerned with the party system and political stability, but the reader must recognize that this problem must be seen in the context of some of the other basic problems facing the country.

ELEMENTS OF INSTABILITY

What are the prospects for political stability in India? To answer this question we must understand what factors mitigate against and what factors contribute to political stability. By "political stability" we mean a situation in which one or a group of political parties can control the government for a reasonable length of time and where change in the governing parties can occur within legally prescribed democratic rules and be tolerated by the defeated groups.

1. The first obstacle to stability is the persistence, in a rather intense form, of the issues in Indian politics discussed above. Unless these problems are astutely handled, they present the basis for widespread political and perhaps even violent protest. These issues call our attention to the considerable social tensions in Indian life—tensions between the Westernized and the non-Westernized, between various linguistic and provincial groups, between North and South India, between the rich and the poor.

2. These tensions have to be worked out in a political system which is relatively new and which has not yet won firm acceptance from all elements in Indian society. The Hindu communalists and the Communists, to mention the two most obvious groups, do not accept the basic political framework. The growth of such groups would make it increasingly difficult to find a workable government majority. Already there are several states, especially in South India, where democratic and secular groups have a shaky combined majority and where groups which disagree on many issues must make the choice of working together or allowing anti-democratic or anti-secular groups to assume power. The danger exists, therefore, not only of unstable government but of "immobilism" similar to that of France, where widely divergent groups are often forced to work together to preserve the republic.

3. Even among groups that profess acceptance of the new democratic and secular framework, there is no widespread acceptance of the ways by which change can be legitimately brought about within that framework. For example, discontented groups often resort to civil disobedience against a popularly elected government. Were there in India a widespread notion of the sanctity of law, which underlies the power of most Western democratic governments, occasional violations of law would not constitute a severe threat; but wanton violations of law do constitute a real threat to democratic institutions in a society where

large numbers of peasants and workers apparently do not yet feel the restraints of law.[5]

4. Of the various social tensions in India, special mention should be made of the role of the dislocated educated urban youth and the unemployed, who play such a large part in the opposition parties. The fact that such groups are mainly attracted to the opposition parties indicates the failure of the Congress Party to prepare for the succession to its own leadership of a newer group. While there are some younger men in the Congress fold, Congress has not been nearly as successful in attracting youth as have the opposition parties.

Youth itself is fragmented into widely divergent political groups and ideologies. The ideals of nationalism which tied the last generation together no longer serve to unite the present generation. The inroads of new and often conflicting values, loss of faith in the old values and institutions, dislocations resulting from changes in family life and the like, widespread unemployment, and dissatisfactions with the educational system, all combine to create an intensely discontented stratum in the society. From this group come the organizers of other discontented groups. Rural discontent, as we noted earlier, may be used by one section of the urban intelligentsia to weaken the position of another section. The real question about "mass" discontent is not only how extensive it is, but who organizes it and for what purposes.[6]

ELEMENTS OF STABILITY

1. Since India's Constitution provides for a federal system with powers distributed between the states and central government, the problem of political stability has to be seen as a state as well

[5] For additional discussion of this point see the author's comments on law and civil disobedience in India in his "Struggle against Power: Notes on Indian Political Behavior," *World Politics*, VIII, No. 3 (April 1956), pp. 398-401.

[6] For an interesting discussion of the role of the intelligentsia in organizing discontent for the Communist movement, see Morris Watnick, "The Appeal of Communism to the Underdeveloped Peoples," in the Harris Foundation Lectures entitled *The Progress of Underdeveloped Areas* (Chicago: University of Chicago Press, 1952).

as a central problem. The Emergency Provisions of the Constitution (particularly Article 356) allow the President of India to "assume to himself all or any of the functions of the Government of the State" in the event that "a situation has arisen in which the Government of the State cannot be carried on in accordance with the provisions of the Constitution."[7] When these provisions, which are known as President's Rule, are invoked, Parliament may legislate with respect to matters allocated to the states: land regulations, education, public health and sanitation, local police powers, etc. Under normal conditions the central government must rely very heavily on its influence rather than such coercive powers. But in the event that a state government fails to maintain law and order, or the political parties are not able to provide stable government, the central government may intervene. These safety features in the Constitution ensure, in the event of a state crisis, orderly state government so long as the central government is strong enough to carry them out. During the interregnum, when President's Rule is in operation, there is time for parties to strengthen themselves, to merge, or to enter into agreements with other parties.

It should be pointed out that President's Rule is not, strictly speaking, authoritarian, since the proclamation declaring President's Rule must be approved by both houses of Parliament within two months of its invocation. The proclamation will then expire unless renewed by Parliament within six months.[8] The administration of a state by the central government is thus subject to scrutinization by Parliament.

President's Rule has already been applied to three separate states where the political parties failed to provide stable government: Patiala and East Punjab States Union (PEPSU) in northern India, Travancore-Cochin on the southwestern tip of India, and Andhra in the Southeast. In each of these areas the Congress Party did poorly in the 1951 general elections, and no one party, either by itself or in coalition with others, was

---

[7] *Constitution of India* (New Delhi: Government of India Press, 1951 edition), p. 174.

[8] *Ibid.*, Article 356, Clauses 3 and 4, pp. 174-175.

able to retain control of the government for any length of time. PEPSU was torn by communal conflicts between the Sikhs and Hindus and within the Sikh community itself. Travancore-Cochin, a former princely state with a weak Congress Party machine, has also been torn by caste and religious issues (between Christians and Hindus), and by a dispute between the Tamil- and Malayalam-speaking areas of the state. And Andhra, a new state carved out by the Telugu-speaking inhabitants of Madras State in 1953, has similarly been affected by traditional divisions, largely in the form of caste rivalries.

While three states obviously provide a poor sample for assessing the prospects for political stability on the state level, and while other factors will enter the situation in the future, these three states do throw some light on what the problem has thus far been.

First, in each of these states the Congress Party failed to win a clear majority. In PEPSU and Travancore-Cochin, as in Orissa, Rajasthan, Hyderabad, and other princely states, the Congress Party organization is relatively new and its record of nationalist activity much briefer than in the states of British India. Then, too, in all three states Congress was badly weakened by caste, communal, or linguistic divisions. Other reasons for Congress weaknesses vary from state to state. However, once the Congress Party hold in a state became uncertain, divisions within the Party often increased since dissidents found their strength magnified by the precarious balance. Unstable politics will frequently magnify the strength of those who refuse to bind themselves by allegiances to larger groups; this is one of the self-perpetuating features of political instability—as dissidents jockey for positions their importance to the party as a whole increases and political instability is further magnified.

Second, in each of the three states no single opposition party was able to form a stable government. The PEPSU Akalis were divided into left and right wing parties. In Andhra, personal differences separated the Praja Party of Prakasam, the Krishikar Lok Party of Professor Ranga, and the Praja Socialist Party. In Travancore-Cochin, basic differences in ideology stood between the Socialists and Communists. In all three states the absence of a consensus and the unwillingness of many of the party leaders and rank and file to join with others prevented the rise of a strong single opposition party or coalition.

The remarkable similarities in the way in which the resulting instabilities were dealt with by the central government and by the political parties in each of these states illustrate the importance of President's Rule in contributing to stability. In PEPSU the establishment of President's Rule by the central government after a coalition of opposition parties failed to maintain law and order, provided an interregnum during which law and order was restored and the Congress Party was able to reorganize itself to resume office. In Andhra, President's Rule was established for a brief period between the collapse of the government and the completion of special statewide elections which a Congress-sponsored coalition won. In Travancore-Cochin, President's Rule was not established at first, but the threat that it might be was known to the various opposition parties whose united ticket prevented Congress from winning a majority in the special elections. But the government formed by the Praja Socialist Party in the state was short-lived, and some time later President's Rule was put into effect.

2. Standing behind the legal power of the central government to take over the administration of a state lies one of the strongest and ablest administrative services in Asia.[9] The capacity of the administrative system to operate a state government pending the reestablishment of party rule represents a real source of stability in India. And in the event that neither the political parties nor the administrative system is able to maintain law and order on the state level, the central government may make use of the military service.

The military, like the administrative service, is a force for national unity. Both are highly respected throughout the coun-

[9] See Paul H. Appleby, *Public Administration in India—Report of a Survey* (Delhi: Manager of Publications, 1953). Professor Appleby conducted a Ford Foundation survey for the Government of India and concluded that the Indian administrative system is among the several best in the world.

try. The military and the administrative service are recruited from all sections of the country, and past experience has demonstrated that their allegiance is to the central government. Both services accept the leadership of Nehru and the Congress Party and are likely to accept the leadership of any group of politicians who can provide the country with a degree of stability and unity. They were trained to do so by the British, and are apparently prepared to continue.

The effectiveness of the military is further enhanced by the fact that under British rule the Indian armed forces were utilized not only for defense but for maintenance of internal law and order. When the police failed to restore peace, especially during Hindu-Muslim riots, the military generally succeeded. In the post-partition disturbances and the crises in Hyderabad and Kashmir, the Indian government made effective use of the military.

As long as one party or a group of parties has firm control of the government, both the military and administrative services can be relied upon to support the government and the system. In addition, although many administrative and military officials command considerable respect in India, none of them has the national prestige or popularity which is accorded Nehru or, for that matter, dozens of other state and central government figures. In fact it can be hypothesized that *the future role of the army and administrative system in Indian politics is probably less a function of the situation within the services than of conditions in the larger society.* As we noted in an earlier chapter, one effect of colonial rule was to move politics into the open political arena rather than to leave crucial political decision making within the civil and military bureaucracy as in Thailand and Japan. With a strong, stable government in New Delhi, the army and administrative system are likely to be instruments for strengthening the center, especially in its relations with the states.

3. In the final analysis, however, perhaps the single most important factor presently affecting the stability of the central government in India is the strength of the Congress Party. So long as the central government is under the firm control of a single

party or group of parties, instabilities on the state level can be dealt with by the center. What, then, are the prospects of the Congress Party's continuing as a force for stability, and what are the prospects for the emergence of a strong democratic opposition which might assume power if Congress were defeated?

CONGRESS PARTY PROSPECTS

The position of the Congress Party is a unique one. Few democratic countries in the world have a political party in as dominant a position as the Congress Party enjoys today. While India by no means has a single-party system, Congress stands as the largest and most powerful party in India and, as we have seen, is probably the single most important force contributing to political stability in the country.

What are the elements which contribute to the present strength of Congress and why has the Party been able to maintain its popularity? Partly it is because the "freedom movement" is so closely associated with Congress and because the Congress organization, having reached the villages before other parties, is strongly entrenched. Partly it is because Nehru is adored by the masses for having made such great personal sacrifices and for having been so closely associated with Gandhi and with the freedom struggle. Partly it is because, while there has been no revolutionary change in the economic system, the Congress government has successfully reached a large number of villages through its community projects and river valley development schemes. If progress has been slow, at least there have been no major economic crises. The favorable food situation resulting both from development work and good monsoon weather has also been an asset to Congress. Partly it is because the values and language of socialism, which have been widely accepted throughout the country, have remained the avowed ideals of the Congress Party. And in part it is because of the weakness and fragmentation of the opposition. As a result, Congress is able to win seats with a plurality vote and the voters cannot readily see an alternative to a Congress government. Finally, Congress strength can in part also be attributed to a kind of inertia which is prevalent in the centuries-old villages of India. No one and no party has been able to overcome that inertia and mobilize the masses as Gandhi once did.

It would be a mistake to believe, therefore, that the strength of Congress rests solely on the popularity of the Prime Minister. One of the factors of Congress strength which deserves special emphasis is the ability of Party leaders to reconcile conflicting points of view within the Party. More than any other party in India, Congress has successfully placated conflicting interest groups and ideologies. Nehru's point of view has been sufficiently broad to retain the support of very divergent groups, which, even when they disagree with Congress policy, see in Nehru the expression of their views. The Muslims in Congress, for example, view Nehru's emphasis on secularism as a protection against the Hindu-minded groups inside Congress. The Hindu-minded, while critical of Nehru on many issues, are attracted by his recent firm policy toward Pakistan, especially since the United States–Pakistani pact. The Gandhians are pleased by Nehru's attacks against the "coat and necktie" mentality of many government officials, his emphasis on village development, land reform, and cottage industries. Labor members and leaders of the Congress-sponsored Indian National Trade Union Congress view the Prime Minister as an exponent of socialism. The business community, once fearful of Nehru's socialist outlook, recognizes the sympathetic attitude of the government toward it and is especially pleased by Nehru's attacks against the Praja Socialist Party, which calls for the nationalization of industry.[10]

But it is not just Nehru who has reconciled these intra-Party differences. The government's Five Year Plan, with its "mixed economy" approach, is essentially an attempt at balancing various points of view. And then there are the large number of Party "compromisers," men who are known to be honest and undogmatic. Several of these men are state Chief Ministers, in the central government, or high up in the Congress Party, and

10 For a description of the various points of view of the Congress Party, see Myron Weiner, "Prospects for India's Congress Party," *Far Eastern Survey*, XXIII (December 1954), pp. 182-188.

are potential Prime Ministers after Nehru. Although none of these men can possibly compete with Nehru in popularity at this stage, there are a number of figures some ten years or so younger than the Prime Minister who have achieved local stature or recognition within influential groups.

The greatest threat to the Congress Party so far has come not from ideological conflicts but from other divisive tendencies. "Communalism, casteism, and provincialism," to use Nehru's own phrase, along with the drive for status and recognition, have been disruptive influences in the Congress organization, as well as in other parties.

We have already seen that there has been a progressive deterioration of the Congress Party since independence with the wholesale withdrawal of many political groups. Although the mass defections from Congress which occurred before the 1952 elections have now stopped, conflicts within the Party continue, especially between Congress governments and the Party organization. On the national level this began with the resignation of Kripalani as President of Congress in 1947 and continued in 1951 when the Prime Minister forced the resignation of Tandon. The Prime Minister's assumption of the office of Congress President ended such conflicts on the national level, but on the state level they have been frequent ever since the general elections: in Hyderabad, Delhi State, Madras, Bihar, etc.

At one time or another nearly every state in India has witnessed a conflict between the Chief Minister, who runs the government, and the President of the Pradesh (State) Congress Committee (the PCC), who controls the Party organization. Factions form around these men based on personal allegiances which are sometimes, but not always, reinforced by caste, linguistic, or area identifications. These factions have often developed a permanence and cohesiveness that have intensified the conflicts between the various state leaders. Disagreements between the PCC Presidents and the Chief Ministers rarely involve differences in policies, although they may be expressed in such terms. Generally the PCC President wants to provide patronage for his supporters or seeks the prestige of holding the highest office in the state. High status rather than financial reward seems to be the dominant motive.

The continuance of factions within the Party is a source of weakness which, if given an ideological overtone or a major issue on which factions differed, would sharpen the lines of division and seriously injure the Party. Agitation for the redistribution of states along linguistic lines has sharpened the factional divisions in some areas, but at the moment no other issue of state policy seems likely to provide a basis for the further development of factions.

On factionalism within Congress, two final points should be noted. First of all, as we have seen, the problem is not confined to the Congress Party alone but exists in virtually every political party. This does not, however, lessen the problem for Congress. And second, more than any other party, Congress has thus far been able to mitigate the divisive effect of factional disputes. Factional groups hesitate to break away from the party in power and enter the political wilderness. Furthermore the Congress Party, as we noted earlier, has had considerable experience with the problem of factionalism and has developed party machinery and a group of party "trouble shooters" to deal with many of these disputes. Finally, more than any other party, Congress has considerable tolerance for divergent views and factions. This tolerance and this intra-party diversity are what give the Congress Party its national character. Perhaps the tolerance and diversity are not as comprehensive as in the days of the national struggle, but they are still broader than those of any other party in India today.

What are the prospects for Congress? This is very difficult to predict, but many factors are on the side of continued Congress strength. A capable party leadership, well-entrenched and well-financed party organization, and a fairly successful program of economic development combine to make Congress prospects hopeful. Since 1952, Congress has done well in by-elections as well as state general elections. In the 1957 elections Congress retained her dominant position in Parliament and again won a clear majority of seats in all but a few state assemblies.

On the debit side has been the failure of the Congress Party to attract large numbers of young people. The top leadership of the Congress Party is growing old, and unless replacements are found, within ten to fifteen years, the Party may not have the leadership to move forward. There is also the problem, as we noted earlier, of a fairly large unemployed educated class, which is being attracted to opposition parties.

But there is good reason to believe that, in spite of these difficulties, the Congress Party will maintain its strength in the central government and in most of the states for at least a decade or so, barring, of course, an internal leadership dispute, a major party split, or some unforeseen domestic or international crisis.

Nevertheless the Congress Party is not likely to continue in its present position indefinitely. As long as democracy flourishes, no one party can dominate the country permanently. The questions therefore are: How long will Congress retain its present lead? and What will happen after that? It is not our intention here to make predictions, but rather to explore the prospects for the rise of a national democratic party capable of providing stable government in the event of a Congress defeat.

PRAJA SOCIALIST PARTY PROSPECTS

An examination of possible alternative democratic governments in India must, at this time at least, begin and end with a discussion of the Praja Socialist Party. No other party in the opposition approaches the PSP as a potential democratic alternative to Congress. It is the second largest party in India in popular votes. The 17.4% of the popular vote which the Socialist Party and the KMPP received in the 1952 elections (in subsequent by-elections the Praja Socialist Party has also been receiving about 17 per cent of the popular vote) is far ahead of the 5.4% which the Communists received or the 3.1% of Jan Sangh. There are a few small democratically oriented parties, but none of these received even the 3% of the popular vote needed for recognition as a national party by the Election Commission.

Of the opposition parties, the PSP has the most complete national coverage. It has a party organization and some popular appeal in virtually every state. Its 18 million voters gave the PSP seats in all but a few small states. The Party has a nationally known leadership and a number of popular state leaders. It also has a substantial following among youth. Most of the important second-rank and many fairly high positions in the Party are held by young people.

There seems to be little possibility of the Socialists winning a clear majority of legislative seats in any state for some time to come. Only in Vindhya Pradesh, Bihar, and Mysore did the Socialists and the KMPP together poll more than 20 per cent of the vote in the '52 elections. Even in Travancore-Cochin, where the PSP formed a minority government, the Socialists received only 16.2% of the popular vote. In the states of Uttar Pradesh and Assam they won slightly under 20% in 1952.[11]

The Socialists have a long way to go before they can replace the Congress Party and provide stable democratic government, but the potentiality exists. Although the PSP has many assets, which we have already described, there are also many stumbling blocks within the Party. Internal differences and inadequate organization have thus far been major obstacles to its growth. Differences toward the Congress Party and toward the PSP Ministry in Travancore-Cochin badly divided the Party through 1953 and 1954. Party issues were publicly debated, and virtually the entire energies of the Party were directed toward these internal disputes. Furthermore disputes and indiscipline within

[11] The overall position of the PSP was not materially changed by the 1957 elections. The PSP won 19 seats in the new Parliament, compared with 21 in the old Parliament in spite of a substantial loss of votes to the splinter Socialist Party of Rammanohar Lohia. For the state legislative assemblies, the PSP did well in the north—especially in U.P., West Bengal, and Bihar— and grew considerably in Bombay, but made a poor showing in the south Indian states. The major results of the 1957 elections are these: (1) Congress again emerged as the most powerful political party in India, with no parties, except in two or three states, in a position to offer a serious challenge; (2) the PSP held its own nationally, having lost considerably in the south but gaining in the north; (3) the CPI increased both its popular vote and its seats in the various legislatures, emerging as the largest party in the new state of Kerala (formerly Travancore-Cochin); (4) the number of seats held by the Hindu parties has decreased; (5) similarly, the number of seats held by independents and by smaller opposition parties has decreased.

state bodies have also been a problem, and the Party has not yet been able to create an effective machinery for dealing with intra-Party disputes. The 1955 breakoff of Rammanohar Lohia and many of his supporters to form a new Socialist Party has further weakened the PSP.

Second, while Party leaders have called for greater constructive work in the villages by Party members, no major constructive work program has yet been launched. There have been a number of local agitations which have added to the Party's local popularity, but there has been little of the sustained village constructive work which helped to build up the Congress Party.

A third obstacle to the growth of the PSP, and one which confronts every opposition party, is the superior finances, organization, and leadership of the Congress Party and the fact that Congress, by virtue of running the government, has no need to prove its distinctiveness.

But if Congress is an obstacle to Socialist strength, the reverse is not necessarily true—that a Congress defeat necessarily means a Socialist victory. The fact is that wherever Congress is weak, non-democratic forces rather than the Socialists have moved ahead. In PEPSU, Andhra, and Travancore-Cochin, where Congress governments collapsed, and in Rajasthan, Hyderabad, Madras State, and Bengal, where Congress does not have a strong hold, Communist and communal elements are strong while the Socialists are not. In the North Indian states where the Socialists are the major force confronting Congress, anti-democratic and anti-secular forces have little influence. This suggests that communalism and communism are as much political dangers to the Socialists as they are to Congress. The destruction of these groups would probably be as politically advantageous to the Socialists as to Congress. It would be foolish for the Praja Socialist Party to try to destroy the Congress if the results were victory for anti-democratic or anti-secular forces. In the long run these forces are a greater danger to the Praja Socialist Party than is Congress.

In those North Indian states where the Socialists are strong and anti-democratic parties are not, the PSP can afford to oppose

Congress militantly and offer itself as a democratic alternative with what it feels is a more progressive economic program. But in those South Indian states where anti-democratic or communal or provincial elements are strong and the Socialists are not, the Socialists are faced with the dilemma of how to appear different from Congress and yet at the same time prevent Congress from being replaced by anti-democratic elements.

CONCLUSION: PROSPECTS FOR THE FUTURE

It has been a thesis of this book that political parties, by providing a range of choice to the electorate and providing the machinery for the peaceful transfer of political power from one group to another, are essential to any democratic system; and furthermore that the party system has an enormous impact on the stability of government. The number of parties involved in the party system is often less important than the relationship among them: a two-party system in which one party is democratic and the other totalitarian is hardly viable, whereas the multiplicity of parties in Sweden, for example, based as the parties are upon agreement on basic questions, has provided that country with considerable stability.

A two-party system is not a prerequisite for political stability, but agreement on the basic structure of government is. As long as the political parties agree that India ought to remain a democratic and secular republic, then there is wide room for differences on specific questions of public policy. Agreement on the *means* to be employed to effect change is what gives a system its stability. "It is not the legislative product," wrote William Ebenstein, "that distinguishes a democratic body from a non-democratic one, but the difference of *procedure.*"[12] And it is agreement on this procedure which is essential to stability.

For the moment, at least, India could be described as having a one-party democratic system, based not on the coercion found in one-party dictatorships, but on consent. The opposition parties in India, although small in comparison with Congress, have the right to organize, agitate, and express their views freely. As long

12 William Ebenstein, *Today's Isms* (New York: Prentice-Hall, 1954), p. 96.

as these freedoms exist, and as long as the ideal continues of a party system in which an opposition party or group of parties may assume power, then democracy will continue in India. The real test of the system will come, not when or if leadership of the Indian government shifts from one set of Congress leaders to another, but when control moves from the Congress Party to one or more of the other political parties.

The problem in India, therefore, is how to strengthen those parties which accept the democratic system and how to weaken those which do not. If either or both the Socialists and Congress can maintain stable government, there may be time to provide the conditions under which some of the smaller parties disappear and non-democratic groups lose strength. Time itself may be on the side of building a democratic order if stable government is maintained. With political stability, people are likely to grow accustomed to democratic rules, and political groups may learn to calculate accordingly. Some parties may merge, and others may be killed off by the electorate. But if the non-democratic parties are to be weakened and the democratic parties strengthened, a consensus on the basic issues of nationalism, secularism, and democracy must be established in Indian society.

To help achieve a consensus, both the Congress and Praja Socialist parties must be prepared to admit other parties into their fold. They must be prepared to treat the programs of some of the smaller regional and communal parties as specific grievances rather than personal or ideological differences. The Scheduled Caste Federation and the Jharkhand Party (a tribal party in Bihar), for example, could be assimilated into the Praja Socialist Party without any compromise on basic principles. There is no reason why the discontent of some of the smaller minority groups cannot be expressed through a large political party. American political parties, for example, have been ready outlets for the discontent of minority groups, helped them satisfy their political wants, and in turn aided them in adjusting to the society. The Congress Party ought to encourage opposition political parties to put forward specific grievances rather than sweeping ideological demands. Whether this will be done depends in large measure upon whether the government is receptive to dealing with specific grievances which are called to its attention by political parties, organized pressure groups, or discontented peasants or workers. *Once ideological questions can be reduced to specific issues, compromise and discussion are possible and prospects for a stable political party system will improve.*

The growth of pressure groups which advocate specific changes in public policy could also serve as a stabilizing force. If pressure groups can achieve some of their objectives through the democratic structure, then they are likely to develop a stake in that structure. The existence of independent and voluntary pressure groups in agriculture, handicrafts, cottage industries, cooperatives, industry, and so on—that is, organizations under the control neither of government nor of parties—is likely to result both in greater governmental responsibility and in greater concern by political parties for concrete issues of public policy. As interest groups organize and make demands on the government and on parties, especially if the demands are with reference to specific issues of state policy rather than broad ideological positions, then the parties themselves are likely to become more compromising. As we have already noted, the extent to which a party is "ideologically" rather than issue oriented may in large measure be due to whether decisions are made with reference to internal needs rather than external considerations. We have seen in the case studies how small a part external considerations have played in party splits and attempted mergers. What factors are likely to affect the growth of interest groups free from control by the government or by parties is beyond the scope of this study; but it is important to note that the role of interest groups in Indian politics and their relationship to political parties is a factor of considerable long-range importance in the development of a stable political system. But, given the party system as it now is and is likely to be for some time, there is the immediate problem of maintaining some measure of stable democratic government.

As we have already noted, the threat to stable government is greatest in the southern states. In these areas the linguistic province issue, the extensive activity of the Communists, the weak-ness of the national movement during the freedom struggle (especially in Hyderabad and Travancore-Cochin, both princely states at the time), strong anti-northern feelings, and intense caste conflicts within Congress, have combined to weaken the hold of the Congress Party. It is in these states, especially Hyder-abad, Madras, Andhra, and Travancore-Cochin (which have now been reorganized into the states of Madras, Andhra-Pradesh and Kerala), that the multiplicity of political parties threatens to de-stroy stable government. It is in these states, along with Bengal to the northeast, that the Communists and other anti-democratic forces have thus far been most successful.

Two developments in the states—the success of non-democratic parties in winning control of state governments, and the forma-tion of unstable governments in which no one party or group of parties can operate the government effectively—are both dan-gerous for the future of democratic institutions in India. Whether these developments can be avoided depends on the ability of the Congress Party to cope with some of the basic problems we have discussed earlier in this chapter as well as the willingness of the Socialists, Congress, and other democratic groups to co-operate. In some situations it may be politically necessary for Congress to stay out of the government but support the Socialists; in other instances, the reverse; and, in still other instances coalitions may be necessary. What is essential, however, is that anti-democratic, anti-secular, and anti-national forces be pre-vented from winning control of the government machinery.

Essentially our argument is that the Congress Party and the Praja Socialist Party (or any other democratic parties which develop) must become the bulwark of the democratic, secular, and nationalist order. They may, and in fact ought to, differ on economic issues, but where the society is threatened by the opponents of a democratic and secular state, then the two parties must stand together. Stable government requires neither a two-party system nor a multi-party system, but it does require a party system in which the major political groups agree on the fundamental nature of the state.

In the final analysis a stable party system, and consequently a stable government, can develop in India only when political polarization is between parties which agree on basic values. Without strong, democratic parties capable of providing the nation with political stability, it is hardly possible for India to carry through a program of social and economic change within the democratic framework.

Bibliography

GENERAL BOOKS AND ARTICLES ON INDIAN POLITICS

Appleby, Paul H. *Public Administration in India—Report of a Survey.* Delhi: Manager of Publications, 1953.

Asia Guide to the First General Elections. Bombay: Asia Publishing House, 1951.

Blunt, Sir Edward. *The I.C.S. (The Indian Civil Service).* London: Faber and Faber, Ltd., 1937.

Brown, D. Mackenzie. *The White Umbrella—Indian Political Thought from Manu to Gandhi.* Berkeley: University of California Press, 1953.

Brown, W. Norman. *The United States and India and Pakistan.* Cambridge, Mass.: Harvard University Press, 1953.

Chhabra, Hari Sharan. *Opposition in the Parliament.* Delhi: New Publishers, 1953.

Desai, A. R. *Social Background of Indian Nationalism.* Bombay: Popular Book Depot, 1954.

Election Commission. *Report on the First General Elections in India 1951-52* (two volumes). Delhi: Manager of Publications, 1955.

Farquhar, J. N. *Modern Religious Movements in India.* New York: Macmillan Co., 1915.

Gledhill, Alan. *The Republic of India.* London: Stevens and Sons, Ltd., 1951.

Government of India. *The Constitution of India.* Delhi: Manager of Publications, 1951.

Government of India. Ministry of Information and Broadcasting. *India, A Reference Annual 1953.* Delhi: Publications Division, Government of India, 1953.

Jennings, Sir Ivor. *Some Characteristics of the Indian Constitution.* London: Oxford University Press, 1953.

Kabir, Humayun. *Student Indiscipline.* New Delhi: Ministry of Education, Government of India, 1954.

Lewis, Oscar. *Group Dynamics in a North-Indian Village.* Programme Evaluation Organisation, Planning Commission, Government of India. Delhi: Manager of Publications, 1954.

Majumdar, B. B. (ed.). *Problems of Public Administration in India*. Patna: Bharati Bhawan, 1954.

Masani, M. R. *The Communist Party of India—A Short History*. London: Derek Verschoyle, 1954.

Murphy, Gardner. *In the Minds of Men—The Study of Human Behavior and Social Tensions in India*. New York: Basic Books, Inc., 1953.

Nanavati, Manilal B. and Vakil, C. N. (eds.). *Group Prejudices in India*. Bombay: Vora and Co., Ltd., 1951.

Park, Richard L. "Indian Election Results," *Far Eastern Survey*, XXI (May 7, 1952), p. 64.

Parliament of India. *Council of States Who's Who, 1952*. New Delhi: Council of States Secretariat, 1953.

Parliament of India. *House of the People Who's Who, 1952*. New Delhi: Parliament Secretariat, 1953.

Raghuvanshi, Dr. V. P. S. *Indian Nationalist Movement and Thought*. Agra: L. N. Agarwal, 1951.

Rajkumar, Dr. N. V. *Indian Political Parties*. New Delhi: All India Congress Committee, 1948.

Singh, Khushwant. *The Sikhs*. London: George Allen and Unwin, Ltd., 1953.

Singh, Trilochan. *Indian Parliament (1952-57)*. New Delhi: Arunam and Sheel, 1954.

Smith, William Roy. *Nationalism and Reform in India*. New Haven: Yale University Press, 1938.

Weiner, Myron. "India's Political Problems: The Longer View," *The Western Political Quarterly*, IX (June 1956), p. 283.

Weiner, Myron. "Prospects for India's Congress Party," *Far Eastern Survey*, XXIII (December 1954), p. 182.

Weiner, Myron. "Struggle Against Power: Notes on Indian Political Behavior," *World Politics*, VIII (April 1956), p. 392.

Windmiller, Marshall, "Linguistic Regionalism in India," *Pacific Affairs*, XXVII (December 1954), p. 291.

SOCIALIST AND CONGRESS PARTIES
Books and Pamphlets

Ali, Sadiq. *Cottage Industries.* Bombay: Praja Socialist Party, 1953.

Ali, Sadiq and Limaye, Madhu. *Report on Kashmir.* Bombay: Praja Socialist Party, 1954.

Banerjee, Anil Chandra (compiler). *The Constituent Assembly of India.* Calcutta: Mukherjee and Co., 1947.

Banerjee, Anil Chandra and Bose, Dakshina Ranjan (compilers). *The Cabinet Mission in India.* Calcutta: Mukherjee and Co., 1946.

Bhargava, G. S. *Leaders of the Left.* Bombay: Meherally Book Club, 1951.

Bright, J. S. *President Kripalani and His Ideas.* Lahore: Indian Printing Works, 1947.

Dandavate, M. R. *Report: Political and Organizational.* (Report to Bombay City Praja Socialist Party, December 1953). Bombay: Mouj Printing Bureau, 1953.

Dandavate, M. R. *Socialist Challenge to Communists.* Bombay: Praja Socialist Party, 1952.

Deva, Acharya Narendra. *Socialism and the National Revolution.* Bombay: Padma Publications, 1946.

Dhawan, Gopinath. *The Political Philosophy of Mahatma Gandhi.* Ahmedabad: Navajivan Publishing House, 1951.

For a Democratic Government in Madras State. Bombay: Peoples Publishing House, Ltd., 1952.

Gandhi, M. K. *Sarvodaya (The Welfare of All).* Ahmedabad: Navajivan Press, 1954.

Goray, N. G. *Report Presented to the First Conference of the Praja Socialist Party.* Allahabad, 1953.

Indian National Congress. *Congress Bulletin,* No. 4, July 10, 1947. New Delhi: All India Congress Committee, 1947.

Indian National Congress. *Constitution of The Indian National Congress.* New Delhi: All India Congress Committee, 1948.

Indian National Congress. *Election Manifesto—What Congress Stands For.* New Delhi: All India Congress Committee, 1951.

Indian National Congress. *The Pilgrimage and After (The Story of How the Congress Fought and Won the General Elections)*. New Delhi: All India Congress Committee, 1952.

Indian National Congress. *Report of the General Secretaries, January 1949–September 1950*. New Delhi: All India Congress Committee, 1950.

Indian National Congress. *Report of the General Secretaries, November 1946–December 1948*. New Delhi: All India Congress Committee, 1948.

Kisan Mazdoor Praja Party Bulletin, No. 1, July 31, 1951.

Kisan Mazdoor Praja Party. *Manifesto of the Kisan Mazdoor Praja Party*. New Delhi: Kisan Mazdoor Praja Party, 1951.

Kripalani, Acharya J. B. *The Future of the Congress*. Bombay: Hind Kitabs, Ltd., 1948.

Kripalani, Acharya J. B. *The Indian National Congress*. Bombay: Vora and Co., Ltd., 1946.

Kripalani, Acharya J. B. *Presidential Address, Indian National Congress Fifty-fourth Session*. Allahabad: All India Congress Committee, 1946.

Kripalani, Acharya J. B. *Presidential Address. First Annual Convention, Praja Socialist Party, Allahabad*. Lucknow: Jana Sahitya Press, 1953.

Kripalani, Acharya J. B. *Toward Sarvodaya*. New Delhi: KMPP, 1951.

Lakhanpal, P. L. *History of the Congress Socialist Party*. Lahore: National Publishers, 1946.

Lakshman, P. P. *Congress and the Labour Movement in India*. Allahabad: All India Congress Committee, 1947.

Limaye, Madhu. *The Barren Path—A Reply to Aruna Asaf Ali*. Bombay: Socialist Party, 1951.

Limaye, Madhu. *Communist Party Facts and Fiction*. Hyderabad: Chetana Prakashan, Ltd., 1951.

Limaye, Madhu. *Evolution of Socialist Policy*. Hyderabad: Chetana Prakashan, Ltd., 1952.

Limaye, Madhu. *Where Is the Left Going?* Bombay: Socialist Party, 1952.

Lohia, Rammanohar. *Aspects of Socialist Policy*. Bombay: Socialist Party, 1952.

Lohia, Rammanohar. *Fragments of a World Mind*. Calcutta: Maitrayani Publishers, 1951.

Lohia, Rammanohar. *Letters to Party Activists*. Bombay: Praja Socialist Party, 1954.

Lohia, Rammanohar. *The Third Camp in World Affairs*. Bombay: Socialist Party, 1951.

Masani, M. R. *Socialism Reconsidered*. Bombay: Padma Publications, Ltd., 1944.

Meherally, Yusuf. *Leaders of India*. Bombay: Padma Publications, Ltd., 1942. Vols. I and II.

Mehta, Asoka. *Democratic Socialism*. Hyderabad: Chetana Prakashan, 1954.

Mehta, Asoka. *Foreign Policy—A Socialist View*. Bombay: Socialist Party [1951?].

Mehta, Asoka. *The Political Mind of India*. Bombay: Socialist Party, 1952.

Mehta, Asoka. *Politics of Planned Economy*. Bombay: Praja Socialist Party, 1953.

Mehta, Asoka. *Presidential Address to the Seventh National Conference of the Socialist Party, Madras, July 1950*. Bombay: Western Printers and Publishers, 1950.

Mehta, Asoka. *Socialism and Gandhism*. Bombay: Congress Socialist Publishing Co., Ltd., 1935.

Mehta, Asoka. *Socialism and Peasantry*. Bombay: Praja Socialist Party, 1953.

Mehta, Asoka. *Who Owns India?* Hyderabad: Chetana Prakashan, Ltd., 1950.

Mehta, Asoka. *Straws in the Wind—An Analysis of Trends of Public Opinion as Revealed by Recent By-elections*. Bombay: Socialist Party, 1951.

Misra, Rammandan. *Escape and Torture*. Monghyr: Congress Socialist Party [1946?].

Narayan, Jayaprakash. *In the Lahore Fort*. Patna: Sahityalaya, 1942.

Narayan, Jayaprakash. *Jeevandan.* Bombay: Rohit Dave for Janata, 1954.

Narayan, Jayaprakash. *Political Trends.* Bombay: Socialist Party, 1951.

Narayan, Jayaprakash. *The Socialist Way.* Lucknow: Dulabeylal Bhargava, 1946.

Narayan, Jayaprakash. *Towards Struggle.* Bombay: Padma Publications, Ltd., 1946.

Narayan, Jayaprakash. *Will the Socialists Leave the Congress?* Bombay: Socialist Party, 1948.

Narayan, Jayaprakash, and others. *Some Memorable Letters on August Revolution.* Calcutta: Azad Hind Kitab, 1946.

Nehru, Jawaharlal. *Report to the All India Congress Committee, July 6, 1951.* New Delhi: All India Congress Committee, 1951.

Patil, S. K. *The Indian National Congress—A Case for its Reorganisation.* Aundh: Aundh Publishing Trust, 1945.

Praja Socialist Party. *Constitutions, Rules and Code of Conduct.* Bombay: Praja Socialist Party, 1954.

Praja Socialist Party. *Governmental Programme for Socialist India.* Bombay: Praja Socialist Party, 1953.

Praja Socialist Party. *The Merger: How and Why.* Bombay: Praja Socialist Party, 1952.

Praja Socialist Party. *Nehru-Jayaprakash Talks.* Bombay: Praja Socialist Party, 1953.

Praja Socialist Party. *Political Perspective and Programme of Work.* Bombay: Praja Socialist Party, 1953.

Praja Socialist Party. *Report of the Special Convention Held at Betul, Madhya Pradesh, June 1953.* Bombay: Praja Socialist Party, 1953.

Praja Socialist Party. *Two Years of the Praja Socialist Party.* Bombay: Praja Socialist Party, 1954.

Ramabhai, Suresh. *Vinoba and His Mission.* Sevagram (Wardha): Akhil Bharat Sarv Seva Sangh, 1954.

Ranga, Professor N. G. *Kisans and Communists.* Bombay: Pratibha Publications [1946?].

Ranga, Professor N. G. *Outlines of National Revolutionary Path.* Bombay: Hind Kitabs, 1945.

Rajkumar, Dr. N. V. *Development of the Congress Constitution.* New Delhi: All India Congress Committee, 1949.

Sahai, Govind. *'42 Rebellion.* Delhi: Rajkumal Publications, Ltd., 1947.

Sitaramayya, Dr. B. Pattabhi. *History of the Indian National Congress* (two volumes). Bombay: Padma Publications, 1947.

Sitaramayya, Dr. B. Pattabhi. *Presidential Address, Indian National Congress Fifty-fifth Session.* New Delhi: All India Congress Committee, 1948.

Socialist Party. *Concerning Organisation.* Bombay: Socialist Party, 1951.

Socialist Party; Draft Constitution of Indian Republic. Bombay: Socialist Party, 1948.

Socialist Party. *Forward to a Mass Party.* Bombay: Socialist Party, 1949. (Includes Constitution passed at the Patna convention in March 1949.)

Socialist Party. *Policy Statement (Adopted by the General Council in August 1947 and Revised in October 1949).* Bombay: Socialist Party, 1951.

Socialist Party. *Report of the Sixth Annual Conference of the Socialist Party, Nasik, 1948.* Bombay: Socialist Party, 1948.

Socialist Party. *Report of the Seventh Annual Conference of the Socialist Party, Patna, 1949.* Poona: Sangam Press, Ltd., 1949.

Socialist Party. *Report of the Eighth National Conference, Madras, 1950.* Bombay: Socialist Party, 1950.

Socialist Party. *Report of the Special Convention Held at Pachmarhi, Madhya Pradesh, May 1952.*

Socialist Party. *We Build for Socialism (Election Platform of the Socialist Party).* Bombay: Socialist Party, 1951.

The Socialist Party's Programme for National Revival. Hyderabad: Chetana Prakashan, Ltd., 1951.

Tandon, Purushottamdas. *English Rendering of President's Hindi Address, the Indian National Congress Fifty-sixth Session.* Bombay: Akhil Bharat Printers, Ltd., 1950.

Articles

"After Gandhiji—What?" *Janata*, III (February 8, 1948), p. 7.

Ali, Aruna Asaf. "The Second Party," *Janata*, III (March 7, 1948), p. 5.

Ali, Aruna Asaf. "Time to Decide," *Janata*, III (February 29, 1948), p. 3.

Ali, Aruna Asaf. "Why I Must Join the Socialist Party," *Janata*, III (March 14, 1948), p. 3.

"The Betul Convention," *Janata*, VIII (June 28, 1953), pp. 9, 10.

Bhasyam, K. "Post Election Set-up in Madras State," *Swatantra*, VII (March 1, 1952), pp. 24-26.

"Bihar Letter: Vested Interests Misinterpret JP's Association with Kripalani," *Janata*, VI (July 8, 1951), p. 8.

"The Birth of a Party," *Vigil*, II (June 23, 1951), pp. 3-4.

"Bright Prospects for Andhra Praja Party," *Vigil*, II (October 6, 1951).

Deva, Acharya Narendra. "The Common Man and Congress," *Janata*, I (February 10, 1946), p. 2.

Deva, Acharya Narendra. "Congress and the Social Change," *Janata*, VIII (August 30, 1953), pp. 4-5, 19.

"Firm Faith in Unity of India—Report on Meeting of National Executive of SP in Delhi on June 8, 9, 10," *Janata*, II (June 15, 1947), p. 7.

Gyanchand, Dr. "Politics of Planned Economy," *Janata*, VIII (August 23, 1953), pp. 6-8.

Hayat, Abud. "Election Prospects in West Bengal," *Vigil*, II (December 15, 1951), p. 17.

"Helping the Third Party," *Vigil*, II (December 22, 1951), p. 17.

"Independence Day," *Janata*, III (January 26, 1948), p. 5.

"Jawaharlal Nehru and Socialism in India," *Janata*, VIII (June 14, 1953), pp. 5-6.

"KMPP-Socialist Alliance," *Vigil*, II (September 22, 1951).

Kripalani, Acharya J. B. "Confusing the Issues," *Vigil*, II (January 12, 1952), pp. 5-6.

Kripalani, Acharya J. B. "Gandhiji and Marx," *Vigil*, II (May 5, 1951).

Kripalani, Acharya J. B. "KMPP-Socialist Alliance," *Vigil*, III (June 7, 1952), pp. 2-3.

Kripalani, Acharya J. B. "The Merger," *Swatantra*, VII (September 20, 1952), pp. 39-42.

Kripalani, Acharya J. B. "The Merger," *Vigil*, III (October 4, 1952), pp. 5-7.

Kripalani, Acharya J. B. "Party Alliances," *Vigil*, III (March 29, 1952), pp. 12-13.

Kripalani, Acharya J. B. "Praja Party's Political Alliances," *Vigil*, II (August 11, 1951).

Kripalani, Acharya J. B. "The Socialist-KMPP Merger," *Swatantra*, VII (September 27, 1952), pp. 30-33.

Kripalani, Acharya J. B. "Socialist-KMPP Merger," *Swatantra*, VII (October 4, 1952), pp. 20-23.

Kripalani, Acharya J. B. "Why the Democratic Front?" *Amrita Bazar Patrika*, December 24, 1950.

Krishna, Raj. "Beyond Politics and Economics," *Janata*, VIII (September 13, 1953), pp. 15-16.

"Leaders of the SP," *Janata*, II (October 19, 1947), p. 1.

Lingamurty, V. "Parliamentary Government and Political Parties," *Swatantra*, VI (January 5, 1952), pp. 15-16.

Mehta, Asoka. "Composition of the Party Elite," *Janata*, VIII (July 5, 1953), pp. 7-8.

Mehta, Asoka. "Election Manifesto," *Janata*, I (February 24, 1948), p. 2.

Mehta, Asoka. "Is Merger Decision Undemocratic?" *Janata*, VIII (September 14, 1952), p. 12.

Mehta, Asoka. "Objectives of Labour—Can the INTUC help to Achieve Them?" *Janata*, II (May 25, 1947), pp. 1-7.

Mehta, Asoka. "Six Years of Freedom," *Janata*, VIII (August 16, 1953), pp. 5-6.

Mehta, Asoka. "Smash U.D.F.," *Janata*, VII (September 7, 1952), p. 1.

Mehta, Asoka. "The Underground," *Janata*, I (February 10, 1946), p. 2.

Mehta, Asoka. "The Why and How of the Merger," *Janata*, VII (August 31, 1952), p. 1.

Mehta, Asoka and Dave, Rohit, "Congress in Crisis—New Problems, New Methods," *Janata*, II (May 4, 1947), pp. 1, 7.

Mishra, Rammandan. "Congress-Socialist Party Relations," *Janata*, II (December 21, 1947), p. 11.

Mohan, Vishnu. "KMPP-Socialist Merger: Will it Last?" *Swatantra*, VII (September 6, 1952), pp. 39-43.

"The Momentous Merger," *Janata*, VII (August 31, 1952), p. 1.

Nanda, Gulzarilal. "Future Role of Indian National Congress," *Amrita Bazar Patrika*, May 11, 1947.

Narayan, Jayaprakash. "The Fast," *Janata*, VII (July 20, 1952), p. 1.

Narayan, Jayaprakash. "KMPP and UDF," *Janata*, VII (September 7, 1952), p. 12.

Narayan, Jayaprakash. "The Merger," *Janata*, VII (September 7, 1952), p. 1.

Narayan, Jayaprakash. "The Party and the Congress," *Janata*, II (March 30, 1947), p. 7.

Narayan, Jayaprakash. "Reorganize Congress," *Janata*, I (May 5, 1946), p. 7.

Narayan, Jayaprakash. "The Structure of the Socialist Party," *Janata*, III (November 21, 1948), pp. 3, 8.

Narayan, Jayaprakash. "To All Fighters for Freedom," *Janata*, I (July 28, 1946), p. 6.

"Ninety-five Percent Rise in Party Membership," *Janata*, VI (June 10, 1951), p. 4.

Patwardhan, Achyut. "Congress and the CSP," *Janata*, II (January 16, 1947), p. 15.

Patwardhan, Achyut. "Parties within the Congress," *Janata*, II (February 2, 1947), p. 7.

Patwardhan, Achyut. "Parties within the Congress," *Janata*, II (February 16, 1947), p. 7.

"The Proper Perspective," *Vigil*, III (July 5, 1952), p. 3.

"PSP—Forward Bloc Merger," *Janata*, VIII (July 19, 1953), p. 3.

Rao, Khasa Subba. "Spotlight on Men and Politics," *Hindu*, October 1, 1953 (Andhra State Supplement).

Rao, M. Venkata. "A Gandhian Socialism," *Vigil*, II (June 23, 1951).

Roy, Samaren. "West Bengal's Politics X-Rayed," *Thought*, V (September 19, 1953), p. 5.

Sachar, Rajendra. "Congress and the Socialist Party—The Case for Separation," *Janata*, III (February 22, 1948), p. 12.

Sampath, P. N. "After the Merger," *Swatantra*, VII (October 11, 1952), pp. 32-33.

Sampath, P. N. "KMPP-Socialist Merger," *Swatantra*, VII (September 13, 1952), p. 37.

"Sardar Patel and the Socialists," *Janata*, III (February 1, 1948), p. 4.

Shastri, Hariharnath. "Should Socialists Support the INTUC?" *Janata*, II (May 18, 1947), p. 3.

"Socialist Party New Orientation—Report on Cawnpore Conference," *Janata*, II (March 9, 1947), pp. 1-2.

"Socialist Party's Election Plans," *Janata*, VI (October 7, 1951), p. 1.

"Stooping to Conquer?" *Vigil*, II (September 8, 1951), p. 3.

"Three-fold Task before Socialists," *Janata*, VI (August 5, 1951), p. 1.

"The Week in India," *Janata*, I (September 1, 1946), p. 1.

Verghese, B. C. "Asoka Mehta's Thesis Must Wait," *Janata*, VIII (August 16, 1953), pp. 8-10.

MARXIST LEFT PARTIES

Books and Pamphlets

All India Forward Bloc. *Constitution of the All India Forward Bloc.* Ludhiana (East Punjab): Secretary General, All India Forward Bloc (Marxist), undated.

All India Forward Bloc. *Draft Thesis—The All India Forward Bloc (Marxist).* Calcutta: General Mohan Singh [1951?].

All India Forward Bloc. *Election Manifesto of the All India Forward Bloc (Marxist).* Ludhiana (East Punjab): General Mohan Singh, 1951.

All India Forward Bloc. *Election Manifesto of the All India Forward Bloc (Subhasist).* Calcutta: All India Forward Bloc, 1951.

All India Forward Bloc. *From Arrah to Chandernagar*. Calcutta: All India Forward Bloc [1949?].

All India Forward Bloc. *Ideology of Netaji—Thesis of the All-India Forward Bloc*. Calcutta: R. S. Ruikar, All India Forward Bloc, 1949.

All India Forward Bloc. *Programme and Policy of Netaji's Party —What Forward Bloc Stands For*. Nagpur: V. R. Ruikar for All India Forward Bloc, 1948.

All India Forward Bloc. *Programme of Post-War Revolution— Draft Manifesto of the Forward Bloc*. Bombay: All India Forward Bloc, 1946.

Bhattacharya, Nepal. *Address to All India United Trades Union Congress*. Calcutta: Barada Mukutmani, 1953.

Bolshevik Party of India. *Political Statement of the Central Committee of the Bolshevik Party of India*. Calcutta: Bolshevik Party Central Committee, undated.

Bose, Bejoy Krishna. *The Alipore Bomb Trial*. Calcutta: Butterworth and Co., Ltd., 1922.

Bose, Sarat Chandra. *Selected Speeches and Writings, 1947-1950*. Calcutta: Thacker's Press and Directories, Ltd., 1954.

Bose, Subhas Chandra. *The Indian Struggle, 1920-1934*. Calcutta: Thacker, Spink and Co., Ltd., 1948.

Bose, Subhas Chandra. *The Indian Struggle, 1935-1942*. Calcutta: Chuckervertty, Chatterjee and Co., Ltd., 1952.

Bose, Mrinal Kanti. *Address to United Trades Union Congress*. Calcutta: UTUC, 1949.

Bose, Mrinal Kanti. *Annual Report to United Trades Union Congress*. Calcutta: UTUC, 1953.

Bose, Mrinal Kanti. *Efforts for Trade Union Unity*. Calcutta: UTUC, 1954.

Chatterjee, Jogesh. *Presidential Address to Second Annual Conference, United Trades Union Congress*. Calcutta: Kranti Press, 1953.

Chaudhury, Sanat Rai. *Tito-Stalin Conflict*. Calcutta: Ganavani Publishing House, undated.

Chaudhuri, Tridib. *The Swing Back—A Critical Survey of the*

Devious Zig-zags of CPI Political Line (1947-50). Calcutta: Revolutionary Socialist Party, 1950.

Chintamani, C. Y. *Indian Politics since the Mutiny.* Allahabad: Kitabistan, 1947.

Chirol, Sir Valentine. *India Old and New.* London: Macmillan and Co., Ltd., 1921.

Chirol, Sir Valentine. *Indian Unrest.* London: Macmillan and Co., Ltd., 1910.

Dasgupta, Sudhirkumar. *Pakistan and Self-Determination.* Calcutta: Ganavani Publishing House, 1946.

Ghosh, Ajoy. *Some of Our Main Weaknesses.* Bombay: People's Publishing House, Ltd., 1952.

Government of India, Home Department. *Sedition Committee 1918 Report.* Calcutta: Superintendent, Government Printing, 1918.

Ker, James Campbell. *Political Trouble in India 1907-1917.* Calcutta: Government Printing Office, 1917.

Lattimore, Eleanor H. *Labor Unions in the Far East.* New York: American Council, Institute of Pacific Relations, 1945.

Masani, M. R. *The Communist Party of India.* London: Derek Verschoyle, 1954.

People's United Socialist Front. *Election Manifesto.* Calcutta: Probhat Sen for the PUSF, 1951.

Raghuvanshi, Dr. V. P. S. *Indian Nationalist Movement.* Agra: Lakshmi Narain Agarwal, 1951.

Rai, Canpat (ed.). *Famous Speeches and Letters of Subhas Chandra Bose.* Lahore: Lion Press, 1946.

Ramgarh to Delhi via Nagpur. Calcutta: Popular Printing Works, 1941.

Revolutionary Communist Party of India. *Revolutionary Communists—The World and India (Political Thesis of the Seventh Conference of the Revolutionary Communist Party of India).* Calcutta: Ganavani Publishing House, 1951.

Revolutionary Communist Party of India. *The Struggle for Socialism (Political Thesis of the Sixth Conference of the Revolutionary Communist Party of India).* Calcutta: Ganavani Publishing House, 1950.

Revolutionary Communist Party of India Central Committee. *Thought for Communists.* Calcutta: Sudarshan Chatterjee [1948?].

Revolutionary Socialist Party. *Election Manifesto—Revolutionary Socialist Party.* Calcutta: Kranti Press, 1951.

Revolutionary Socialist Party. *For Socialism, Toilers' Democracy and Freedom!—RSP Theses and Statement of Policy on National Situation.* Delhi: RSP Central Office, 1954.

Revolutionary Socialist Party. *Forward to Socialist Revolution—Statement on National Situation.* Basti (U.P.): Revolutionary Socialist Party, 1948.

Revolutionary Socialist Party. *The Leninist Way—RSP Statements of Policy on International and National Situation.* Kanpur: RSP Central Office, 1950.

Revolutionary Socialist Party. *On National Struggle—Thesis of the R.S.P.I.* Calcutta: Revolutionary Socialist Party, 1942.

Revolutionary Socialist Party. *On Russo-German War—Thesis of the R.S.P.I.* Calcutta: Revolutionary Socialist Party, 1941.

Revolutionary Socialist Party. *Political Situation and Statement of Policy of the R.S.P.I. Central Committee.* Revolutionary Socialist Party, 1947.

Revolutionary Socialist Party. *RSP: What It Is and Why?* Delhi: Revolutionary Socialist Party, 1953.

Revolutionary Socialist Party. *Second All National Party Convention of Revolutionary Socialist Party of India—Speeches and Resolutions.* Muzaffarpur: Hindustan Press, 1947.

Revolutionary Socialist Party. *War Thesis of the R.S.P.I.* Calcutta: Revolutionary Socialist Party, 1940.

Revolutionary Socialist Party. *What Revolutionary Socialism Stands For—The Thesis and Platform of Action.* Calcutta: Revolutionary Socialist Party, 1946. (First impression in 1938.)

Roy, Anil. *Party and Leadership.* Calcutta: Jatiya Sahitya Prakasani, undated.

Roy, Anil. *What Netaji Stands For.* Calcutta: Sunil Das, undated.

Roy, Leela. *We Shall Not Stand It.* Calcutta: Jagaran Publishing House, 1945.

Ruikar, R. S. *Netaji's Politics and Ideology*. Nagpur: Nagpur Forward Bloc, 1948.

Singh, General Mohan. *Presidential Address to the Sixth Plenary Session of the All India Forward Bloc*. Cuttack: Dibakar Patnaik, 1952.

Socialist Republican Party. *What We Believe*. Calcutta: Socialist Republican Party, 1948.

Subuhey, S. *Netaji Speaks*. Bombay: Padma Publications, 1946.

Tagore, Saumyendranath. *Bourgeois-Democratic Revolution and India*. Calcutta: Ganavani Publishing House, 1946.

Tagore, Saumyendranath. *Communism and Fetishism*. Calcutta: Provat Sen, 1940.

Tagore, Saumyendranath. *Congress Socialism?* Lucknow: Jagriti Publishing House, 1942.

Tagore, Saumyendranath. *The Constituent Assembly*. Calcutta: Ganavani Publishing House, 1940.

Tagore, Saumyendranath. *Gandhism and the Labour-Peasant Problem*. Gauhati: Radical Institute [1940?].

Tagore, Saumyendranath. *Hitlerism or the Aryan Rule in Germany*. Calcutta: Ganashakti Publishing House, 1933.

Tagore, Saumyendranath. *The Hour Has Struck*. Calcutta: Ganavani Publishing House, 1949.

Tagore, Saumyendranath. *Permanent Revolution*. Calcutta: Samar Bose, 1944.

Tagore, Saumyendranath. *Post-War World and India*. Calcutta: Ganavani Publishing House, 1947.

Tagore, Saumyendranath. *Revolution and Quit India*. Calcutta: Ganavani Publishing House, 1946.

Tagore, Saumyendranath. *Sahajanand, Kornilov, and Peoples' War*. Lucknow: S. M. Jaffar, 1942.

Tagore, Saumyendranath. *Tactics and Strategy of Revolution*. Calcutta: Ganavani Publishing House, 1948.

Tagore, Saumyendranath. *The Treacherous Marsh*. Calcutta: Avijan Publishing House, 1948.

Tagore, Saumyendranath. *Stalin, Truman Hands Off Korea*. Calcutta: Ganavani Publishing House, 1951.

United Trades Union Committee. *Constitution.* Calcutta: United Trades Union Committee [1948?].

Why R.C.P.I., Prof. K. T. Shah and Purnananda Das Gupta Resigned from U.S.O.I. Calcutta: Ganavani Publishing House, 1951.

Williams, L. F. Rusbrook. *India in the Years 1917-1918.* A report prepared for presentation to Parliament in accordance with the requirements of the 26th section of the Government of India Act. Calcutta: Superintendent of Government Printing, 1919.

Yagee, Sheel Bhadra. *Presidential Address at the Fourth Party Conference.* All India Forward Bloc. Ingohta (U.P.), 1949.

Articles

Banerjee, Shibnath. "Plea for United Socialist Bloc—No Bloc but Platform," *Nation,* July 10, 1949.

"Call to Left," *Nation,* June 1, 1950, p. 4.

Chaudhuri, Tridib. "Plea for Socialist Unity," *Nation,* July 17, 1949, pp. 4, 6.

Choudhury, Sanat Roy. "Role of the USO," *Nation,* November 22, 1949.

Das Gupta, Purnananda. "Left Unity vs. Socialist Party—Revision of Stand Urged," *Nation,* September 17, 1949.

"Leftists in Maharashtra," *Thought,* v (June 27, 1953), p. 17.

Manusri (A Worker). "Review of the Left Forces and Revolution," *Nation,* August 25, 1950, p. 4.

"Towards National Leftist Front," *Nation,* November 21, 1948, p. 1.

"United Socialist Bloc," *Nation,* June 26, 1949.

"USOI Draft Election Manifesto," *Nation,* October 24, 1950.

HINDU COMMUNAL PARTIES

Books and Pamphlets

Akhil Bharat Hindu Mahasabha. *Constitution, Aims, Objects and Rules.* New Delhi: Hindu Mahasabha, 1951.

Akhil Bharat Hindu Mahasabha. *Election Manifesto.* New Delhi: Hindu Mahasabha, 1951.

Akhil Bharat Hindu Mahasabha. *Full Text of the Resolutions Adopted by the Akhil Bharat Committee on 23rd August 1953.* New Delhi: Hindu Mahasabha, 1953.

Akhil Bharat Hindu Mahasabha. *Full Proceedings of 28th Session, Calcutta.* Calcutta: Hindu Mahasabha, 1949.

Akhil Bharat Hindu Mahasabha. *Text of Resolutions at 29th Session, Poona.* Poona: Hindu Mahasabha, 1950.

Akhil Bharat Hindu Mahasabha. *Full Text of Resolutions Passed at the Special Convention Held at Jaipur.* Delhi: National Printing Works, 1951.

Akhil Bharat Hindu Mahasabha. *Full Text of Resolutions, 30th Session, Bhopal.* New Delhi: Hindu Mahasabha, 1953.

Akhil Bharat Hindu Mahasabha Central Parliamentary Board. *Mahasabha and Its Ideals.* Calcutta: Bharat Publications, 1950.

All India Hindu Mahasabha. *Full Text of Resolutions Adopted by the Working Committee on 10th and 11th September 1949.* New Delhi: Hindu Mahasabha, 1949.

All India Hindu Mahasabha. *Full Text of Resolutions at 27th Session at Gorakhpur.* New Delhi: Hindu Mahasabha, 1947.

All India Hindu Mahasabha. *The History of the Bhagalpur Struggle (The 23rd Session of the A.I. Hindu Mahasabha, 1941).* Bhagalpur: Madhukari, 1942.

All India Hindu Mahasabha. *Hindu Mahasabha on Cabinet Mission Proposal.* Calcutta: Hindu Mahasabha, 1946.

All India Hindu Mahasabha. *Resolutions of the Working Committee Meeting Held on 7th, 8th and 9th May, 1949.* New Delhi: Hindu Mahasabha, 1949.

All Jammu and Kashmir Praja Parishad. *Jammu Fights against Separatism, Communalism and Totalitarism.* Delhi: Publicity Secretary, All Jammu Kashmir Praja Parishad, 1953.

All Jammu and Kashmir Praja Parishad. *New Jammu.* Jammu: Praja Parishad, undated.

All Jammu and Kashmir Praja Parishad. *A Plea to Understand Praja Parishad.* Delhi: Bharat Mudranalaya, 1952.

All India Ramarajya Parishad. *Election Manifesto.* Delhi: Nigambodha Ghat, 1951.

Bharatiya Jan Sangh. *Kashmir Problem and Jammu Satyagraha.* Delhi: Bharatiya Jan Sangh, 1953.

Bharatiya Jan Sangh. *Manifesto and Constitution.* Bombay: Shivaji Printing Press, 1951.

Bharatiya Jan Sangh. *Our Kashmir.* Calcutta: Bharatiya Jan Sangh, 1953.

Chatterjee, N. C. *Awakening of New India—Problems of Today.* New Delhi: Rashtriya Sahitya Mandir, 1952.

Chatterjee, N. C. *Demand for Enquiry into the Detention and Death of Dr. Syama Prasad Mookerjee.* New Delhi: Hindu Mahasabha, 1953.

Chatterjee, N. C. *Democracy in Peril—Problem of Jammu.* New Delhi: Hindu Mahasabha, 1953.

Chatterjee, N. C. *Hindu Politics.* Calcutta: R. C. Banerjee, 1944.

Chatterjee, N. C. *Presidential Address to All India Hindu Mahasabha 30th Session, Bhopal.* New Delhi: Hindu Mahasabha, 1952.

Curran, J. A., Jr. *Militant Hinduism in Indian Politics—A Study of the RSS.* New York: Institute of Pacific Relations, 1951.

Deshpande, Professor V. G. *Why Hindu Rashtra?* Delhi: Hindu Mahasabha, 1949.

Farquhar, J. N. *Modern Religious Movements in India.* New York: Macmillan Co., 1915.

Golwalkar, M. S. *We or Our Nationhood Defined.* Nagpur: Bharat Publications, 1945.

Keer, Dhananjay. *Savarkar and His Times.* Bombay: A. V. Keer, 1950.

Khare, Dr. N. B. *Presidential Address, Akhil Bharat Hindu Mahasabha 28th Session, Calcutta.* Calcutta: Hindu Mahasabha, 1949.

Khare, Dr. N. B. *Presidential Address, Akhil Bharat Hindu Mahasabha 29th Session, Poona.* Poona: Hindu Mahasabha, 1950.

Khare, Dr. N. B. *Presidential Address, Akhil Bharat Hindu Mahasabha Special Session, Jaipur.* Jaipur: Hindu Mahasabha, 1951.

Lahiry, Ashutosh. *The Moslem Minority Problem*. New Delhi: Hindu Mahasabha, 1948.

Madhok, Balraj. *Dr. Syama Prasad Mookerjee—A Biography*. New Delhi: Deepak Prakashan, 1954.

Madhok, Balraj. *Kashmir Problem—A Story of Bungling*. New Delhi: Bharti Sahitya Sadan, 1952.

Malaviya, Shri Govind. *Hindu Code Bill*. Calcutta: Anti-Hindu Code Committee, 1951.

Malkani, K. R. *Principles for a New Political Party*. Delhi: V. P. Bhandar, 1951.

Malkani, K. R. *The Rise and Fall of the Congress*. Delhi: V. P. Bhandar, 1951.

Mookerjee, Dr. Syama Prasad. *Integrate Kashmir*. Delhi: Shartiya Jan Sangh, 1952.

Mookerjee, Dr. Syama Prasad. *Presidential Address to 26th Session of All India Hindu Mahasabha, 1944*. New Delhi: Hindu Mahasabha, 1944.

Mookerjee, Dr. Syama Prasad. *Why Bharatiya Jana Sangh?* Delhi: Bharat Mudranalaya, 1951.

Mookerjee, Nehru and Abdullah Correspondence. *Integrate Kashmir*. Lucknow: D. Upadhyaya, 1953.

Prakash, Indra. *A Review of the History and Work of the Hindu Mahasabha and the Hindu Sanghatan Movement*. New Delhi: Hindu Mahasabha, 1952.

Savarkar, V. D. *An Echo from Andamans*. Poona: R. J. Deshmukh, 1947.

Savarkar, V. D. *Hindu Rashtra Darshan (A Collection of the Presidential Speeches Delivered from the Hindu Mahasabha Platform)*. Bombay: L. G. Khare, 1949.

Savarkar, V. D. *Hindu Rashtravad—Being an Exposition of the Ideology and Immediate Programme of Hindu Rashtra*. Collected and edited by Satya Parkash. Rohtak: Rohtas Printing Press, 1945.

Savarkar, V. D. *Hindu Sanghatan—Its Ideology and Immediate Programme*. Bombay: Hindu Mahasabha Presidential Office, 1940.

Savarkar, V. D. *Hindutva*. Poona: S. P. Gokhale, 1949.

Savarkar, V. D. *Presidential Address to All India Hindu Maha-sabha 24th Session, Cawnpore.* Poona: G. V. Ketkar, 1942.

Varma, Durga Dass. *We Chose Sacrifice.* Jammu: All Jammu and Kashmir Praja Parishad, 1953.

Articles

"The Country First," *Organiser,* v (October 29, 1951), p. 4.

"Glimpses of a Glorious Life," *Organiser,* vi (July 6, 1953), p. 5.

"Guruji on the Ills of the Nation," *Organiser,* v (February 25, 1952), p. 9.

Lahiri, Ashutosh. "Immediate Problem Before the Mahasabha," *Hindu Outlook,* May 3, 1953, p. 2.

Moonje, Dr. B. S. "Hindu National Ideas and Ways to Achieve Them," *Mahratta,* October 22, 1943.

"A New Party Is Born," *Thought,* iii (October 26, 1951), p. 4.

Prakash, Indra. "Liquidation under the Garb of a United Front," *Hindu Outlook,* August 30, 1953, p. 3.

"Savarkar-Mukherji Talks," *Hindu Outlook,* September 7, 1952, p. 3.

"A United Front," *Organiser,* v (May 12, 1952), p. 8.

Index